My Body, My Earth

Also by Ruby Gibson

Home is the Heart

My Body, My Earth

The Practice of Somatic Archaeology

Ruby Gibson

iUniverse, Inc.
New York Bloomington Shanghai

My Body, My Earth
The Practice of Somatic Archaeology

Copyright © 2008 by Ruby Gibson

All rights reserved. No part of this book may be used or reproduced by any means, graphic, electronic, or mechanical, including photocopying, recording, taping or by any information storage retrieval system without the written permission of the publisher except in the case of brief quotations embodied in critical articles and reviews.

iUniverse books may be ordered through booksellers or by contacting:

iUniverse
1663 Liberty Drive
Bloomington, IN 47403
www.iuniverse.com
1-800-Authors (1-800-288-4677)

Because of the dynamic nature of the Internet, any Web addresses or links contained in this book may have changed since publication and may no longer be valid.

The information, ideas, and suggestions in this book are not intended as a substitute for professional advice. Before following any suggestions contained in this book, you should consult your personal physician or mental health professional. Neither the author nor the publisher shall be liable or responsible for any loss or damage allegedly arising as a consequence of your use or application of any information or suggestions in this book.

The term Somatic Archaeology is a registered trademark of Ruby Gibson. All rights reserved.

The essential oil blend names used in this book are registered trademarks of Young Living Essential Oils. All rights reserved.

ISBN: 978-0-595-48823-0 (pbk)
ISBN: 978-0-595-49076-9 (cloth)
ISBN: 978-0-595-60858-4 (ebk)

Printed in the United States of America

Cover photo
Spirit of the Spring
By Hailey Nicole Martinez

Chapter icon photo
Siete Moai de Rapa Nui
By Ola Faye Thompson

Section icon drawing
The Medicine Shield
By Reynel Martinez

For my parents
Bob and Gloria

For my children
Jinji, Ola Faye, and Michael Mateo

And for the next seven generations
who will hear the heartbeat of Mother Earth
and remember her boundless stories.

Somatic: relating to or affecting the body, especially the body as considered separate from the mind

Archaeology: the scientific study of ancient cultures through the examination of their material remains, i.e., buildings, graves, tools, and other artifacts usually dug up from the ground

Somatic Archaeology: unearthing in the human body those remains and artifacts of our familial, ancestral, and spiritual lineage in order to uncover our myths and remember our stories for personal and planetary evolution

Contents

Acknowledgments xv
Preface xvii

The Concept

CHAPTER 1   The Archaeology of Healing 3
    Remember Your Story. 5
    Heal Your Story 5
    Body Talk. 11
    What's Right With You?. 13
    The Myth of Duality and Healing 14
    My Story as a Healer. 16
    Sift Through Your Buried Treasure. 20
    Historical Amnesia 22
    Change the Big Story 23

CHAPTER 2   Somatic Storykeeping 30
    Chronicle Your Stories 33
    Sacred Stories 34
    My Sacred Story 35

CHAPTER 3   Remember and Embrace Your Past 39
    A Skill for Life. 40
    Global Remembering 41
    Seven-Generation Memory 43
    Storing Memories 45
    Types of Memories 46
    Excavate Your Chakra System. 50

The Preparation

CHAPTER 4 Prepare for a Somatic Excavation 59
  Safety. 60
  Addictive Behaviors 61
  Empowerment. 62
  Somatic Filters. 62
  Planning a Somatic Excavation 67
  Long-Term Excavations. 69
  Benefits of Digging 69

CHAPTER 5 Aromatherapy for Balancing Brain and Body 71
  What Are Essential Oils? 72
  Essential Oils Are Not All the Same. 73
  Aromatherapy and the Brain 74
  Essential Oils and ADHD 76
  Essential Oils as Energy Medicine 78
  Aroma Memory. 79
  Application of Essential Oils 80
  Aroma-Mood Reference Guide 82

CHAPTER 6 Tools to Excavate Your Story. 93
  Fear of Your Story 94
  Somatic Excavation Techniques. 95

The Practice

CHAPTER 7 Somatic Breathing Techniques. 113
  Breath Assessment 114
  Four Basic Soma-Breaths 115
  Somatic Archaeology Breathing Exercises. 118

CHAPTER 8 The Five Steps of Somatic Archaeology 127
  The Five Steps 129
  Somatic Archaeology Protocol 136

Chapter 9   Self-Care for the Somatic Archaeologist......... 141
    Self-Care Suitcase 142
    Self-Sabotage... 148
    Black Holes.. 149
    Your Touch Story 150
    Heal Your Sexual Story.. 152
    Maintain Healthy Boundaries................................ 155

The Way of Life

Chapter 10   The Circle of Life 161
    The Sacred Medicine Wheel................................... 162
    A Personal Medicine Wheel 162
    The Alchemy of Healing.. 165
    Balancing the Four Worlds 169

Chapter 11   Mend the Circle 175
    Somatic Archaeology Wheel of Suffering.............. 176
    Somatic Archaeology's Wheel of Healing 184
    Somatic Archaeology Wheel of Transformation .. 191
    Recreate Yourself with Earth Passages 194

Chapter 12   A Life Worth Living 199
    Your Life Circle... 200
    Healing Between Worlds....................................... 201
    Archaeology of the Soul 209
    Closing the Circle.. 209
    Advice from Somatic Archaeologists 210
    Bring Joy into Your Story..................................... 213
    Take Your Story into the World 214
    The Gift of Suffering 215
    Conclusion 216

About the Author 219

Appendix

Somatic Glossary 223
Essential Oil Information 227

Acknowledgments

With gratitude and profound respect, I acknowledge my ancestors and all of those, seen and unseen, that guide the healing of this planet and her people. This work is birthed through the inspiration of many grandmothers and grandfathers who are the storykeepers of our great awakening, and is a testament to their bottomless compassion and endless love. Thank you always to Mother Earth for her patience, tolerance, harmony, and remarkable splendor.

This book could not have been written without the courage of my Somatic Archaeology clients, who, over the years, have been willing to share their stories and trust their bodies to the somatic healing process. They are my greatest teachers, and have given me the perspective and understanding to put these thoughts and concepts into words. Thank you all.

I am grateful for my somatic students and colleagues whose wit, depth, and capacity have supported and encouraged me through the toughest and the most magnificent of times. Your beauty, essence, and smiles shine through as a dear reminder of genuine friendship and devotion to healing in its truest sense.

With appreciation I honor the artists—Ola Faye Thompson, Hailey Nicole Martinez, Reynel Martinez, and Sue Scudder—who have contributed by creating Earth-inspired symbols and photographs that add beauty to this book. Special thanks to Susan Bridle for her editorial talents and timely assistance.

I am indebted to my teachers and friends who have guided me with their beautiful hearts: Megan, Allyn, Suzanne, Carl, Olena, Kimie, Ric, Jay, Rhonda, Thaayrohyadi, and Tulley Spotted Eagle Boy. I honor Eagle Star Blanket, whose teachings and love of the Medicine Wheel have provided invaluable insights to develop the wheels of Somatic Archaeology. Many thank to Dennis Simpson and the Colorado School of Healing Arts for providing a platform to encourage my awareness of somatic therapy.

Finally, I am grateful for the unwavering support, laughter, and wholesomeness of my family: Gloria, Bill, Celeste, Judy, George, Glo, Jinji, Dominic, Ola Faye, Sheena, Mateo, and of course Michael James, who helped me to grow up and find my truth. I thank *Mi Corazon de Oro*, Hakita, whose generous heart and spirit is a guiding beacon in my life. Always remember that your love is the glue that holds these pages together.

Preface

Fondly do I remember the spring of my youth—vines escaping, waters running, flowers blooming, and the fertile smells of delicate growth. It was a magical time on the eastern seaboard, when innocence prevailed and Mother Earth was my primary teacher. The lessons learned were instinctual then, and reflective of the interplay between the Earth and the waters and the sun and the wind.

As children with ambitious dispositions, my sisters and I would diligently place ourselves at the creek's edge in our backyard and crown each other as queen of the waters. Strong stick in hand, it was our responsibility to clear the water's path of any old leaves, rocks, trash or other debris that kept the water from flowing smoothly. It was a job that required constant attention, for it seemed there was always something that would deter the precious, natural flow.

My sisters and I would check on the waters every day, and although no one else paid much attention to this creek, we knew that this was our most important job. The creek's headwaters came from three large ponds on our neighbor's property. The neighbor, a well-to-do old lady, did not pay much attention to the waterways. A chain link fence with pointy barbed wire at the top surrounded her yard—a large, sweeping, well-manicured lawn. After doing such a thorough job cleaning our portion of the creek, we would find ourselves jabbing our sticks under the fence to attempt to clean out the neighbor's clogged canals. We were appalled that she could allow her creek to be so unattended!

Day after day, I would sit patiently, eyeing the ignored side of the fence, watching the water struggle around piles of leaves, broken twigs, and misplaced rocks. And then one day I could stand it no longer! Her congested artery, although not my responsibility, was dragging accumulated debris into our clean and tidy creek. With a determination beyond my years, I piled some rocks close to the fence and carefully jumped into the forbidden territory.

Treading quietly and stealthily, I stayed close to the ground to avoid anyone seeing me from the large house that sat amidst the three ponds. I went as far up the creek as I dared to go and began using my stick to drag clumps of soggy leaves out of the water. The creek immediately responded with a gentle gurgling sound and a gush, as the swiftness of the current gratefully increased. As I worked, the waters began washing away years of junk that had stifled its flow, and the stream and I rejoiced in the movement.

Immersed in my self-proclaimed duties, I was shocked as a voice suddenly disturbed my purging, yelling at me loudly, "Get off my property!" I turned to see a hunched-over, wicked-looking woman galloping toward me with stick in hand. It was obvious that she was not going to join me in my venture, but rather was chasing me away. I was far upstream and knew that I could not make it back to my pile of rocks, so I ran into the forest adjacent to the ponds. To my dismay, she followed me. I ran in fear of my life, for we had spent many nights with neighborhood children sharing horror stories about the old lady—and they were all about to come true.

Coursing through the trees, I lost a shoe on a root, but did not stop to pick it up—the back fence to our property was in sight. As I threw my small body over the barbed wire, my shirt caught on a barb and I found myself hanging from the fence with the old lady still in pursuit. Ripping my shirt to escape, I fled just in time to the safety of our house, frantically breathing, my heart beating wildly, to hear the woman yelling threats to my retreat. It took me weeks to recover.

That was the last time that I even thought about messing with someone else's waterways. Although apprehensive at first, with my tail between my legs, I eventually made my way again to our backyard, the creek, and my mission. I continued to keep our side of the creek as swift flowing and clean as possible—right up to the fence line. As the neighbor's inaccessible leaves drifted under the fence, I begrudgingly cleared them away without hope of ever completing my task. Her muddy waters would always affect mine, no matter how pure or well tended my creek was.

As I grew up, contemplating my fascination with keeping things clear, I began to recognize that the creek waters represented my spiritual source, symbolizing the ever-present flow of life that connects all of us. A part of me has always strived to keep the connection unhindered, to keep myself open, to move gracefully with inspiration. Those childhood creek waters represented my soul, and I was a good caretaker of my soul. So good in fact, that I could not tolerate those who were not good caretakers and allowed their neglect to overflow into mine.

In essence, that is what this book is about. It is the result of the many years I have been seasoned as a custodian of my soul. It is the accumulated effect of constantly paying attention to those things that muddy my waters. My once-small quick running creek has widened into a slow, constant waterway that now resembles a river. I still struggle a bit when I see another riverbed that is dry, or is dammed, or is full of debris. But I don't try to clean it. I learned my lesson. I just show the owners how I keep mine clean and free running. And I show them what I do when my waters get clogged—for they still do. Even with constant attention, the storms of life deposit new obstacles to overcome. I never feel weary in this work, though, for I know the satisfaction and joy of an unhindered flow.

Ruby Gibson, Shadow Mountain, 2007

May you begin your somatic excavation
with tenderness and consideration
for all that has transpired before you.

The Concept

1

The Archaeology of Healing

So many of us do not know our own story. A story about who we are, not what we have done. About what we have faced to build what we have built, what we have drawn upon and risked to do it, what we have felt, thought, feared, and discovered through the events of our lives. The real story that belongs to us alone. Until we stop ourselves or, more often, have been stopped, we hope to put certain of life's events "behind us" and get on with our living. After we stop we see that certain of life's issues will be with us for as long as we live. We will pass through them again and again, each time with a new story, each time with a greater understanding, until they become indistinguishable from our blessings and our wisdom. It's the way life teaches us how to live.

—Rachel Naomi Remen, *Kitchen Table Wisdom*

Everybody is born with a story, one that is wise and profound and mysterious. The beauty of our individual stories stretches from a time far before us, and travels far beyond us. As a parable fabricated from the myths of others, these stories help us to develop, test our character, and validate our truths. Our stories construct the reality that we experience and they help us invent our future. We live them, dance them, and dream them as the main character, director, and producer.

Stories are the footholds of the past that mold us, and we make them each day. Stories can blind us and bind us to repetitive circumstance, as well as embolden us to rise above adversity. Some are sweet, some tragic, but all stories are teachers and have hidden meanings for us to explore. Potent and accessible in our bodies, we can remember our stories, uncover their trail, and find their origin with Somatic Archaeology.

Although it may appear that the words *somatic* and *archaeology* are an odd combination, they weave together into a model of healing that impacts our past, present, and future. Our bodies, like the Earth, are the keepers of memory. Just as the Earth contains the historical library of life in its ruins, graves, trees, rocks, and oceans, our bodies inherit the archives of our ancestors in their cells, muscles, blood, and bones. Adopting the attitudes, patterns, and dynamics of our families, communities, and environment, these elements shape and define us. We become what we've inherited, what others have said we are, what our teachers have taught us, and what Earth rhythms have modeled for us. Our Earth, our body, remembers all.

When we wish to examine how we evolved as a culture and a species, we dig in the Earth. The Earth is the link to times past and the battleground for our personal evolution. The Earth stores the symbols, the skeletons, and the shadows of our lives. Excavating the information the Earth stores helps us to piece together our lineage and illuminates for us the wisdom of the ancients, the fruits and folly of our forefathers.

To examine how each of us evolved as individuals or as family systems, and to explore the social and spiritual influences that have shaped us, we excavate our bodies. Our bodies provide the link to our inherent wisdom, cycles, and perfection, and as well, they store the symbols, skeletons, and shadows of our personal lives. The stories in our body furnish us with understanding to witness the imprints of memory that have manifested into our accomplishments, struggles, symptoms, emotions, beliefs, and limitations, as well as our tenacity, courage, and potential.

In this archaeological excavation of our bodies, we find that the search itself is as valuable as the artifacts that emerge; that our desire to know more about ourselves is the true driving force. History may predispose the future, but *examining* history gives alternatives to the future. The remains in our bodies directly influence our personal health, thoughts, relationships, and actions—and unearthing these memories can eventually lead to our greatest well-being, and hence, to social change and global harmony. Where we have been can tell us much about where we are going.

Remember Your Story

The practice of Somatic Archaeology, simply stated, is the process of becoming whole by curing your amnesia and remembering your stories. When you dig, you remember, and when you remember, history is revealed, and when history is revealed, you clearly recognize the trail of stories that formulate your life. This knowledge affords you choices and restores to you the power to manifest your unique destiny in a conscious way.

Right now, you are simultaneously making stories and history. You are living and breathing within the blueprint of your ancestors, and modifying it with each choice and action you take. You are a living testament to your words, your beliefs, and your family. Each day you move within the expansion or restriction set forth by your past, diligently establishing it in your future. Life exists as a mirror image of your efforts, influenced by those around you, those before you, those above you, and the Earth beneath you.

To address the accumulation of history that is perpetuating our collective distress and personal anguish, we must approach healing from this circular point of view. Often, we spend so much time suppressing our stories and sidestepping our afflictions that our lives are spent in recovery rather than in living. We have effectively forgotten how to remember the genesis of our suffering and the origins of our truth.

The occupation of our generation is to remember. As a bridge between the ancient Medicine Wheel, human behavior, spirituality, and bodywork, Somatic Archaeology can help you unearth in your body the origins of your stories in order to create awareness and reconciliation of tragedies, life patterns, and cultural myths. With recognition and resolution of your past, you can move forward and heal your life story.

Heal Your Story

The essence of healing is really quite simple. What it all boils down to is that you must learn to love your story. You know what I mean—the personal issues, the family dynamics, and the burdens of humanness. You may not like your story or think you deserve what you've inherited, but you've got to learn to love it in a way that transforms it. Otherwise, you will keep passing the unhealed or fragmented stories forward, generation to generation, until someone grabs a hold of them and decides that they have the capacity to remember the truth, heal the wounds, and create a different story.

Typically, in each generation there is someone in the family who seems to have the courage and insight to pay attention to the stories. I call these people *storykeepers*. Storykeepers are the ones who have an inherent need to speak with honesty, to remember the stories, to remedy what ails the family system, and to attend to this as if it is their most important job in life. You may very well be one of them. If so, this book is written for you.

Are you the black sheep of your family, the one who rocks the boat, the peacekeeper, or the instigator of change? Then, celebrate! Learn to love it! Although healing your story may seem like an endless task, or a bottomless pit, or that you are the only one that seems to care, it is a great honor to be a storykeeper. The sooner you embrace your role, the easier it will be. The sooner that you recognize who you are, the more empowered you will feel.

This book will teach you how to excavate your history through your body. You are going to have to dig in and get your hands dirty, and as we all know, digging in the dirt is messy work. But think what you will find—secrets and truths, remnants of childhood, artifacts of ancestors long passed, auspicious events, tidbits of memories, loose ends of unfinished business, misplaced power—just the things storykeepers love. Whether it is challenging or enjoyable to witness, it is what has been passed forward to you, and your story cannot be avoided.

Most of us have the Humpty Dumpty syndrome. Remember when all the king's horses and all the kings men couldn't put Humpty back together again? Well, the moral of this story is that it wasn't the king's job to begin with! The trails of our lives have been ruptured and broken because of tragedy, heartache, and a loss of continuity—having to abandon our homeland due to war or genocide, losing our loved ones to catastrophe or disease, giving our creativity and integrity to drugs and alcohol, severing our spiritual relationship to our Creator—an endless list of traumatic events. We are carrying the fragments of these events and the rubble of memory within our bodies, and therefore we are the only ones who can put ourselves back together again.

Somatic remembering is extremely personal. If you feel as if you don't know who you are, what you are passionate about, or how to find meaning in your life, unfolding your story will help you see the significance of all that has led you to this moment. As a storykeeper, you have the responsibility to mend the circle of life for yourself, for your family, and for your Earth. Within this book, you will find the tools and techniques to do it well and to do it gracefully. Sometimes all you need is a plan, a step-by-step procedure to give order to the chaos.

And the plan is this: dig within. Unearth yourself. Even if you don't like what you find, keep digging. There is something beautiful underneath. Eventually you will expose the joy, love, dignity, and sweetness that are yours by birthright. You will also find your passion and the innate potential to co-create a future where your deepest dreams can come true, at the same time, establishing wholeness for yourself, your ancestors, and your children. It only takes one person rocking the boat for change to ripple in many directions.

I invite you into the pages of this book. My prerequisite for writing is that I had to unearth my own story. I am an observant digger and have clearly marked the path for you. I can show you how to begin, explain the fundamentals of digging, teach you how to recognize potential hazards, and draw upon hidden clues, but your excavation will differ from mine. Your mountains may be higher, your valleys deeper, the paths overgrown or well traveled. It will all have meaning to you. The stories and treasures you unearth will be for you to understand.

Nonetheless, all our stories are human stories. Underneath the relics of our lives, we each will eventually find forgiveness, acceptance, compassion, gratitude, and peace. These blessings were there all along, but may have been buried by grief, regret, resentment, or indifference. May you begin your somatic excavation with tenderness and consideration for all that has transpired before you. It's really quite simple to heal your story—just begin digging.

Who Can Benefit from Somatic Archaeology?

Whether it is his-story or her-story, we all come from somewhere. So the answer is: Everyone! For some people the past is riddled with heartache and violence, and for others historical memories are fond and cohesive. Our stories, whatever they consist of, are not a departure from normalcy; they are not an aberration of moral character; but they are the foundation of our past and the fertilizer of our future. Remembering and unearthing your story is a sign of courage, and brings authenticity to this Earth journey.

I believe in the inherent goodness of human nature, and hold fast to the conviction that we have all done the best we could to get to this moment in time. Although we may have veered from our morals, made mistakes, or squandered our precious resources, an innate harmony binds each heart to the forces of creation. The perfection of our transgressions, however large or small, historical or current, will be revealed as a process of evolution. The forces of the past always propel us full circle back to the source of suffering—those moments or experiences that are infused with fear.

Unraveling your story all the way to that origin of fear, whether it is personal or inherited, will provoke the awakening of love. Like a great mother of countless children, our Earth earth has woven a web of love that holds us accountable to our choices. Even in the advance of technology, we cannot remove ourselves from the cycles of Earth and creation. Our pain is planetary suffering, and likewise, our joy comes from the harmony of the Earth. Our personal stories are composed by the joy and suffering of our collective stories—memories of Earth changes and shifts, wounds of war, misfortunes and accomplishments, spiritual and cultural traditions, art and music—and will be unearthed, remembered, and healed simultaneously within the rhythms of universal love.

> *Wherever a story comes from, whether it is a familiar myth or a private memory, the retelling exemplifies the making of a connection from one pattern to another: a potential translation in which narrative becomes parable and the once upon a time comes to stand for some renascent truth. This approach applies to all the incidents of everyday life: the phrase in the newspaper, the endearing or infuriating game of a toddler, the misunderstanding at the office. Our species thinks in metaphors and learns through stories.*
>
> —Mary Catherine Bateson, *Peripheral Visions*

Let's begin by tending to the microcosm of your personal history. The practice of Somatic Archaeology provides tools to explore your body's warehouse of memory in order to decipher the cause and effect of your experiences and patterns. When your personal stories go unremembered or become dormant, they will typically translate into a symptom, which is your body talking to you, saying, "Wake up, pay attention, don't forget about this!"

Unfortunately, when we experience this symptom as painful or unacceptable, many of us are taught to suppress or ignore it. Doing this for long periods aggravates the symptom and drives it in deeper, creating chronic physical or emotional conditions. Expressing or tending to the symptom through the process of somatic remembering helps to relieve the pain, producing well-being, optimism, and freedom. This somatic healing story from one of my students demonstrates the connection between a current symptom and a buried, historical trauma.

Alysson's Story

"I had a colonoscopy and my doctor found an ulcer at my ileocecal valve. Oh, my God, please don't let this be Crohn's disease! Crohn's disease is an autoimmune inflammatory bowel disease that can affect the digestive track from mouth to anus. Most commonly, it shows up in the small intestine. Does this one ulcer hint at the presence of many ulcers within my small intestine? That possibility terrifies me since my Uncle Elmer suffered horribly from Crohn's disease, which he was diagnosed with in his early twenties. He moved back home, never left, had many surgeries, and ended up with a colostomy. He died a young man at the age of forty-nine.

"I decided to do a Somatic Archaeology session that focused on my small intestine. I placed my left hand on my solar plexus and my right hand above my ileocecal valve on the lower right side of my abdomen. I started to breathe deeply, in through my nose and out through my mouth. After a few minutes of slowing down, becoming present with my body, and feeling into the sensation, I asked myself: What do I notice? First, I noticed the prominent aortic pulse under my left hand. I checked in with the area below my right hand. Not much seemed to be happening there. Just as I was about to settle on working in my solar plexus area, I noticed sensation building under my right hand. It felt hot and cold at the same time. Icy hot. I brought my awareness there and focused my breath on the icy hotness.

"An image came into my mind's eye of hot red and white liquid, oozing in a straight, slightly diagonal path, with the right end higher than the left. The red was red, and the white was white, but they commingled in a lightening bolt pattern. To release the heat, I began with the fire-breathing dragon breath (see chapter 7)—in through my nose and out through my mouth, imagining myself exhaling fire like a dragon. After a few minutes, I felt my face contort into a dragon face, fierce and angry.

"As I continued to breathe, I spontaneously started to scan my internal horizon, left to right, right to left. One thought kept coming to me: I am protecting my family, I am protecting my family. I asked myself, from what? From the invaders. I then could see small figures far off in the distance at the edge of the horizon. They were advancing with spears, bows, and arrows toward my family and I. A battle was about to begin. I felt fear trembling in my chest, but I was determined to protect my family. The icy hot feeling in my body spread upward in my abdomen, so I placed my left hand above my right.

"Suddenly I knew: I am protecting my family, not just my immediate family, but also my entire tribe. For a few moments I felt helpless. Tears came. What am I supposed to do? How can I stop these invaders from killing us? Then, I realized that I am powerful, and can burn them to death with my fire breath. When the invaders were halfway to us from the horizon, I blew my fire toward them, left to right, right to left. I burned them all, and they fell dead to the ground, covered with gray and black ashes.

"Tears continued to fall. I suddenly realized: They are all my family, not just my tribal members, but these other Indians, too. We are all family. And I just killed some of them. How could I have done that? What am I to do now? As the answer came, 'We come together as one,' the Indians I thought were dead stand up, leave their weapons on the ground, and brush the ashes from their bodies. They walked toward my tribe. With respect and kindness, we greeted each other. One Indian grasped the upper arms of another and moves his head and upper body to the left and then to the right of the other. We commingled and greeted each other in this welcoming, warm way, until each person from my tribe has greeted each person from the other tribe. After all the greetings are done, we meet in a large circle. My tribal members sat in a semi-circle, and the other tribal members sat across from us in a semi-circle. We were all one family. Our leaders sat in the center, sharing prayers and pipes. The occasion was joyful.

"I checked back in with my body. My hands were abuzz with energy. Is the energy coming from my hands or my abdomen? I briefly lifted my hands from my body. The feeling of moving energy greatly diminished, so I placed my hands back on my right abdomen and the buzzing feeling returned. I realized that it's the interaction of the two that's facilitating the energy movement. My sense was that I was injured during an actual battle between the Mohegans and the Pequots that most likely occurred during the Pequot War that began in the fall of 1636. My sense was that I was Mohegan.

"I had heard that an autoimmune disease suggests an internal conflict within, like me attacking myself in some way. I am both Mohegan and Pequot by birth. Though I usually identify myself as one-fourth Mohegan, I am actually three-sixteenths Indian, one-sixteenth Pequot and one-eighth Mohegan. Hundreds of years ago, Mohegans and Pequots fought to the death. Having the blood of both within me, I can now feel that I've carried that conflict in my body, which has manifested in the form of digestive woes, possibly to the point of having developed Crohn's disease. My Uncle Elmer has twice as much Indian blood as me. He was one-eighth Pequot and one-fourth Mohegan. The two bloodlines came back together as recently as my great-grandmother Alice, who was Pequot and white. She married my great-grandfather, Lemuel, who was a Mohegan chief. They birthed my grandfather, Elmer Sr., who was then both Mohegan and Pequot. His son, my Uncle Elmer, was also both.

"At the end of the Somatic Archaeology session, I asked my body, 'What else do I need to know?' The answer came: Move back to Connecticut to be with your people. Be both Mohegan and Pequot, and help bring your two tribes together. They will be stronger as one, as they were before the Europeans came when they were one tribe. They have much healing to do. And so do I.

"Can I heal this ulcer and any others that might be hiding in my small intestine? I believe I can, but certainly not in western medicine ways. Recently, some initial testing indicated that I do not have Crohn's disease, but my doctor is ordering more tests. I await the final word while I continue my Somatic Archaeology excavations. The affirmation I have received from this somatic session is, 'I am in harmony with all that is.' I will continue to speak this as I travel forward in my life."

Consider that for every physical symptom you have, there is an emotional, mental, spiritual, and collective counterpart. What an enormous amount of interwoven information your body holds! In Alysson's story, this information was remarkably detailed and vividly catalogued. Her mind did not have the capacity to remember it all. That is why she came to her body. It is the vessel through which she followed her symptom to sensation, and while exploring sensation remembered a great and tragic story. Remembering this story exposed underlying emotions and conflict that had been fused to her symptoms. Now her body can heal, and her newly found insights can change the future.

Body Talk

Your body does not speak in English or a modern language; the language of the soma is sensation. This is a physical feeling, sometimes vague or general, and sometimes distinct and reoccurring. Sensations can be subtle or demanding, loud or as soft as a whisper. Whether an impression is coming from your body, heart, mind, or soul, it holds a profound amount of information when we *feel* it and *respond* to it. Somatic dialogue ensues when the conversation goes both ways—your body talking and your consciousness listening. Your body is always speaking to you, but you need to pay attention and listen with sensitivity and mindfulness.

Your body also communicates its story to you through symbols, pictures, colors, patterns, and feelings. The first step in hearing your body language is to notice where energy is blocked, or where movement is stifled or restricted. This is usually most apparent as pain, inflammation, tension, or contraction. A repetitive injury site, chronic disease, or a distressed area is a telltale sign. X marks the spot! The areas where you feel discomfort is your body telling you, "This is a good place to begin your excavation."

Your body facilitates the excavation of your story through breath, sound, and movement. Inhaling and exhaling fully while giving your body a voice through words, sounds, or sighs uproots buried memories. Allow tension to move and unwind through your spine and neurology as you shudder, shake, contract, relax, freeze, thaw, and kick it out. Each time you encourage movement, you shift how you are holding onto your story, supporting an internal swing from the flight/fight/freeze response of the sympathetic nervous system into a parasympathetic state of relaxation and safety. Allow your body to follow an instinctive rhythm of empowered release—it already has an inborn wisdom that guides the healing of your story when it is given the opportunity and attention to do so.

If your heart is in turmoil and is conveying depression, unexplainable anxiety, grief/loss, anger, confusion, guilt/shame, apathy, or hopelessness, you may have inherited emotional patterns of suppression, denial, and withholding that are keeping you hostage. An emotion is always rooted in a physical symptom or sensation. You can follow the felt sense of the emotion to a body area. Once you have located the emotion, breathe into it in a way that makes room for it rather than suppresses it, thus exposing the sensations that are the guardians of that memory. There is always a good reason for repressing emotions. Search for the fear associated with the containment and make sure you feel safe to become vulnerable enough to let it be exposed and released.

On a mental level, if your psyche and mind replay images, nightmares, words, statements, and beliefs that create distress, distrust, and insecurity, you are holding fear-based thoughts or visual imprints in your body. Possibly, you have become heir to social, cultural, racial, and familial stories that adversely shape your success, your dreams, and your self-esteem with negative self-talk and judgmental attitudes. Unearthing the imprints of critical or pessimistic memories in your body will reveal a trail leading you to the origin of the fear—which may be many generations removed. Verbalize the thought or word repeatedly, and it will lead you to a sensation. Then use your breath to expand into the sensation, sifting through remnants of the past that perpetuate the negativity. Once the negative belief is acknowledged, replace it with a positive, enlivening statement that is in alignment with your highest intent and divine well-being.

When your soul has a backlog of experiences that are seeking resolution, this burden can get heavy. You may have a proverbial "U-Haul of Stories" that you have been dragging around. If you have lost your connection to Mother Earth and her stories, been uprooted from ancestral lands, dulled your mystical spark with addictions, or have forgotten your destiny, you may have spiritual amnesia. This causes feelings of emptiness or powerlessness. If you find yourself caught in a web of social, political, or spiritual dynamics that involves a group and influences you adversely, you may be locked into a contract or archaic agreement with them. The tools of Somatic Archaeology can help you remember and heal spiritual or past life dynamics that repeat patterns of suffering.

Keep in mind that we all hold body memories that are positive and uplifting. These are typically more accessible, but they may be buried under fear-based memories. Stories that are filled with devotion, passion, and happiness cause our soma to feel alive with possibility and freedom. These can promote health, heal wounds, and create generational patterns laced with abundance and honored traditions. Follow sensations that are tingly, expansive, and full of mobility and infused energy to reveal where joy lives in your body. Humans are connected through stories of love, as much as they are bound through stories of suffering. Joy and suffering are embodied side by side, establishing the duality of life. Your body holds all memories as sacred; whether they are light or dark, following your body talk will lead to illumination.

What's Right With You?

Frequently we are asked, "What is wrong with you?" Doctors ask this when we are sick; parents ask this when we misbehave; partners ask this when we don't get along. This question deceives us into orbiting around the problem and not the solution. But how often are you asked, "What's right with you?"

You can get so lost in the complexities of what is wrong that you can spend years swimming in your oppression, consumed with your offenses, transgressed with your struggles. What a shame. If you pay more attention to what is *right*, you save precious time living rather than suffering. Keep in mind that the goal for healing is to find the joy and perfection that reside within your story. Uprooting memories of suffering or pain is a by-product of that process.

This culturally pervasive question, "What's wrong with you?" is an ideology that prohibits your self-knowing and restricts the full measure of your power. It holds you to the premise that you are flawed. While it is certainly important to acknowledge your imperfections and attend to your misbehavior, this is not the state of mind upon which dreams are built. You must embrace all you are to become all you want to be.

With the generous helping of global challenges that face our generation, it seems only fitting that you be not only encouraged, but also wholly supported, to explore and genuinely exhibit your *rightness*. With that in mind, I encourage you to put much more emphasis on your delight then on your drama.

The Myth of Duality and Healing

The myth of duality is the baseline for our current human story, emphasizing right versus wrong, good versus evil, yin versus yang, science versus spirituality, hero versus villain, etc. In the words of Ram Dass, "The heart surrenders everything to the moment. The mind judges and holds back. Across planes of consciousness, we have to live with the paradox that opposite things can be simultaneously true." Unifying these polarities—a theory that is central to many religious teachings and spiritual systems—is thought to liberate human beings from their own suffering, by bridging God and human, or feminine and masculine, together for the purpose of self-realization and enlightenment.

Our human pendulum has swung from patriarchy to matriarchy many times over as we renegotiate interactions with each other. Most recently, here in America, we have learned to live in a hierarchal system of power in which the ladder is the symbol of achievement. Since only one person can sit at the very top and be triumphant, others vie for power and define strategies for success. This unfortunately leaves the rest dangling off the rungs or complacent with being at the bottom, accepting the consequences, choices, and actions of those above.

When we bring this patriarchal model into Earth consciousness or matriarchal symbolism, the structure changes to a wheel. The circular model of human interaction allows for a group goal or collective vision to be placed in the center, while everyone sits around the wheel, offering wisdom and contributing skill toward a goal that is mutually beneficial. This model takes into consideration all life forms and elements that construct a synchronistical blend for well-balanced living.

Duality is about entitlement and power. And the origin of power is sexual in nature because intercourse—the merging of male and female—is the action of creation. When we are at odds with our self, we can't create or manifest because our masculine and feminine aspects are divided. This is particularly evident in those who parents were argumentative, embittered or opposed to each other.

Children absorb the duality into their bodies and minds, and establish relationships that repeat or mimic their parent's struggles in an effort to heal the duality held within. This struggle then lives on in our marriage, our community, our job, and our children.

Unity is about respect and balance. The old adage "As above, so below" offers the perfect insight for understanding that unity on a spiritual level translates into physical balance. You create a bridge from the myth of duality to personal harmony when you align yourself with heavenly principles that represent unification of the divine masculine and feminine. By identifying with Father Sky/Mother Earth, Jesus/Mary, Buddha/Tara, or whatever spiritual symbols characterize the sacred balance of masculine and feminine for you, wholeness or perfection can be experienced conceptually and energetically. Continually raising your thoughts and dreams to the divine blend will ease your need to act out archaic imprints of duality, and as well to hold them in your body.

The darkness fears the light, and the light fears the darkness. If there is no fear, there is no division. Yet, the darkness needs the light and the light needs the darkness. Otherwise they could not define themselves. They would not know who they are. The journey, then, toward an existence in light, must be through the darkness. There is no other way to accomplish resonance with that which we seek. Pain erupts only when we lose our way, forget our destination, and linger too long in the duality. What a relief to finally break through the confines of dualism and rest at last in the heart of hearts, in the grace of knowing both and choosing one! I imagine it is like kissing the brilliance of a star while surrounded by the dark void of the heavenly sky.

This myth also sets the stage for our modern healing experience—mind versus body. Most of us have been raised in a culture that fractures the aspects of human experience into four quite distinctly different quadrants—physical, emotional, mental, and spiritual. Over time, we have developed a system that encourages this separation by teaching specialized education in one quadrant and relying on professional partners in the other categories to fill in the blanks of knowledge and expertise; e.g., oncologists, psychologists, podiatrists, neurologists.

This myth of human division has also created the platform for the healing of our story: most of us proceed down the road of recovery acting as if we can only heal one aspect of ourselves at a time, or assuming that we are not educated enough to trust our own instincts without the assistance of a trained professional, or believing that *our* story has nothing to do with *their* story, or Mother Earth's story, or feeling that we are, in fact, not whole. And so the myth is perpetuated.

In alignment with this mythical system, we manifest body splits that separate our right side from our left side, above from below, physicality from luminosity, and mind from affliction. We are afraid to link our intuition to our power, or our past to the present time. The big picture gets lost in the fractionalization, and we disregard our relationship not only to our bodies, but also to the Earth as a primary measure of wholeness.

> *Viewing our bodies and the Earth as mirrors of one another, they suggest that the extremes witnessed in one may be considered metaphors for changes within the other. This thinking relates destructive weather patterns and storms, for example, to the unsettled consciousness of people where the storms occur. At the same time, such holistic views suggest that the extremes of earthquakes, life-threatening storms, and disease may be eased, or even eradicated through subtle shifts in our belief system.*
>
> —Gregg Braden, *The Isaiah Effect*

Wholeness happens when we begin to unite our dualistic parts, consciously merging hemispheres of our brain, blending left and right into the centerline of our bodies, or, on a larger scale, observing Earth changes as they parallel our diagnoses and spiritual awakening. Simple somatic awareness skills, augmented by prayer and intuition, allow us to get out of the way of needing to *know how* to blend ourselves with our world or our story, and then we can simply *allow* the inborn rhythms of our body wisdom to dominate our healing experience and bypass our fractured conditioning.

My Story as a Healer

While being trained as a body worker and certified massage therapist in the late 1970s and early 1980s, I was instructed not to cross the line between mind and body, or spirit and body, or emotion and body—to pass the baton of healing should anything happen outside the scope of my training. I soon learned that this was a very fuzzy line indeed. This line continued to get exceedingly blurry as clients prayed during sessions, or cried when parts of their bodies were touched, or recalled traumatic events while unwinding certain muscle groups.

I felt stymied by this invisible therapeutic line, but instead of scaring me off, it encouraged curiosity. Every time that I touched someone's body, I felt, saw, and sensed things that I was not taught to professionally address. It was this curiosity about my clients' stories that pushed me to look under the surface of anatomical structures and into the blueprint of the bones, muscles, and rhythms of the body. I began to recognize the deeper paths of energy, thought, feelings, and history that establish our physical form, and I began touching clients as four-dimensional beings.

I became like a somatic detective, encouraging clients to breathe more deeply and feel consciously into their tissues. As they did so, they began to describe vivid scenes that arose, which then evoked memories and emotional responses, and consequently their muscles relaxed or their headaches went away. At first, it was like something magical was happening, but then this unwinding process—which I came to call Somatic Archaeology—began to follow a pattern and I developed a method.

As the director of a massage school for several years, I witnessed students with abusive touch histories who were drawn to hands-on training to find a way to be in control of touch, to display and learn healthy boundaries, to feel the power deep inside them that had been smothered from overbearing, absent, or violent caretakers. I saw that, as they were being touched in class, the students' memories were erupting like bubbles that had been buried at the bottom of the ocean floor.

When these memories were disregarded or treated with indifference, they perpetuated the myth of division and actually reinforced the students' physical pain and holding patterns. When these memories were honored and addressed, the students developed the ability to feel and understand the stories that had brought them to this day. This knowledge furnished them with the ability to do things differently in their lives. It was as if the remembering allowed them to unlock chains that had bound them to the past—chains that had been completely forgotten!

We do experience very valid physical pain that is real and treatable. But there is also an energetic force that establishes symptoms and feelings that are invisible and intangible. This is sometimes referred to as phantom pain or somaticized pain. The myth of duality assumes that there is no connection between the real and the phantom pain, or between the energetic force and the symptom, yet the myth ceases to exist when we feel the truth of the connection between the individual mind, heart, body, and soul.

This awareness began my passionate journey to educate body workers to enhance their clinical training by including somatic therapy techniques. I codeveloped a national certification program designed to educate massage therapists on how to touch clients who had unhealthy touch histories. I studied with numerous therapists, healers, and indigenous spiritual teachers who offered wisdom, depth, stories, and techniques to help me see through the externalization of symptoms and into the core causes of suffering. I also relied on ancestral wisdom to guide me within, to awaken the scope of my healing work and the fulfillment of my personal destiny.

Eventually I translated thirty years of experience and knowledge as a somatic therapist, holistic student, spiritual seeker, ceremonialist, and educator—and of course as a storykeeper—into the development Somatic Archaeology. The years of hands-on experience allowed me to search beyond what I knew in order to find that which I sensed, felt, and remembered. I then became my own bridge between what I felt and thought, and I began to heal side by side with my clients. This process dissolved the myth of duality even further, allowing me to feel whole again. I found that in myself, as well as in my clients, the blueprint of wholeness was still intact deep inside, despite the reinforced conditioning of the myth of duality. It had simply been buried underneath the rubble of westernized cultural deception.

Consequently, I learned that we do not heal in isolation. We heal in relationship. Every person that I come into a somatic session with becomes a mirror for my process, and I for them, allowing both of us to see more clearly into the underlying causes of symptoms. My joy becomes their joy, and their pain becomes my pain. We share tears, laughter, and emotional intimacy as we recover stories and release them. Afterward, we both feel better and more empowered. Recovery and healing are always reciprocal.

> *I would say that the thrust of my life has been initially about getting free, and then realizing that my freedom is not independent of everybody else. Then I am arriving at that circle where one works on oneself as a gift to other people so that one doesn't create more suffering. I help people as I work on myself and I work on myself to help people.*
>
> —Ram Dass

Here are a couple of stories from my somatic clients who have begun to erase the myth of duality, and therefore mend the stories held within their bodies. As you can tell from reading the stories, the process is effective, compassionate, and sometimes swift, but it requires consistent, repeated, and deliberate attention to digging.

Pam's Story

"I first experienced Somatic Archaeology in May 2007 for chronic pain, which I had felt for years. I had been to massage, chiropractors, and acupuncturists to try to elevate what seemed to be something that I would have to just *live with*. After the first Somatic Archaeology session, which was subtle, I was totally relieved from my pain! I am to this day pain-free. I was so impressed that I went back for another Somatic Archaeology session and although the outcome took some days, my second concern began to dissipate. I believe that Somatic Archaeology has had a profound effect on my journey. It is intuitive, provides a safe place, and guides me through my own healing as can only happen when true openness occurs. The connection that Ruby has access to, and the unspoken allowance of that which can take place with Somatic Archaeology, is all that matters."

Danyel's Story

"I was very seriously abused as a child by my father. I had great success working on the trauma using EMDR (Eye Movement Desensitization and Reprocessing) with another therapist. We were able to get at and clean up the horrors I lived through. But we reached a point where I hit a wall and could not get at this terrible pain in my gut. I searched and searched for help. Then I found Somatic Archaeology.

I started working with Ruby about eighteen months ago. But, time being relative and all, especially when in pain, I'd swear it has been more like a hundred and eighty years. After the first couple sessions I knew *I did not want to work with her anymore*. This is why I have continued to work with her. We were getting to the grief, the terror, the pain, and the rage. It hurt like hell. I wanted to run for the hills. I still had very deeply repressed memories, and every week I wanted to quit, and every week I dragged myself up the mountain to her office.

"There is nothing *magical* about Somatic Archaeology. It is not an easy, painless solution, and it is hard for me to put into words. I have to do the work. It may sound like a never-ending source of hard work and pain, but the opposite is true. The progress of the work done to date has shown up in every part of my life. Eighteen months ago I was in so much emotional pain I was prescribed Vicoden just to take the edge off. I needed 500 mg just to get through a day. Now, if I use 500 mg a week it is unusual.

"My health is better. All areas of my life are better just due to the somatic work we have done so far. Without the help, strength, support, and guidance of Somatic Archaeology, I would not be very functional today. In other words, for the first time in my life, I awaken every morning thrilled to be alive."

Diane's Story

"I've spent forty years learning to integrate and heal from a childhood traumatic event. In the last two years, through the work of Somatic Archaeology, I have found tools to learn how to return to my body and excavate the emotions I still held. When I did this, I was able to express and create movement of those old images, sensations, thoughts, and feelings. In trauma, there is a loss of control and safety. With Somatic Archaeology, I learned how to restore that sense of safety in my body where the trauma lives. Drawing from my own healing, I have learned to translate these tools into my work with clients as a psychotherapist specializing in trauma, loss, and catastrophic illness. I have discovered that therapeutic somatic treatments are more holistic than limited stereotypical *talk* psychotherapies. Somatic Archaeology is vital to restoring so many lives within our culture that are frozen and disconnected by traumatic events."

Sift Through Your Buried Treasure

Somatic information is layered in our bodies much the same way geologic information is layered in the Earth—the most recent experiences are closest to the surface, while the older, more historical experiences are deeper underground. All of these experiences become our stories, and our stories become our reality. Once uncovered, our deeper stories awaken us to the cause and effect of our life choices and dynamics, but we must allow this information to come from the wisdom of our bodies. Uncovering the details and emotional memories does not always happen according to a timeline that makes sense to our brains.

Current symptoms can be linked to past situations, accidents or traumas that we have lost the association to—until we begin to excavate body memory. A client who came to me with a severe case of arthritis in her hands was searching to understand why her body had manifested such painful symptoms. While unearthing memory in her bones and joints, she remembered that as a young woman she had loved to play the piano. When she married, though, her husband wanted her to work and raise their children, which allowed her no time to play or pursue her dream of being a concert pianist. The repressed creative urge and accompanying anger had built up in the joints of her fingers and wrists over the years until she barely had use of her hands at all! Through remembering her passion and tending to her needs and emotions, she was able to reverse some of the symptoms, although it would take her body time to undo the physical damage.

Sifting through the treasures of your past can be both enlightening and painful. Keep in mind that you dig it up to let it go! Let the past remind you, teach you, and inform you, but don't continue to hold on to it with vengeance, remorse, or resentment. It is important to create change in alignment with the information that is revealed to you, to honor your truth, to forgive, and to use your newfound wisdom to act accordingly.

> *Stories set the inner life into motion, and this is particularly important where the inner life is frightened, wedged, or cornered. Story greases the hoists and pulleys, it causes adrenaline to surge, shows us the way out, down, or up, and for our trouble, cuts for us fine wide doors in previously blank walls, openings that lead to the dreamland, that lead to love and learning, that lead us back to our own real lives as knowing wildish women.*
>
> —Clarissa Pinkola Estes, *Women Who Run With The Wolves*

It is an archaeological prerequisite to tread lightly. As you uncover treasures, you must handle them carefully, dust them off lovingly, and become a witness to all that has transpired. Do not disregard artifacts because they are small or seem insignificant. Do not dig something up and be in a big hurry to discard it. All memories hold value. Take your time to examine them carefully and welcome their contributions to your landscape. Each piece is important and holds clues that may very well lead you to another treasure.

The origin of a treasure may be clear or unknown. It is not necessarily important, in a therapeutic context, to reveal the full trail of history at once. It is nice to have lucid and rational memories emerge intact, but as with dreams, somatic information erupts from the subconscious. It comes in fragments and waves of impulses, most especially if there has been lying, deceitful or covert behaviors, or if traumatic events have split up a familial or tribal system.

Strong fearful experiences can also cause memories to fragment, and therefore you may be digging up one piece at a time. Be patient with yourself as you put your puzzle back together. Write the memory fragments down to help make sense of them. Your body's wisdom allows you to unearth various aspects of a memory according to your innate capacity to integrate the information. This is a welcome safety mechanism. Faster is not better in Somatic Archaeology. As you dig, you will begin to feel more competent with the excavation tools, you will trust yourself more, and your nervous system will decompress, allowing deep-rooted experiences to surface.

Some memories have been embodied for centuries or generations, and therefore it may also take some time for those treasures to be fully excavated. Your mind may remember fragments of memories, depending upon your age when an event occurred and the severity of the circumstances, but you will not always consciously be aware of treasures that are inherited from your family members. Memories can be so deeply entrenched in your psyche or life that they seem commonplace; they are just accepted as part of life.

It may also be that a treasure is from a different time line or has been carried over from your spiritual lineage, and these memories can be hard for our conscious minds to decipher because they do not make sense in the here and now. Or it could be that past experiences have translated into physical symptoms, as in the story above about the woman with arthritis. Emotional experiences do not somaticize overnight. They can take years or even generations to embody.

Historical Amnesia

When you suppress or forget where you've come from, you cork up a very turbulent and explosive energy that ripples in many directions. Historical amnesia creates inner pressure and external conflict as your soul demands self-expression but your heritage demands compliance. This dynamic is the source of most generational suffering. Often, you receive love and acceptance within compliance, but your unique self-expression threatens the mold. Most of the time, we instinctively choose love and acceptance and follow in the footprints of our grandmothers and grandfathers.

You may experience inherited obligations and patterns in many forms, finding that you are predisposed to certain lifestyles, diets, relationship patterns, customs, and ideas. Your body memory establishes a concept or belief about reality, inhibiting your ability to experience life in a new or different way. When you crave change and try to find your own path, you are really seeking to exhibit your true destiny—one that is not clouded or compromised by the expectations of others.

It takes courage to break the mold. Change is often scary and challenging because the memories, the secrets, and the subtle designs do not want to be exposed. Therefore, we can stay stuck in these dynamics in order not to challenge the status quo, and then we cease to progress. Fear of confronting old models makes it is difficult to advance, and instead we adapt and forget. Historical amnesia then anchors us into the very thing we attempt to avoid—repeating history.

One evening at a book signing for *Between the Stars,* by Deborah Santana, I had the opportunity to listen to the author's famous husband, Carlos Santana, introduce her. He spoke about how his wife had kept him on track over the years, and how they had grown together—and then he told a story. He said that he had a friend who had always baked a ham in a small square pan, cutting the edges of the ham to fit it in the pan. When Carlos asked why she did it that way, the woman replied that her mother and her grandmother always did it this way. So they went to her grandmother and inquired why this was an important tradition. Grandmother answered, "Well, when I was young, we were poor. And we only had one baking pan. So we would have to cut the ham to fit in the pan. I guess we've been doing the same thing ever since!"

The moral of the story? Sometimes we continue to do things just because it is a tradition, even if it is based on poverty, loss, or fear. We need to look carefully at what we are doing and why, questioning our actions to be sure that we are doing things for the right purpose. It may be time to change the story.

Change the Big Story

If the drama being playing out on our planet right now is a reflection of our personal stories, then the key to changing the big story is the healing of our individual stories—reconciling injustice, anointing wounds, recognizing power, finding forgiveness, and becoming whole. This takes vision and dedication. Building our global society into a world of harmonious and peaceful living is the work of all people. Waiting for others to change, for governments to ally, for family disputes to end, or for war to stop before we change our stories is foolish.

Nothing changes unless we change. Unearthing the source of our limitations and predisposed beliefs gives us the opportunity to make a conscious choice about what we decide to carry forward—or leave behind. We perpetuate the healing of our families and communities as we reconcile the past and get to know ourselves fully, bringing unresolved historical challenges full circle to present time.

One of my clients wrote the following poem about her healing journey. The story of her healing journey helps give perspective to the *bigger* picture of healing and the process of Somatic Archaeology. It is each person's responsibility to resolve their own story and add to the beauty and harmony of the global story.

Cathy's Story

Who I Have Been
I have been lost, misguided, disconnected from Spirit.
Wanderer. Chameleon. Whatever you want me to be.
Uncommitted. Unconvinced. Faithless.
Seeker only of pleasure.
Selfish. Dishonest. Judgmental.
A wallower in fear and drama and self-pity.
Angry. Controlling. A master manipulator.
Resentful. Self-righteous. Finger pointer.
Immobilized by perfectionism.
Unwilling to change.
Distraught by comparison of myself to others.
I have been a self-loather with delusions of grandeur.
A giant head rolling around without connection to its body or spirit.
Quick to love. Quicker to run. Fair-weather friend.
An isolator, dictator, procrastinator.
Thoughtless, spineless mimic.
Needy seeker of attention.

Who I Am
I am a seeker of truth.
In transition. Hesitant. Often reluctant.
I am clean and sober.
Opening. Clearing. Filtering light.
I am a seeker of connection. With Self. With Spirit. With others.
I am seeking, but sometimes hiding.
I am awakening, emerging, testing.
I am asking, listening, trusting.
I am willing.
I am an observer, a learner, a server, a nurturer.
I am sometimes lost in my past, sometimes my future.
Yet, I am a believer in the present.
I am strong, then weak.
Certain, then confused.
Peaceful, then irritable.
Open, then shut down.

I am the surveyor and miner of my Spirit and Self.
Measuring, searching, chinking away.
I am making room.
Grateful for the space that is created and for the space that is held.
I am sister, daughter, friend, student, teacher, worker.
Seeker of more accurate definitions of these roles.
I am learning to focus.
I am expanding.
I am hopeful.

Who I Will Be
I will be whole. Full of light and spirit and love.
Confident, certain of myself, connected to Spirit.
I will be a seeker, a creator, an artist.
A dancer, a singer, a comedian, a teacher, and a healer.
I will be a truth-teller, a beacon for Spirit, a keeper of wisdom.
I will be a fearless friend and lover,
A woman of integrity, a person who is honest.
I will be a champion for the downtrodden, a protector of animals,
A worshipper of Mother Earth and all of her gifts.
A reverent grower of life, of flowers and trees and food.
I will live in the present moment, show compassion for all of my brothers and sisters, respect each person's truth and life exactly as it is.
I will forgive at all costs, give love without hesitation, and accept love willingly.
I will be grateful, humble, inspired, enthusiastic.
Giving, gracious, playful.
I will laugh, and laugh, and laugh some more.
I will listen with an open heart.
I will let Spirit guide me.
I will speak my truth to all who will hear.
I will feel my feelings, and I will belong.

Reconcile Your Story

Every story has a twist. The Earth spirals and bends her story every day as weather patterns come and go. Floods change the landscape, fires burn old forests, winds sweep debris from the sky and trees, and earthquakes shake our foundation. The same thing happens inside of us. Our emotions flow and cleanse our hearts, anger burns up our fears, thoughts remodel the design of our lives, and our bodies continually replace cells that alter our structure. Our bodies are adapting to circumstance each moment as we meander through our story lines.

These variations in the story line are accelerated moments when reconciliation can most easily be achieved because movement is already occurring. Accelerated moments typically occur during beginnings and endings—human cycles such as births, deaths, unions, divorces, moves, graduations, or retirement changes; and Earth or celestial cycles such as seasons, solstices, equinoxes, eclipses, and moon phases. You can use these energetically charged times to your benefit to come into relationship with your story in a new way that impacts your ability to rationalize the series of events that led you to this moment. This allows you to catch sight of how your life could be different. Yearn to free yourself, to feel vitality, to follow your bliss—and this yearning will eventually become stronger than the grip of fear.

Reconciliation can be described as the friendly end to a dispute, but in Somatic Archaeology, an internalized conflict is over when you find the power to imagine a difference, or change, in the outcome. Reframe your memories by imagining that you get what you need, that you succeed, or that you find your way to safety. In your mind's eye, visualize that events come out in your favor. Doing this during accelerated times multiplies your efforts.

Many clients ask me, "Can you guarantee me that if I let go of this old story, the new one will be better?"

My answer is always, "No. There are no guarantees in life. Trust that your story is unfolding according to plan, and that it has been choreographed specifically for your learning and evolution. Give yourself permission to dream in something new. And then the only question left to ask is, 'If you truly love yourself, what would you do right now?'"

You know. It all comes down to love. Feeling love for yourself and your journey is reconciliation. Love is something you know inside and feel in your entire being, regardless of other circumstances. Love is something permanent. It never goes away. It may get clouded over with fear or anger or jealousy; nevertheless, it still stays true under the fog. Love will bring out the best in you, and probably the worst. Love may be apparent right away, or you may take years to recognize it, but when all is said and done, love is what stands out, what is illuminated, what is remembered.

As in Cathy's story, you may vacillate between feeling strong and feeling weak, between wanting something different in your life and wanting to continue with the familiar. A story can become so much a part of your life that you can forget how you felt without it. Therefore, repeated excavations in one area of your body may be required for full reconciliation. Each time you dig, you will find more pieces, expose more details, and gain more understanding. Eventually, you will change the configuration of the archaeological site. Then traveling to it and exploring it will no longer carry the emotional charge that it once did. A memory never goes away completely, but unearthing and embracing it can change how it impacts you, and can modify the influence it holds over your life.

A young woman who came to see me revealed that her father had frequently put a gun to her head. When I displayed shock, she explained that it was such a normal occurrence in her family that she did not consider it a traumatizing experience. It was how things were done in her family, and she did not, yet, have the perspective to recognize how dangerous or horrific her father's behavior was. She had been living under duress for so many years that she had grown accustomed to violence.

To completely free herself, she allowed her bones, muscles, and tissues to have a voice, to speak their horror, to raise their objections, to plead for their freedom, and most of all, to wake up. Then, it was important to find a memory that encapsulated respect and safety to her. She found it buried under her fear. Once she unearthed it, she could reconcile her pain because she had something with which to replace the fear.

I received the following note from a client who is a Vietnam veteran. For Ron, reconciliation was his acknowledgement of the pain. He was able to remedy the anger and hurt he felt toward his father by honoring and loving his son. He changed the pattern, and hence began to heal the deeper wound. Shifting his perspective was a bold and necessary step for him to move from being a victim of circumstance to an empowered, vital carrier of history. This occurred because Ron allowed himself to feel and remember his story, to understand it and to change.

Ron's Story

"I have done a lot of reflecting and looking at my motives about my father. As you know, any continued behavior becomes a pattern, and with a pattern, there are paybacks, emotionally and spiritually. My anger toward my father has become part of my identity, and hence I have to look at why.

"Frustration about getting my needs met by him; his lack of acceptance of my love; fear because I won't have any relationship with him if I let the negative feelings go; these are some of the reasons. My anger indicates that that I am still not taking care of myself. I am thankful for my Somatic Archaeology session with you; I left feeling and believing I had been mentored. I have spent thousands on some serious programs that did not help me.

"Enclosed is a simple poem that I wrote for my son after his first tour from Iraq. When you read it the first time, please read it out loud. Sincerely, Ron."

"This has been a long, grueling day and night ... two years and one month. All the feelings on the spectrum have been felt. When I felt despair and helplessness, your knowing that I love you pulled me through. When I was lonesome, imagining your smile and touch filled me with joy. I clutched you hard some times. At times the fear was overwhelming but your confidence and honesty brought me peace. Sadness has been a real struggle as I have watched you mature through the eyes of war. War is so ugly, pathetic and shameful. You have witnessed war's constant companions: lust and pestilence! Yet you still see the good in humankind. A cliché, yet a truth: words alone cannot express my gratitude, my pride, and especially my love for you. Knowledge: you are not alone! A promise: I honor your service to your family and country. I will honor the scars on your heart—as warriors, this is the only way we can raise each other up. Ours is an endless patrol. Never forgetting we are blessed because our tears are the large tears of joy, of happiness ... and not the small bitter tears of heartbreak and sorrow. Thank you for staying alive! I have often thought that some of the most profound blessings by word are: I love you or love one another or peace be unto you. But today you quietly said: Dad, I'm home."

I let go of what I think to remember what I know.
Descend the dusty steps of yesterday to find my memory flow.
I rummage in the darkest spots, sift through broken dreams
Cascading like some liquid jewels that decorate my stream.

The darkness shudders as I set my illumination free.
Shaking off what holds me back from stepping into me.
Tattered remnants fill the cave as I burrow in my Earth.
I cradle relics I have known, shedding tears that hide my worth.

Knowing love transcends the fear, I travel toward my heart.
Hearing whispers of the ancients that were here from the start
I am much more than I can know in this archaic light.
Their pain, their joy, their struggles have now become my plight.

The burden of these artifacts is one I have employed

But woven in my essence is the strength I have enjoyed.
I meet myself with courage and embrace this shadow side
Surrendering resistance to my familial tide.

Circular now, with no beginning and no end,
I sense the structure and the blueprint that have become my blend.
My imprints I acknowledge, my karma I digest
Bringing memories full circle that hence I choose to bless.

I think I know what ought to be, I know I think too much.
Ascending from my murky depths, I recognize love's touch.
Nothing more I need to know, heart rhythm now my voice,
Filling me from the inside out, wholeness is my choice.

—Ruby Gibson, original poem

2
Somatic Storykeeping

If you don't know the trees you may be lost in the forest, but if you don't know the stories you may be lost in life.

—Siberian Elder

One of the most important functions of our bodies is to be the custodian of stories. Our tales are legends that give us direction and help us to feel real. We organize ourselves around them. They also fuel our passion and give meaning to our days. We never move or think or dream without them. When told with respect, stories can honor the characters and imbue delight into the storyteller. When shared as gossip, they dishonor the characters and breed contempt, jealousy, and mistrust in the storyteller.

Somatic storytelling is a sacred job. When you tell your stories, the ones you find deep within the veins of your life, be sure you speak kindly about your ancestors and your relatives. Find their goodness and emphasize it—tell their story as if it is your story. If you must speak of suffering, tell the story with a moral, or with a lesson learned, or with an unexpected turn of fate that helps to reframe the pain. And, of course, seek the spirit of the story by developing objectivity, looking at it through the eyes of an eagle as well as through the eyes of the mouse. Perspective is essential.

One of my dear friends and students had been in the Vietnam War as a Special Operations soldier. He went on very precarious and risky missions. He lived in the jungle for days and weeks at a time, surrounded by danger—jungle rot, leeches, scorpions, poisonous snakes, booby traps, and the most dangerous threat, the North Vietnamese (NVA) soldiers. He survived where many did not, and I applaud his courage for telling his sacred story.

Rey's Story

"The whole dirty business about war is killing. About 2 percent of all the people in a line infantry company (one hundred and thirty men) are trigger pullers—the ones that do the actual killing. But in Special Operations, all of them have to be proficient in the art because members are few on the team and you have to use automatic fire to maximize the amount of targets you are putting down at one time. In other words, you have to be good enough to write your name with your weapon. I was very good at it.

"When I got home, I processed out of the service at Oakland Army Terminal, a joint's ride from Berkley, the Mecca of the antiwar movement. Coming out of the terminal July 4, 1968, we were pounded by tomatoes and other refuse. After getting to the San Francisco Airport, three of us who had served together were assaulted by five bullies who felt we needed a good ass-kicking for killing babies in Southeast Asia. We turned it around but we decided to let them live.

"I think that was the start of my downward spiral into what we call PTSD. I felt a huge loss and alienated, a victim of emotional circumstances of which I had no control. I tried college. My hair was short and my peers seemed to have a radar sense of who I was and where I had been. It seemed to center around big guys that used violence in football to take out their aggression and then being justified to challenge my involvement in 'The War.' This took the form of verbal threats of physical violence. They would be thinking of beating the shit out of me and I would be trying to figure out how to take them out … forever. Scary thoughts for their life expectancy and my mental state.

"I had one particular nightmare that was my constant companion since the day it happened. One day before the start of the 1968 Tet Offensive, we were handed an ambush mission on the approaching trails to our base camp and the small city of Song Be, a stone's throw from the Cambodian border. As we were walking to the ambush site we were forced by the terrain to step onto a trail. My friend Superspade was walking point and I was his slack man. As I got into the dogleg of the trail, I heard a distinct 'pssst-pssst' and two Vietnamese words, and then I saw a smiling NVA (North Vietnamese Army) soldier calling me in.

"He thought I was his friend and I was chewing on my heart. Time went into extreme slow motion. I put a clump of bamboo between us, balanced myself, and came around the bamboo. We were so close that I could see a progression of emotions transform his face and eyes—panic, fear, and the realization he had called in his own death. I knew it was either him or me. We were looking into each other's eyes. As he was raising his rifle, I fired a burst and ended his life. At that exact moment, I sensed this strong exchange of energy. I had shot other people but not like this. It quickly turned into an eight-yard heated firefight as fourteen men blazed away at each other.

"After the firefight, I check his body and picked up his sandals, which he had been blown clean out of. I felt a sense of deep loss. After returning home, this same nightmare would haunt me: the smiling NVA soldier and I would see each other, and we would both raise our rifles, but when I would shoot, only a drop of water would come out the barrel of my gun. I would see these cherry blossoms of fire come out of his barrel and just as I was feeling the bullets thudding into me, I would awake in a drenched, panicked sweat.

"For almost thirty-nine years I had this dream. At first it would come about five days a week but as time went on I committed myself to a healing journey which involved Earth-centered healing techniques, sweat lodge ceremonies, and raising my children. My dreams reduced to about three or four times a month. When I began doing Somatic Archaeology my burden and story was revealed and released. What I recognized was that in the process of our exchange that day, I had picked up what I call a 'dead hitchhiker.'

"When I allowed myself to remember the incident (and this was not easy, it took me a few attempts), I could sense his spirit and the indelible traces of the trauma that bound us together. This process of remembering allowed me to speak with him in Vietnamese, which I don't speak. He told me his name, where he was from, and that he had a son he never got to know, and the sadness and anguish he had because he had called in his own death. He was young. He had thought I was a friend.

"There was something very healing about being able to talk to him. I was able to break the spiritual contract I had made with him to kill him, and allowed myself to feel the grief I was holding. Since that Somatic Archaeology session, I have not had this dream again. It was a very healing process for me. I can sleep now and my PTSD is better. I don't feel the heaviness in the back of my heart like I used to. For years I thought I had a serious heart problem, for which I took a series of tests to determine if I had heart problems. Every time it came back clean. It was a somatic memory. I know it now and I am grateful for my good friend Ruby."

Author and trauma specialist, Robert Scaer, MD, explains, "The military trains men into a pathological state. Soldiers learn to dissociate productively. During a manufactured freeze response, shock is analgesic (numbing) allowing one to continue survival skills. Trauma capsules store information in the brain as repressed memory for future use, and are reflected in the body's motor patterns, smell, and visual responses. Hard-wired cues cause the memory of an event to emerge as an emotionally charged flashback. You can't heal trauma with words alone. You have to include things somatic in nature."

Pain in your body and suffering in your soul are the result of a story that has simply gone underground and needs to be revitalized. Wake up your stories; let them breathe and shake them out. Good or bad, wicked or innocent, loving or toxic, you have done a good job holding them, but now is the time to bring them into the light of day. That is the essence of sacredness in storytelling—by releasing and healing each story within, you also bless it. And you bless the others in your story because it helps them to heal, too.

As a storykeeper you will want to honor and keep track of the stories that surface from the folds of your soma. Organize them to help you remember, and as well to pass the stories onto your children, friends, or family. You can chronicle your somatic stories according to age, prioritize them according to intensity or their ability to illuminate, or categorize them according to cycles.

Chronicle Your Stories

Draw a timeline of your life from birth to present time. Fraction out the line into yearly segments, or design it according to the cycles of your life. It is common to have seven-year or ten-year cycles. As you highlight the events in your life that stand out, you will be able to see the cyclical patterns more clearly.

You will need a large sheet of paper for this—either off a roll of butcher paper or by taping standard size paper together to create a long strip. Begin by marking the day of your birth, and then continue down the timeline noting important experiences and their corresponding dates all the way to the present.

Align with the mouse-eye view and be sure to scrutinize your story. Chronicle little things and big things—births, anniversaries, losses, deaths, marriages, moves, and professional highlights. And then include less well-known data such as rites of passage—when you went to prom, lost your virginity, ran away from home, told your first lie, did a vision quest, or began your spiritual journey. Accidents, traumas, religious holidays, vacations, and auspicious occasions are very important, so include them as well. Be sure to gather information from what your mind remembers *and* what your body remembers, as both are valid in this process.

Notice any patterns that emerge. What stands out to you? Are there any blank segments on the timeline when you had no memory? When do the segments of concentrated events occur? Are there any annual or seasonal repetitions in your timeline? What did you forget to include? The answers to these questions can help you to piece together the fragments of your past and make sense of occurrences. It helps to objectify your experiences and get the bird's-eye view of your story.

If you are an ambitious storykeeper, it would be valuable then to match this up with your children's, parents', or grandparents' timelines to find any corresponding similarities or patterns to help you follow the trail of history. Notice any place in your body that gets triggered or anxious as you do this. If this happens, those areas of your body are probably holding underground memories that are seeking resolution. Go to the Five Steps of Somatic Archaeology to begin excavating your story by focusing on those particular areas of your body.

Sacred Stories

Sacred stories always flow in circles. Many of the stories your body holds are spiritual in nature, transcending time and space and bringing past and present experiences full circle. Round and round, these stories are represented symbolically and mythically in each person, and come with a sense of soul infusion, embodying your spirit's legacy and creative potential.

Remembering your sacred stories help you witness your fate consciously. When you act on purpose, your life force feeds and organizes all the other parts of you into a functional system. When you are spiritually aligned and inspired, a rebirth occurs that is explained as a movement from your karmic path to your dharmic path, manifesting a personal renaissance that is nurtured by alignment with Earth-centered flows. It has its own rhythm and cannot be forced, but rather is nurtured with prayer, meditation, and ceremony.

> *Be still until the waters clear.*
> *Do nothing until the darkness ends.*
> *Rest until the storm clouds pass.*

Wait for winter's breath to die.
Nature does not fight against itself
Nor does it dance when the music ends.

—Ute poem

Karma is a Hindu and Buddhist philosophy described as fate, by which the quality of an individual's life is predetermined by his or her behavior in this and previous lives. Karma is all the issues that you are confronted with in your lifetime—those things that you *have* to work with. Dharma, on the other hand, is the truth about the way things really are in the universe and in nature, and it defines those things that you *want* to work with. Karma is your familial and ancestral path of recovery; dharma is your spiritual path of purpose. Waking up sacred stories assists you to reframe your karma and step into your destiny.

The distinctive design of your sacred stories is also influenced by ancestral prophecies that create a semblance of higher order and compliance to sacred law—the rules that govern harmonious interaction amongst spirits, planets, and the cosmos. As you awaken spiritually, you alter your blueprint in a way that resonates with creative and mystical patterns, helping you to breathe life into global dreams of peace. Utilizing the wisdom and traditions of your ancestors makes sense as we prepare for future Earth changes. The circle of life is the circle of healing, and encompasses all. Everything we do has a cause and an effect. We are all related.

My Sacred Story

"At the turn of the 1900s, my great-grandmother and great-grandfather were living in northern New England, near the Canadian border, or so I am told. As the story goes, my great-grandfather went off to war and returned with syphilis, which was never treated and so he died soon thereafter. My great-grandmother was left alone to care for their two-year-old daughter. Out of grief and despair, she was arrested for drunkenness and lewdness, and placed in prison. Their daughter, my grandmother, was taken into social services and handed over to a Catholic convent to be raised by nuns.

"When my grandmother was seventeen, she was set loose, unprepared, into society. Years of rebellion at her strict Catholic upbringing were unleashed, and she soon got pregnant. The father of the baby died a few months after conception in a car accident, and she was left to birth and raise a child alone in a community that outwardly shamed unwed mothers. Life was hard, my grandmother got sick and she could not get a job. She met a man who wished to marry her, although he would not accept her child. So with a broken heart, she gave up her little son for adoption. Hence, the circle of history repeated itself.

"A distant family member and his wife who were unable to conceive took in the boy and made him their own son. As it was also socially unacceptable to be infertile or to adopt a child, the couple decided to tell the boy that he was their real son, and they went to great lengths to establish this, formulating stories about the conception and delivery and forging the birth certificate with their names.

"My father was raised by this loving and dedicated couple in a small New England town, and by all means and purposes, he led a charmed and simple life full of friends and family, playing in the rivers and farmlands. It was only when he was sixteen years old and overheard his mother and a friend discussing the fact that he was adopted, that his buried memories and feelings erupted. His heart became troubled and his anger flared.

"My father died when he was fifty-five years old from alcoholism. He served in the Korean War, came home, married my beautiful mother, and had four children. But the tragic heaviness of his past could not allow his soul to rest. My parents divorced and then my father remarried twice again. He was a charismatic and gregarious man, smooth at business but smoother at lying. Over his adult years, he dug himself into a hole of deception and remorse that fueled his addictions and distanced him from the people he loved.

"I cherished him despite the craziness and depression that whirled around him. It was as if the generations of loss and suffering that preceded him got lodged in his great big heart, and he did not have the skills or resources to heal the pain. As a young woman, I did my best to help him through suicidal episodes and ruptured conversations, but I did not know about his past. He had kept it a secret.

"By the time I had the ability to somatically excavate my story, my father and his relatives who held the fragments of historical truth were gone. This sacred story was revealed only through my brother and I searching the social services system paper trails, and through excavating my body for the emotional imprints and deep seated memories that I had inherited from him.

"Through years of exploring my childhood story, following the emotional trails of grief and abandonment in my body, I have been able to uproot and reconcile not only my pain, but also the suffering of my father and his ancestors. It has been a long and seemingly endless task that has resulted in the sweetest gifts and the capacity for unconditional love for all that transpired.

"Breaking this cycle of suffering could not have been done without the help of my siblings, but mostly I owe an enormous amount of gratitude to my mother, whose steady, gracious, and forgiving heart has been a beacon of hope in the misty sea of my emotions. She has endured so much with strength and positive energy. Her contributions and support have been immeasurable, and without her, I would not have had the capacity to bring myself full circle in healing this part of my story. She taught me to love myself and, consequently, to love my story."

When I first decided to pursue healing work at the age of thirteen, I asked myself a question: "Where would I make the biggest impact?" I thought about the plight of whales and about homeless people. I considered environmental advocacy and the rain forests. I wanted to help orphaned children or become a spokesperson for indigenous land rights. I reflected on helping those with addictions. All of these grabbed at my heartstrings, but when I looked at the origin of each of these issues (as any good somatic archaeologist would), I found that a pervasive lack of respect was the underlying cause that perpetuated suffering and destruction in the world.

I determined that if I garnered respect for my story, I would more easily respect my family and their story; and if I respect my family's story, then I will respect the story of others, and if I respect another's story, then I will respect my environment, and if I respect my environment, then I will respect all life. It was decided. Self-respect and mutual respect were the goals.

As I matured as a healer, the idea of respect mutated into many things—admiration, compassion, reverence, and, of course, the polar opposites, intolerance, resentment, anger, and apathy for healings I initiated and traumas I witnessed. I think I have felt every emotion imaginable through the somatic excavations of others and myself. I have screamed and cried and laughed uncontrollably. I have gone to the deepest wells of suffering and have climbed peaks of enchantment. I have prayed and I have prayed and I have prayed some more.

I have sometimes lost sight, but more often, I have been strong. You see, I am a sacred storykeeper. I always keep the light at the end of the tunnel as my guide and teacher. I have awakened my stories, my mother's and father's stories, my grandparents' and great-grandparents' stories, and, progressively, my spiritual stories. I have remembered for myself, for my children, my clients, and my community. But now, at fifty years of age, I believe I have found the most sacred story of all. Now I remember Mother Earth's story, for the journey she has taken, and for the wholeness that exists despite the chaos that abounds. Her story ushers in infinite respect for the creation of this beautiful world and the gift of life. What a remarkable place we have to remember and evolve!

> *The warmth of spring melts into the weariness of winter.*
> *I stand patient, ready to bloom,*
> *abandoning last year's style for something a little simpler.*
> *Yellow petals, perhaps?*
> *With a center so black that even I can't find the bottom?*
> *I fear myself.*
> *No, actually, I fear my potency. It rumbles in the blackness,*
> *ready at any moment to show its face and swallow me whole.*
> *I thaw into my destiny.*
>
> —Ruby Gibson, original poem

3

Remember and Embrace Your Past

There is no agony like bearing an untold story inside of you.

—*Maya Angelou*

Each emotion or somatic sensation we experience has a reference point inside us, and speaks to us in energetic terms referred to as vibration. Vibration is the foundational basis for all existence. Sound, color, thought, aroma, food, weather, language, water, fire—all things have a vibration that may be measured, heard, touched, and even seen under the right circumstances, but for the most part, vibration is invisible to the five senses of humans.

Vibration establishes the energetic blueprint of the life force. It is the atmosphere of the invisible. We sense it and respond to it every day; it comes in the form of feelings, intuition, hunches, and memories, yet it defies words or explanation. The entirety of nature speaks this silent language as a dialogue of formlessness. Each world responds to the other, animal to plant, plant to water, water to Earth, Earth to air, air to human, all without uttering one single word. And yet there is a cohesive movement, an unseen intelligence that guides the interaction of all species.

> *There is a voice that doesn't use words.*
>
> —Rumi

Learning to communicate in the atmosphere of the invisible is vital to recalling stories from the past. Memories do not have a voice; they are written in your heart, coded in your cells, dancing in your psyche, dense with emotional energy. The secret to accessing them is to listen with your sixth sense, which is anchored in your soma and designated by your personal blueprint. It is cleverly organized and perfectly designed by the intelligence of creation.

The journey into the atmosphere of the invisible is at once profound and simple, and it is the greatest teacher we have. It can inform you of everything you wish to know about your story, your legacy, your past, and your future. It can also take you into spiritual realms, and into the magical realms of Earth. When you awaken your stories, you enter a world of mystical emotional communication that bypasses the complexity of our human minds. The doorway into the atmosphere of the invisible is your body, and it is from here that you can soar, and remember, and find the truth of your existence.

> *… it's human feeling and emotion that affect the stuff our reality is made of—it's our inner language that changes the atoms, electrons, and photons of the outer world. However, this is less about the actual words we utter and more about the feeling that they create within us. It's the language of emotion that speaks to the quantum forces of the universe …*
>
> —Gregg Braden, *The Divine Matrix*

A Skill for Life

Many people are willing to go into the atmosphere of the invisible and decipher information for you. Although this may give you some insight, there is greater value in accessing this information for yourself. It may take some time and effort to establish the skills to see with your other eyes, or to hear with your other ears, or to feel with all your senses, but it is well worth the investment.

Other people can give you their interpretations, but they will be jaded by their own stories, their own beliefs, and their own fears. If you have the desire to seek within, you as much as any other person have the capacity and ability to access the unseen simply because you have a body and a spirit. The tools are here in this book. Empower yourself to remember your own story and find your own truth. In the long run, no one can really do it for you. No one can feel your feelings for you. Remembering is an essential life skill for every person on the planet, especially during these times of fast-paced evolutionary awakening.

Global Remembering

Memory can be intensely personal, but certain events and eras become shared memory. Familial encounters, communal exchanges, and global happenings all define us in unique ways. They set the stage for relationship dynamics, construct human laws and rules, dictate appropriate action, and link us irrevocably together. When we remember our collective past—community or tribal stories, environmental disasters, or war—we engender meaning in our own lives. We preserve these memories like treasures and cling to them for significance because they remind us of who we are, those we have lost, and where we have been, and they give us structure.

These ancient treasures reveal the shadow and light of humanity and the deep historical roots underlying our own lives. Our forbearers teach us ingenuity and creativity through our memories, creating a trail for evolution. By studying our collective relics, we learn about the traditions of ancient peoples and the values expressed through their artistic symbols, their use of ritual and spiritual ceremonies to fortify kinship, their connection to the Earth and her rhythms, their development of technologies, and the religious and prophetic consequences of their lives.

We remember our history to keep the fires alive. It has been told said that the most important job in any tribe was to carry the fire or coal from camp to camp, because fire allowed for the group's survival. Without the fire keeper, all would perish. Spiritually speaking, keeping that fire aglow translates into keeping the story or heartbeat of a culture from being extinguished. Prophecies are passed down through generations as sacred protected words, and visions are alive as stories in invisible books; they are not always translated in a precise, linear way.

Traditions, myths, and spiritual ways of life are remembered through symbols, sounds, visions, artwork, songs, legends, and through the rhythm of the heartbeat of Mother Earth. The voices of our past lead us into our future. They are both predestined and continually cocreated. Prophecies are as well the memories of Mother Earth, who is simultaneously evoking her intelligence and remembering alongside us, unraveling her pain and finding her balance.

All around the globe, in all cultures and in all facets of our lives, we are confronted with our deepest fears and are asked to be crusaders of our own inner revolution. Under the proverbial microscope of self-reflection, we are acutely aware, now more than ever before, of the imbalance that has evolved through our species, and our individual contribution to this state of affairs. Consequently, we become cognizant of our heightened susceptibility to the backlash of our own actions. Repetitive and unconscious patterns have created an unfolding drama on our planet, and the accountability reflects our stories as a hierarchal mirror of spiritual prophecies.

Spiritual prophecies all lead to the same conclusion: we are in the process of awakening our stories, collectively and, consequently, individually. There is really no way to avoid the great wave of change that, for better or for worse, is revolutionizing our planet and our lifestyle. Although you may feel challenged by the chaos around you, or by your body and the stories within you, this is truly the perfect time to embrace your history. This is certainly not a time to be rigid in your beliefs. It is time to look your fear in the eyes and acknowledge it, let it rattle through your bones and shiver up your spine. Those who chose to remember their stories will have a smoother transition during these changing times.

This awakening can be recognized as the return of the divine feminine—the great pendulum of life swinging back into balance. It denotes a time during which we are weaving instinctual knowledge back into our social fabric. Although we are born through a female human, Earth is our genuine mother, giving us life each day through food, air, water, and shelter. Consequently, it would be safe to say that Mother Earth also has a mother, often referred to as our grandmother or Earth's Mother. And it is her memories—the ancestry of our shared mother—that are emerging through each of us as we excavate our personal stories.

Star Blanket, a Métis shamanic healer, explains, "Earth-based prophecies, designed to bring people together, establish a missing link between many different systems of teaching. It is not an attempt to generate another system of religion or method of healing, but rather creates a world-bridge, allowing diverse beliefs to come together under one roof as a global model for evolution. That universal roof is nature. By employing the wisdom of our collective grandmother, Earth's Mother, we can then create common ground for multi-cultural interaction."

Seven-Generation Memory

Seventh Generation is a precept of the Gayanashagowa, or Great Law of Peace (the constitution of the Haudenosaunee, or Six Nations of the Iroquois Confederacy), in which the chiefs consider the impact of their decisions on seven generations to come.

This spiritual legacy is also reflected in how we store somatic memory. Within your body you hold the stories of seven generations before you, and how you live, think, and behave affects seven generations ahead of you. Therefore, what you heal in the present time you are also healing backward, forward, and horizontally, affecting your ancestors, your children, your great-grandchildren, your immediate family circle, and your tribe or community.

According to Hyemeyohsts Storm in his book *Lightning Bolt*, "The Zero Chiefs were the people who sought to solve the riddle of the language of Space and Time. They would discover the exact measurement of the Earth, the Moon, and the Solar System while they pondered the question of distance ... and for the first time in human history there now existed a language that could describe the invisible. The abstract world could be studied and comprehended by means of mathematics."

The science of numbers, referred to as the Sacred Twenty Count, provides insight into the concept of seven generational healing. According to this system, seven is the number for the Dream of Life, for all things that are made within beauty, or that are broken and thrown away. We look to our past to learn what we have built. The number seven evokes the seven ages of man, the colors of the rainbow, the day god rested, the number of orifices in the human head, the pillars of wisdom, and the seven notes of the diatonic music scale.

When we are healing familial patterns, our body memory reaches back seven generations, but when we are healing global patterns, our body holds memories for eight or nine generations. Eight is the number for all natural laws and the Circle of Law. The eight guides the forming of all that is within the future, and gives us a way to reappear each day. Nine is the spiral, the number for the moon and for movement. The moon moves the tides of the earth and the blood within all living things. Somatically remembering for ten generations or more includes cosmic memories connected to the stars and planets, your higher self, and memories from other timelines and lifetimes.

Access seven-generation memory in your body by slowing time down, allowing your awareness to come into relationship with the pace of your body, your soma. Time is a linear mental construct designed to help you orient and organize your physical and material life. The presence of the clock gave birth to the notion that time lies outside our bodies, yet all of nature, plants and animals alike, is instinctually calibrated by an intrinsic sense of time and movement, and the needs and impulses of their bodies.

Humans have this same inherent ability, which they can activate through their sixth sense. This is the ability to go underneath the awareness of the present moment into the vastness of cellular and somatic memory. Imagine that your body is like a house; the attic is your head (super conscious), the living room is your heart (conscious), and the basement is your belly (subconscious). This is the framework of somatic memory.

You may avoid some rooms in your body because they hold painful memories, while you can more easily occupy other areas. Unearthing seven-generation memory with Somatic Archaeology is like entering the subconscious rooms in your body in order to bring your stories upward into your heart consciousness, and finally into your super conscious to be integrated and assimilated spiritually.

The process of exploring these deeper recesses of your body is available any moment that you choose. Through this exploration, the voices of your past will become familiar again. The genetic potential you are born with is lying dormant within you, waiting to be turned on. Your memories may be vague or distinct, acutely clear with intense emotion, or like distant, archaic feelings.

In the book *Grandmothers Counsel the World*, by Carol Schaeffer, Yupik Grandmother Rita Blumenstein explains, "The past is not a burden. It is a scaffold that has brought us to this day. Within this understanding, we are free to be who we are. We create our lives out of our past and out of the present ... We are our ancestors when we heal ourselves. When we heal ourselves, we also heal Mother Earth and we heal all future generations."

Our ancestors are crying out to "set things right." There is much injustice to attend to. This is the work of all people. It can be done through our bodies and through our hearts. Within each human vessel is the matrix of all creation. As you release your historical obligations, you make room for the future. You now have space to glance forward into a new reality. Imagine that what you choose to awaken, reconcile, and release today ripples out forward for seven generations, and backward for seven generations. What a profound impact one courageous person can have!

The spiritual occupation of this generation is to be the bridge between yesterday and tomorrow. It can be difficult to let go of where you have been until you know where you are going. Your power lies in the present. By bringing your past and your future into this present moment, you expand into your timeline and energetically connect with any emotions, experiences, wisdom, or traumas you have repressed or adopted. When you align properly and accept yourself in totality and with objectivity, then you have the capacity to reconcile your past and to dream about who you are when you are emancipated from suffering.

In his book *The Four Insights*, Alberto Villoldo writes, "In sacred time, the future as well as the past is available to us and everything is happening at once—and we can only dream the world into being from this place of timelessness. As we raise our perception to that of the eagle, we get closer to experiencing this sense of infinity. Rather than waiting for a far-off day in the future when we can recover our original nature and return to Eden, the Earthkeepers say that now is the perfect time to step into infinity and recover our divine self and walk with beauty in the world."

Storing Memories

You may remember the physical details of your historical experiences, but may have forgotten the emotions that went along with them. Sometimes you can have body memories with no pictures at all. Flashbacks may be accompanied by the feelings that were felt at the time, or by visual pictures. Due to factors such as age, dissociative tendencies, or drug/anesthesia use, you may not always remember specific events.

These variables occur because the process of storing memories is complex and very individual. You store different experiences in the right and left halves of your brain. The left brain stores the sequential, logical, language-oriented experience; the right brain stores perceptual, spatial experiences. When you attempt to retrieve right-brain information through left-brain techniques, such as logic and language, you sometimes hit a blank. You are simply not going to remember all stories in a precise, orderly way.

The left brain is logical, theoretical, detail-oriented, factual, communicates with words and language, in tune with present and past, applies to math and science, can comprehend, acknowledges information, perceives through order/pattern, reality-based, forms strategies, pragmatic, goal-directed, and practical.

The right brain is feeling-based, "big picture" oriented, imaginative, communicates with symbols and images, in tune with present and future, philosophical, non-rational, aligns with spiritual beliefs, appreciates, perceives spatially, fantasy-based, presents possibilities, creative, intuitive, and impetuous.

Somatic Archaeology relies on the right side of the brain to evoke generational memories in a non-linear manner. By deactivating your nervous system through deep breathing, aromatherapy, and brain integration (see Breathing Exercise 10 in chapter 7), barriers to memory soften and you can access emotional memories directly without having to detour through your intellect. Your mind is selective, but your body remembers everything. With body memory, it is irrelevant whether your story is real or imagined or historically imprinted. If you find yourself questioning the accuracy of your memories or if you feel that you have been influenced by other people's stories, turn to your body for clarity.

When it comes to memories there is also a big difference between women and men. "Women remember more detail. It is in fact the biggest difference between how men's and women's brains operate," noted John Gabrieli, PhD professor of psychology in the neurosciences program and in radiology at Stanford University. "When people in a brain scanner look at pictures that spark emotion, for instance if they are frightening or tragic, men end up storing the information on the right side of the brain where they can separate the emotion from the details. Women keep the memories on the other side. For women, there is much more of an integration, literally in the brain, physically in terms of brain anatomy, where emotional feelings and emotional memories occur."

As our understanding of the neuroscience of emotion and cognition grows, it is increasingly apparent that the myth of division which branches human behavior into two separate categories—emotion and cognition—is not as clear as previous philosophical and psychological investigations have suggested. The mechanisms of emotion and cognition appear intertwined at all stages of stimulus processing, and their distinction can be difficult. It is also apparent that, much like the study of cognition is divided into different domains, such as memory, attention, and reasoning, the concept of emotion has a structural architecture that may be similarly diverse and complex (Russell & Barrett 1999, Scherer 2000).

Types of Memories

There are many kinds of memories. We have given them names to pacify our need to analyze them. These designations may have spiritual or religious value, or may be familiar to certain cultures or ethnic groups, so if they do not fit in your language system, please rename them. Keep in mind that we are using common words to categorize something that defies labeling. Classifications are only for presenting a variety of possibilities.

Body Memories

Body memories are either love-based or fear-based. Love-based memories are typically accompanied by feelings or physical sensations of expansion, warmth, safety, generosity, fondness, freedom, or passion. Fear-based memories are usually accompanied by feelings or physical sensations of pain, tension, contraction, anxiety, being overwhelmed, oppression, or inflammation.

These memories, held over a period of time, eventually translate into your physical symptoms, your health, or disease processes. Our bodies all degenerate as we age, but the degree of severity or suffering you experience is measured by the body memories that you hold.

Unreconciled, fear-based body memories are rich with toxic emotions such as anger, guilt, fear, grief, resentment, regret, jealousy, animosity, and greed. Embodied for a long time, they suppress your life force energy. Compounded with a stressful lifestyle, toxic chemicals in your environment, a processed-food diet, a lack of exercise, and a disconnection from Earth energies, this leads to the many health crises that we face today.

Love-based body memories are rich with enlivening emotions such as tenderness, gratitude, patience, bliss, courage, forgiveness, humor, compassion, and abundance. Embodied for a long time, they create mobility of your life force energy and fluidity of your emotions. Compounded with a low-stress lifestyle, minimal toxicity in your environment, a fresh-food diet, joyful movement and exercise, and a connection to the Earth and her rhythms, this leads to buoyant health and prosperity.

All body memories carry emotion with them. They are typically from this present timeline or are carried over from recent generations. Many of these stories contain pictures, aromas, a unique resonance, and a tangible sensation. The most intimate type of recollection, body memories can be sexual in nature, can recall your birth or your childhood, can make you easily laugh, smile, or cry, and can alter the entire structure of your life. They are made daily and are the most accessible type of memory.

Family Memories

Family memories are stored as belief systems or traditions. These imprints designate how you should operate in order to fit in, to be loved/accepted, or to validate familial dynamics. They make up the status quo. Typically they will have some sort of religious or spiritual influence, will reflect addictive tendencies and emotional ground rules, will form the basis for cyclical patterns, and will mirror patriarchal or matriarchal lineages. Family memories set the stage for the drama of your life.

Family memories hold the blueprint for large systems and so can be passed on for many generations. These stories embody grudges, feuds, creative talents, clan hierarchy, professions, legends, compliancy, prejudices, and cultural pride. They are sometimes remembered externally as kinship stories, as family shields, as dwellings or homes, as land or territory, as tributes, and as gravesites or burial grounds. These memories are fierce, because, as they say, blood is thicker than water.

Passed forward with dedication, they design your myths and diligently require obedience. Most of us comply with them whether or not we know it or like it. Family memories mold you on all levels and fashion your subconscious. They are the platform for dreams and the fuel for our personal growth as we seek to find our own distinctive path in life.

Family memories are deeply instinctual, filled with emotion, and influence our health and predisposition to disease. They bind us as one and keep us tethered to our bloodline.

Ancestral or Seven-Generation Memories

Ancestral memories are designed around the need to perpetuate healing and pass forward the wisdom and recklessness of your forbearers. They are often confused with past life memories because they are so perceptually vivid they feel like your own. You may mistake them for your own personal or spiritual stories.

Ancestral memories are the seeds of your Earth-based existence. Nurtured over many years and seasoned with many trials and tribulations, they quantify and qualify your deepest urges and survivalist tendencies. They can be both sweet and bitter, but they always carry strength, perseverance, and tenacity. They are carried in the blueprint of your DNA.

A generation is typically designated as thirty years. Multiply this times seven generations and the result is two hundred and ten years. That would mean that approximately two hundred years of ancestral memory reside in your body to teach you, support you, and evolve you. Then imagine that the actions you take today will create another two hundred years of memory for future generations.

Seven-generation memory implies that the experiences of your ancestors are active within you; they travel close beside you with love and heal as you heal, restore as you restore, and progress as you progress. They help to relieve you of their burdens, to mend their errors, to manifest collective dreams that may have gotten waylaid during times of war, genocide, poverty, or trauma. For the family system moves forward as a group and can leave none behind in order to excel as one. Each one carries another. Ancestral memory is designed so that we will not forget our lineage, our potential, or what we leave for our future generations.

Collective/Tribal Memories

Collective memories are founded on Earth spirituality and are primarily symbolic. The vibration of the invisible world translates into signs and codes that speak to your higher self through energetic form. Symbols are something visible representing something invisible. They are characterized by association, resemblance, or convention, and are imbued with rich layers of meanings.

Symbols define us. Deeply mythological and prophetic, symbols, totems, glyphs, and artwork are the messengers of the spirit world. They instruct us about the passages and phases of life, linking us to past cultures and giving us vision for the future. Whether it is a cross, an animal, or a cultural design, we use symbolic images in our governments, flags, sports teams, clubs, schools, clothing, and even in our cars to keep us connected to our memories.

Tribal or group memories hold the alchemy of creation stories, and, as ancestral memories do, they bind us together. The guardian of tribal memories is the star nation who use designated symbols to open doors to original wisdom. These memories are most often accessed as spiritual visions or in the dreamtime when one is aligned with group rhythms. They also are invoked through initiations. Remembering collective stories furnishes you with power and imbeds deeper meaning into your life story. They can also bring deep sorrow and grief if the memories include cultural loss, genocide, or oppression.

Past Life Memories

Past life memories can erupt from a somatic excavation swiftly and without warning, and shape your dharmic path. Many are not tangible to the present timeline. They may be vague or distinct, full of emotion, or like wisps of mental pictures, hard to grasp. They typically involve an unresolved traumatic event of some sort, and can be triggered by a present-day event that has trailed from the past, by meeting a person who has links to that era or timeline, or by seeing a symbol that opens the doors of your consciousness.

Past life memories often come forward as part of a healing cycle initiated by the recovery of antiquated stories. Annual cycles or seasons influence these memory patterns, as well as deaths, births, and life passages. Also, watching historical programs or reading historical texts can awaken past life memories.

They are important because they can influence how you express your power in this timeline by binding you to certain contracts or obligations, and therefore keep you from your full potential. Past life memories gush from the folds of other memory patterns that are layered in your soma, and are the result of gratifying personal growth work. This type of recall happens typically in dreams and in déjà vu moments.

Spiritual Archival Memories

Spiritual archives are referred to as Akashic records, or the memory bank of the cosmos. The Akashic records are a collection of mystical knowledge that is encoded in the ether. They are thought to have existed since the beginning of Creation and even before. It is held that the ancient Indian sages of the Himalayas knew that each soul or entity recorded every moment of its existence in a "book." They believed that if one attuned oneself properly, one could access that book.

Accessing memories from the Akashic records is a skill that is learned from dedication to self-awareness and meditation techniques, and is supported by certain spiritual alliances and rituals. The doorway to these universal stories is the energetic system of your body, up and through your chakra system to the refined vibrations of etheric pulsations. The cosmology you explore in this dimension is beyond human comprehension, as you find your destiny woven into the movement of the stars, the moon, and the galaxies beyond.

Excavate Your Chakra System

At the core of your memory banks is your chakra system. Your chakra system holds the imprints, dynamics and essence of all your experiences, present, past and future. It is the main framework of your psyche and your ego, and reveals to you where specific memories or imbalances are held in your body. A fabulously simple energetic map of your incredibly complex self, it provides the chart by which you can plot your somatic excavation. It holds all the clues and landmarks for a successful healing journey to the atmosphere of the invisible.

Chakra is a Sanskrit word that means "wheel of light." Chakras regulate, maintain, and manage the physical, emotional, mental, and spiritual aspects of your being. The vibration of a chakra is depicted by its color, sound, and content. If you could see into the atmosphere of the invisible, a chakra would look like a funnel of energy spiraling clockwise or counterclockwise depending on whether you are taking energy in or extending it outward. Each one has a unique vibration, color, and cellular structure.

I invite you to breathe into each chakra, expand in all directions, and encourage the flow of energy. Imagine the energy spiraling clockwise to draw in or close a chakra, or counterclockwise to release or open it. Imagine the associated color pulsing in the chakra, or flood it with vibrational frequency by giving voice to the sound. Focus on the content or description. Directly apply plant, mineral, and animal energies for greater enhancement. (See Aroma-Mood Reference Guide in chapter 5 for essential oil application and description of oil blends.)

Below is a brief outline of the chakra system to facilitate deciphering where you hold memories in the body. The chakra system also generates awareness of your body flows and allows access to the mysteries you have stored inside. There is a whole universe waiting to be explored! There are seven chakras in your human anatomy, and two that rest above your body. For the purposes of Somatic Archaeology, we will be describing all nine chakras.

First Chakra—Also know as the root or base chakra.
Sanskrit name: Muladhara
Element: Earth
Gland: Adrenal
Vibrational Frequency: Keynote C, C#, Vowel Sound Hu
Plant World: Essential oils of black pepper, cedarwood, Grounding, Ruta VaLa, Valor
Mineral World: Agate, bloodstone, hematite, garnet, ruby, red jasper
Animal World: Snake, lizard, alligator, and all crawlers
Located at the base of the spine near the perineum, this chakra contains your base survival instincts. It holds unconscious symbols and memories regarding life or death circumstance, safety, and basic maintenance of life. This chakra gives vitality and stability to your physical body. Your fight-or-flight response is established here, as is your resistance to being grounded in your body. Address this chakra when working with security, courage, patience, and autonomy, or with loss of homeland. It's associated with the color red and is the slowest or densest energetic center in the body. Physical complaints associated with an imbalance in this chakra include constipation, rectal problems, sexual frigidity, unexplainable anxiety, spinal pain and tension, addictions, and compulsions.

Second Chakra—also known as the sacral or navel chakra.
Sanskrit name: Svadisthana

Element: Water
Gland: Ovaries, womb, testicles, prostate, genitals
Vibrational Frequency: Keynote D, D#, Vowel Sound O
Plant World: Essential oils of Clarity, Forgiveness, geranium, Inner Child, lavender, SARA
Mineral World: Carnelian, coral, calcite, amber, citrine, moonstone
Animal World: Dolphin, whale, swimmers, otter, beaver, turtle, frog, bat

Moving upward in the body, this chakra is located just below the navel, in your reproductive center. This wheel reflects your relationship to your sexuality and your mother, and enfolds memories and dreams of the divine feminine. It's the seat of creative power and holds your potential for intimacy. Issues around nurturing and self-approval are established here. Enter this chakra when working with giving and receiving, tolerance, jealousy, assimilation, and creativity. It's associated with the color orange and the vibration begins to quicken in this chakra, bringing your unconscious energy into the subconscious. Physical complaints related to this chakra include bladder infections, kidney stones, reproductive problems, impotence, menstrual fluctuations, sexual dysfunction, low back pain, and intestinal issues.

Third Chakra—also known as the solar plexus chakra.
Sanskrit name: Manipura
Element: Fire
Gland: Adrenal
Vibrational Frequency: Keynote E, Vowel Sound Ah
Plant World: Essential oils of Abundance, peppermint, Peace & Calming, Purification, Sacred Mountain
Mineral World: Citrine, gold topaz, amber, tiger's eye, gold calcite, gold
Animal World: Badger, raven, elk, coyote, skunk, mountain lion

Continuing upward in the body, this chakra is located in the solar plexus. It defines your relationship to your power and to your father, and embraces memories and dreams of the divine masculine. It is the seat of anger, fire, will, and addictions. In this chakra you take your creative energy and actualize it in the world. This is where you demonstrate self-protection and leadership. Address this chakra when working with your neurological system, personal mastery, sacred law vs. human law, physical transformation, anger, and self-control. It's associated with the color yellow and the vibration quickens again, bringing your subconscious energy into the conscious. Physical complaints related to this chakra include liver, spleen and gall bladder problems, ulcers, ineffective digestion, flatulence, burping, hernias, chronic fatigue, and any symptom related to energy, metabolism, addictive patterns, high blood pressure, weight, and body temperature issues.

Fourth Chakra—also known as the heart chakra.
Sanskrit name: Anahata
Element: Air
Gland: Thymus
Vibrational Frequency: Keynote F, F#, Vowel Sound A
Plant World: Essential oils of AromaLife, Forgiveness, geranium, Hope, Joy, rose, Valor, White Angelica
Mineral World: Emerald, green and pink tourmaline, malachite, green jade, green aventurine, chrysoprase, kunzite, rose quartz, ruby, moldavite
Animal World: Deer, elk, horse, buffalo, dog
Continuing upward, this chakra is located in the middle of your chest, in your heart and lung area. It is the center of love and compassion, which also holds memory of loss, grief, regret and resentment. In this chakra you express your self worth and align with your personal truth. Your physical and spiritual bodies unite in this chakra. Enter this wheel to learn about group consciousness, understanding, harmony, emotional instability, and acceptance. It's associated with the color green, raising the vibration a notch, bringing consciousness to maturity and oneness. Physical complaints related to this chakra include bronchial problems, heart disease, heart palpitations, circulatory concerns, thymus problems, breathing issues such as asthma and pneumonia, and smoking addictions.

Fifth Chakra—also known as the throat chakra.
Sanskrit name: Vishudda
Element: Ether
Gland: Thyroid, parathyroid, hypothalamus
Vibrational Frequency: Keynote G, G #, Vowel Sound I
Plant World: Essential oils of Believe, Harmony, lemon, Present Time, Release, Ruta VaLa, ylang ylang
Mineral World: Turquoise, chrysocolla, chalcedony, blue sapphire, celestite, blue topaz, sodalite, lapis lazuli, aquamarine, azurite, kyanite
Animal World: Moose, elk, antelope, dolphin, spider, songbirds
Moving into the throat and neck area, this chakra is the center of self-expression. It is where you voice your truth and declare your value. You are empowered here when you remember to sing praise to your Creator. In this chakra you manifest

your creativity and inspiration. Address this chakra when working on integration, communication, honesty, discernment, and speech problems. Once again there is a quickening of vibration in this conscious wheel. It's associated with the color blue, and is the place where we communicate our dreams, humor, and emotions. Physical complaints related to this chakra include thyroid imbalances and metabolism problems, tinnitus, sinus infections, olfactory dysfunction, ear infections, sore throats, TMJ, whiplash, and difficulty swallowing.

Sixth Chakra—also known as the third eye chakra.
Sanskrit name: Anja
Element: Light
Gland: Pineal and pituitary
Vibrational Frequency: Keynote A, A# Vowel Sound Ee
Plant World: Sage, and essential oils of Acceptance, cedarwood, frankincense, Palo Santo, patchouli, Surrender, vetiver
Mineral World: Lapis lazuli, azurite, fluorite, sodalite, quartz crystal, sapphire, tourmaline
Animal World: Eagle, crow, owl, wolf, grouse, dragonfly
Progressing into the third eye, this chakra is the seat of the intuition. It represents your mental capacity, your vision, and your cognitive clarity. For most people in our culture, it is the helm of operation. In this chakra you can remember clairvoyant and telepathic skills, which sit alongside perceptions of your reality. The amygdala, the emotional center of your brain, is located in the frontal lobe that is at the core of this wheel. Come to this chakra to work with imagination, concentration, nightmares, detachment, fragmentation, PTSD, or ADHD. It's associated with the color indigo, which raises the vibration, opening our awareness to the non-physical worlds. Physical complaints related to this chakra include headaches, vision problems, pituitary imbalances, and issues with concentration, such as spaciness.

Seventh Chakra—also known as the crown chakra.
Sanskrit name: Sahasrara
Element: Spirit
Gland: Pineal
Vibrational Frequency: Keynote B, Vowel Sound Ohm
Plant World: Cedar, and essential oils of Awaken, Gathering, Gratitude, Into the Future, Release
Mineral World: Amethyst, alexandrite, purple fluorite, diamond, selenite

Animal World: Whale, turtle, hummingbird
Ascend into the crown chakra, which sits just above the top of your head. Akin to a lotus flower, this spiritual center of your physical body is the place where you connect with your higher self and your Creator. It holds your relationship to the divine and the potential for abundance and prosperity. It also contains ancestral memory. Come to the chakra to address lack of inspiration, disconnection, hesitation, spiritual will, idealism, and depression. The doorway to your dreams, it's associated with the color violet, which is the highest vibration of your physical chakra system. Physical complaints related to this chakra include out of body experiences, alienation, pineal imbalances, sleep problems, and nervous system imbalances.

Eighth Chakra—also called the memory chakra.
Element: Ether
Vibrational Frequency: Keynote High C, Vowel Sound Hu
Plant World: Sweetgrass, and essential oils of frankincense, Idaho balsam fir, Palo Santo, rose
Mineral World: White or clear quartz
Animal World: Mythological animals, unicorn, dragon
This chakra is located about six inches above your crown chakra. It is associated with the color silver, and holds the knowledge of your life purpose and it is the access point to the Akashic records. Memories of spiritual symbols are stored in this wheel, along with your sense of a non-linear time continuum. This is where communication with your spirit guides and loved ones takes place. Enter this wheel to find lost fragments of collective memory, to discover the process of manifestation, and to bring spiritual clarity. You may want to have safe boundaries when working with this chakra, restricting access to communication with non-familiar spirits or energies. Just as you would keep the front door of your home closed to keep strangers from wandering in, playing with your eighth and ninth chakras requires great discernment and discipline.

Ninth Chakra—also called the soul chakra.
Element: Love
Plant World: Essential oils of rose, spikenard
Mineral World: White or clear quartz
Animal World: None
This chakra is associated with the color gold, and sits at the apex of your aura, above the eighth chakra. It holds the memory of your soul purpose and life con-

tracts. It is an all pervading and synergistic center of bliss and enlightenment, and connects you with the cosmos—the Milky Way and the movement of the stars and moons. Establishing oneness with source, the vibration is very refined, and will be unfamiliar to most people unless they deliberately focus on it. Explore this chakra for illumination, fulfillment, memories of harmonious interaction, universal truth, integration with your nine spirit selves, the capacity for co-creation, and to attain spiritual unification with the cosmic flows.

The visible world is a mirror of the invisible world. As above, so below. Your design, impulses, visions and actions in this third dimensional world are simply a reflection of the vibrations that exist around you in the ether and live within the energetic system of your body.

The energetic system of your body is impressionable and fragile, yet very hardy when it comes to holding memories or stories. It is unique to each individual, and, much like a thumbprint, it has its own patterns and movement. The flow that creates your luminous body is called the life force or *prana*, the source of all existence. When you feel at peace, it is essentially this force flowing through you in a generous, harmonious manner.

When you feel distress, this flow of life force is disrupted or interrupted. While exploring your chakras, utilize the Somatic Breathing Techniques and the Five Steps of Somatic Archaeology to assist you to recreate a harmonious flow. Expand into the blueprint of energy around you and inside you to feel and sense where there are blockages and to release them. When you first begin doing somatic excavations, it may feel awkward or unfamiliar to explore the atmosphere of the invisible. The more you practice it, the stronger the "muscle" of your sixth sense will get, and the easier somatic exploration will become. The best way to think about it is to "feel yourself from the inside out."

> *I embrace the familiar with reluctance. I fear I will be here, think here, feel here, and die here, forever. What if the inside of me changes and the outside remains the same? I am a slave to conformity of desire. I want to live brand new, sing a different song, relocate the view, breathe fresh air, walk naked in the northern sun, write ideas, create visions of potential, love my man without reservation, night and day, day and night, fondle joy, arch my back for another, be seen, leave tracks, make noise, dream out loud, cry my passion to the sea, worship my truth—that's all ...*
>
> —Ruby Gibson, original poem

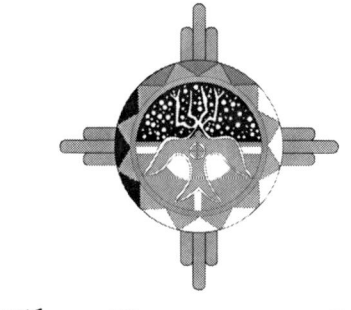

The Preparation

4

Prepare for a Somatic Excavation

Those who do not have power over the story that dominates their lives, the power to retell it, rethink it, deconstruct it, joke about it, and change it as times change, truly are powerless, because they cannot think new thoughts.

—Salman Rushdie

I had a client who experienced a horrific gang rape at a young age. This event followed him into his adult years, manifesting as severe dissociation, panic attacks, disabling seizures, and extreme PTSD that prohibited him from living a normal life. There was no safe place in his mind or body, and his medications were the only thing keeping him at all functional.

The first time he came to my office was by a referral from a psychologist. He could barely make eye contact with me, could barely breathe, could barely talk, was scared and shaking, and spent a good portion of our time together curled up in a ball in the corner. This began a three-year therapeutic relationship that would eventually allow him to lose fifty pounds, have an intimate relationship, write a book, play the guitar, hold a job, and travel around the United States.

He was an extremely bright and creative man, with a heart of gold and a sweet disposition. I have never seen someone so wounded with such a strong will to survive. Every week, inch by inch, he excavated his body until he worked his way back to the rape, and to the familial stories that had predisposed the traumatic experience. Together we sifted courageously through the crime scene in his body, unearthing the good and the ugly, unleashing the pain and the terror, and we were finally able to reorganize the pieces of his past into some semblance of sanity. Somatic Archaeology helped him find the power he had misplaced and the smile he had forgotten.

A predominant factor in the success of our work was that he had a great healing team. His primary care physician, his psychologist, his friends, and his family all contributed support, care, and advice that emboldened him to believe in himself. They gave him safety—emotionally, financially, and morally. This container of safety helped him to access painful memories, to trust in himself, to improve his self-esteem, and to absorb the loving energy that permitted him to let go of the anger his perpetrators had transferred into his body.

If necessary, I invite you to create an excavation team that offers you a variety of therapeutic approaches to enhance a holistic approach. Self-reliance can isolate you. Get support from friends and family to establish a sense of safety, to become aware of abusive tendencies, to make sense of your story, to have a shoulder to cry on, to feel the impact that you have on others around you, and to develop a deepening of the dreams or ambitions that you have for yourself.

Safety

Many times your body and mind can go on acting as if you are threatened long after a threat has passed. Feeling safe is different for everybody—it is a personal perspective and is relative based on your story. Establishing a sense of safety in your daily life is essential to the healing process. If you are unstable or have experienced a recent trauma, it may be dangerous to excavate and add new information to an overwhelmed body.

You will heal when you feel safe enough to do so. Have a home environment that is soothing and nurturing, and remove yourself from close proximity to threatening people, chaotic or unpredictable circumstances, and abusive dynamics. Recognize unhealthy patterns and relationships that you have established, and take steps to change or eliminate them.

Regain a sense of control and stability over your daily schedule to establish a foundation from which you will move forward. Current problems and life upheavals such as job changes, moving, family crisis, or divorce may cloud your goals and progress, accelerate worrying, and make it difficult to find the time to pay attention to your story or allow time for changes and integration.

Create safety by establishing sobriety in your life and relationships, maintaining positive thoughts, following your instincts and intuition, paying attention to symbolic or synchronistic events, actively visualizing the success of your goals, and maintaining a disciplined spiritual practice that allows you to feel connected to a higher order of things. Safety comes with faith that all life is choreographed for your learning and evolution. Make room to pay attention to the cycles and events happening within and around you.

Addictive Behaviors

It is essential to discontinue, or to be in the process of discontinuing, addictive or numbing activities that may hinder your excavation. These behaviors include addictions to alcohol, drugs, sex, food, or gambling. When you use drugs or alcohol to numb or dull sensation, you will have a very difficult time making progress with any type of therapy, but particularly with Somatic Archaeology. Addictions will keep you cycling round and round in your old story, and prohibit you from awakening to a new story.

Some people are obsessed with risky activities such as road rage or dangerous acts that continue to traumatize them by releasing adrenalin and keeping their nervous system activated. Be careful of any reenactment activity that creates sensations or dynamics similar to that of a traumatic event.

Self-medicating is self-sabotage. With addictive behaviors, physical detoxification is hindered and each day is about recovering from the one before. Emotionally disengaged from your feelings, you can lose the desire and will to become well or to change habits, and you remain spiritually detached and weakened. If you find that you are unable to stay clear on a regular basis, I encourage you to reach out for counseling or a rehabilitation program before you begin somatically excavating your stories.

In addition, you must be willing to establish new patterns. It is helpful to have a payoff, or a goal that is enticing enough to encourage you down a road that, although it leads toward well-being, may temporarily heighten sensitivity and increase your awareness of struggles or problems. Incentives to be sober and create a new story may include the longing to be in a healthy relationship, relief from physical pain, the desire to end the cycle of suffering and not pass on the legacy to your children, establishing power and control of your life/destiny, and creating spiritual awareness and harmony.

Empowerment

Many years ago, a group of school children were kidnapped from a bus. The kidnappers put them in a cave and left them there while they went to get their ransom. All the children were huddled together, scared and cold, worrying that they would never be found. They were certain they were going to die, and so awaited their terrible fate.

All of them—except for one child.

One young boy decided that he wasn't going to take it! He decided to get out of there and so he began to dig. He dug and dug and dug. This boy dug his way out of the cave and eventually rescued all the children. The parents came and got their children, a little bruised, scared, and hungry, but otherwise fine, and took them home. As it turned out, everyone was okay.

Follow-up studies on these children determined how they coped with the event. All of the children had difficulty sleeping, nightmares, anxiety, panic, etc. They were still processing and wrangling with their fear every day. Except one child; the boy showed no signs of PTSD. Why? Because he moved his fear through his body by acting in an empowered and self-protective manner. He extended his energy into positive movement that reconciled the situation.

This story is very important because it clearly outlines the manner in which we can protect ourselves from the devastating aftereffects of traumatic events. This story also displays one of the most fundamental principles of Somatic Archaeology—that healing comes as a direct result of empowered action, of recognizing our choices, and of making change. Again, we heal and we remember when we feel safe enough to do so. Empowerment is safety.

While it is best to act in an empowered, self-protective manner during threatening events in an effort to reduce the embodiment of fear, it is not always possible. For some, it would put them in greater danger. If this was true in your case, you can still, at any time, revisit the memory of the event in your body and use your somatic imagination to do what you needed to do at the time to change the outcome and reframe the experience. (See the Five Steps of Somatic Archaeology in chapter 8 for the protocol.)

Somatic Filters

We all develop somatic filters to sift through stressful or emotional stories. Filters help us to block, avoid, or alter certain memories to comfort us and to make it easier to feel safe. Filters only let some of the story through, leaving the rest buried. Somatic filters, used long term, create barriers that insulate you from reality.

We learn early in life to adapt to our families—we mind our manners, we are seen and not heard, we manage our emotions, and we sidestep certain people. We also cope with challenging and dangerous situations in a number of ways. Our innate reactions are to flee, to fight back, to faint, to freeze, or to talk our way out of it.

When we are unable to follow our reactions and remove ourselves from danger, there results a state of helplessness. This was the case in the story about the schoolchildren. They lacked the power and capacity to protect themselves. Consequently, they embodied the story, their fear incubated, and they began to cope with the threat. They filtered the fear through their dreams, their bodies, and their neurology.

Recognizing the somatic filters that you have developed over the years offers insight about how your system adapts to current events, and how it adapted to historical events. Even if it has been years since you felt threatened, you may still keep your filters securely in place. To address these filters somatically, you must first become aware of them. The goal is not necessarily to eliminate them, for they will diminish when you no longer need them. Just begin to recognize when you use them. Generally, they will become pronounced on the verge of crisis or when you feel threatened or fearful. Pay attention and let your somatic filters teach you about yourself.

The following is a basic overview of somatic filters that may perpetuate your story and therefore become obvious during somatic excavations, as well as tactics you can employ to support yourself. Honor, respect, and appreciate each of these filters because they are strategies created by you to endure your experiences and mask your stories.

Dissociation

When we become overwhelmed, we face the tendency to dissociate or split off from our acute awareness or presence in our bodies. It is a very effective filter that allows you to deal with stress. Almost everyone does it—sometimes it is referred to as being spacey, or as daydreaming, or being out of your body. When certain memories are evoked in somatic excavations, you can filter your awareness by falling asleep, "zoning out," or disconnecting from your body temporarily. Most people can come back from dissociation to present time easily and quickly.

Dissociation also occurs when we must endure experiences that are not endurable. In this case, we may dissociate permanently, filtering big gaps of memory, especially from certain areas of our body. In some cases, this effect can become chronic, lingering long after the experience has ended. If you have adopted dissociation as a means of filtering past stories or events, you have done so for good reason. It has helped you to get through a difficult time.

But long-term dissociative tendencies can be damaging, not because they insulate you from your pain, but because they keep you cut off from your passion and aliveness. Dissociation can filter out your power and keep you from recognizing your ability to change your story. Some people have a consistent and generalized sense of dissociation, and others only dissociate when triggered or when excavating certain body memories.

If you know that you dissociate during times of stress, you will want to proceed slowly with your excavation. If you find that you have difficulty staying present while doing the breathing exercises or somatic meditation, then you will need to enter your body and story gradually and deliberately. And keep breathing. Breathing is the easiest way to stay present in your body and will help to keep you connected.

Avoidance

As issues or fears arise during a somatic excavation, be sure to address them. Generally, the issues that you wish to avoid or detour around hold the most information and healing potential. Be honest with yourself, speak your truth, and clarify difficult topics. Reach out for help. Avoidance stifles authenticity and can restrict you from experiencing your whole story.

If you notice that you are avoiding an area of your body that is charged or potent with emotion, take time to pay loving attention to it. Imagine that you embrace this area and are curious about what it holds. Trust your instincts and be kind to yourself. Send love and appreciation even if you dislike this part of your body. Be prepared to find some wonderful buried treasures. Gratefully encircle even the most remote parts of yourself instead of filtering them out.

Denial

Denial is a common and effective way of ignoring your story, operating on a subconscious level. It is influenced and modeled by familial patterns. Denial is primarily a cognitive process that can interrupt the course of a somatic excavation. The process of developing somatic awareness is, in itself, motivation enough to challenge this coping mechanism. Notice the areas of your body that you avoid excavating. When in doubt, you can ask someone you trust to tell you what you

Phobias

Phobias are very complicated and sometimes irrational fears or dislikes. It is important to address *where* in your body the phobia lives, rather than *why* the phobia exists. A strong somatic component operates alongside the fear. Remember the last time the phobia occurred. Bring it to mind, then explore the particular sensations that arise when you imagine this fear. This will give you a physical link to your phobia and will help you recognize the prephobia sequence of events that leads to the fear. Encourage yourself to breath, to stay aware of sensations. Follow the Five Steps of Somatic Archaeology to release buried memories that reinforce the phobia.

Shame and Guilt

Shame is a filter for someone else's guilt or disgrace. People project shame onto another person or story in order to alleviate responsibility. Guilt is when you do something wrong and you know it; but shame is when someone else tells you that what you are doing is wrong. Embarrassment, unworthiness, and dishonor combine to entrench shame and guilt in our memory banks for a considerable amount of time. Conchita's story clearly defines the toxic effects of blame and shame to avoid accountability or honesty.

Conchita's Story

"So many times, instead of relating to others through a clear, realistic sense of self, I play relational hide-and-seek, evading what I am certain will be judgment or rejection should I get caught being 'It'—my real self.

"I have been playing this game my entire life. My family made up the basic rules, and I have perfected them over time and through much practice. I have been on the receiving end of so many looks of rejection from those close to me that it is difficult to even look others in the eye. My over-familiarity with the game often brings me to the point where I don't recognize it as a game at all. At this point, I simply call the game life. In actuality, the name of the game is shame.

"Shame is just another word for that inner voice of condemnation that pervades my consciousness from time to time. It is often accompanied by physical manifestations such as tightness in my chest or intestinal aching. It differs from a healthy conviction of wrongdoing or embarrassment resulting from being human, as it is about my personhood, my value, and my worth. I often feel unloved and unlovable, rejected and rejectable.

"Shame causes me to hate who I am. It is attached to things about me that are intrinsic to my personhood, such as my gender or ethnicity. It leaves me in a place of self-loathing which no amount of affirmation can rescue me from. My inner dialogue becomes one of endless evaluation, scrutinizing my every move, my every word, judging everything along the 'good/bad' continuum. In this place of self-hatred at my perceived deficiencies, I live from a place of judgment, and grace becomes my greatest deficiency.

"Shame makes me want to hide who I am. It is imperative to conceal the defects, often behind veneers of a false 'goodness.' These false selves, who require considerable energy to maintain, consist of a collection of placating, people-pleasing behaviors, designed to evoke admiration, sympathy, and/or perceptions of likeability. The downside of this perpetual smokescreen is that others can never meet me in my sadness, anger, and weakness. Because I falsely believe that those parts of my real self will immediately elicit rejection, I cut off from them, and it becomes overwhelmingly painful or anxiety producing to deal with these emotions. Untreated shame can and will kill.

"I grew up relating defensively, cautiously, censoring, and mistrusting the sincerity of others. As a result, my ability to meaningfully connect was stunted. I also cut myself off from my Creator. I find myself wandering off into distant lands, searching for that ever-elusive panacea for the sickness in my soul. Chemical addictions, relational addictions, thought addictions, or feeling addictions—I search in vain for the missing piece/peace that would quiet the continually running monologue in my heart.

"For me, the way out of shame began by focusing away from the hell of self and self-consciousness. I chose to leave my hidden-ness, renounced self-hatred, and extended forgiveness to those who wounded me. While excavating my body with Somatic Archaeology, I forgive myself over and over again for bitter reactions that rise up from my unhealed heart. These are the slow, painful steps toward the land of the living. Walking away from the familiarity of established dysfunctional patterns of relating is a long, arduous process. It is hard work excavating what lies beneath the layers of shame, but well worth the effort. I now have insights on where this originated, and because of this I make different choices, I stand up for myself and I give myself a voice."

Planning a Somatic Excavation

A Somatic Archaeology excavation cannot be completed all at once. It requires time, patience, diligence, and most importantly, continuity. Once you start digging, more will be revealed. As more is revealed, your somatic filters are less effective and your awareness is heightened. Symptoms and memories can become exaggerated or emphasized. It is important to keep digging—don't stop halfway through an excavation. Stay with the process.

Create an excavation plan to monitor yourself and log what you unearth. Stories take time to become imbedded, and they will take time to be exposed. Refer to the suggestion to chronicle your stories in chapter 2. This activity will give you added insight for your excavation plan. The amount of time it will take for you to unearth your story is dependent upon many things.

Age of Experience

The age at which a storyline began is extremely important information. Powerful events that happened during the formative years from ages zero to six impact your level of safety, your self-esteem, your stability, and your relationship to your mother. Experiences from ages seven to twelve influence your sexuality, your work ethic, your creativity, and your relationship to the world and your father. From age thirteen on, you will be swayed by stories of religious and spiritual experiences, addictions and drug use, peer and social dynamics, and your professional drives. Of course, this is all based on the stories you were born into and the events that influenced you.

Family Patterns

How your family copes with stressful events or upheavals is also an important thing to consider when creating an excavation plan. Did they talk it out? Look for solutions? Or did they drink it away? Fight and blame? Sweep it under the rug? What kind of filters were you exposed to as a child? Learned behaviors of avoidance will generally lengthen the time it takes to unearth your stories, while open, proactive, and solution-based family attitudes will allow you to excavate your past more easily. Observe yourself carefully to avoid slipping into unhealthy family patterns, and make a conscious decision to change.

Resources

Another important consideration is the support and resources that were available to you during a crisis or trauma. If you were isolated and had nobody to talk with about your feelings, or were forced into secrecy and covert behaviors, it will be more difficult to access storylines and the experience will be imbedded under fear. Alternately, if you had a shoulder to cry on, a special person or relative who befriended you, and you were able to speak openly and honestly about the experience, the story will be more accessible and less entrenched somatically.

Length of Time and Storyline

Consider the length of time since a traumatic event occurred, and subsequent events that have been layered on top of the experience. One woman came in for a Somatic Archaeology session to explore some pain in her neck that she assumed came from a whiplash injury sustained in a recent car accident. While exploring the area she found that she was withholding a great deal of repressed anger in her neck from a sexual molestation she had experienced as a child. Upon release of the anger, she became aware of a family storyline designed to keep her from speaking up for herself. With further digging, she realized that her mother had the same tendency. She was able to follow the symptom (in this case whiplash) all the way back to her mother's and grandmother's inhibitions and conditioning, and hence release the imprint and the pain in her neck.

When you follow the symptom, you will discover the true storyline. Generational or long-removed patterns can be so thoroughly woven into your story that they get buried or masked by other events. Or they might be catalyzed by traumatic events. Car accidents, falls, and injuries are notorious instigation of the revelation of a buried trauma. Let the wisdom of your body guide you. Never make assumptions from a mental determination about the origin of the symptom, for you will only get a small part of the answer. Be sure to ask your body as well—it holds the records of your life. Be curious and dig. The trail of history will expose itself before your eyes.

Your spiritual consciousness, the amount of recovery/healing work already done, the depth of healing you desire, your current lifestyle, health, and addictive tendencies, and as I have said, the level of safety in your life right now are all factors to consider when designing an excavation plan. Use this information to pace yourself and set realistic goals. It is important to take time to assimilate the stories and emotions that emerge before bringing more memories to the surface through further somatic excavations.

Long-Term Excavations

Long-term excavations are very important in somatic recovery work. Our society's desire for quick-fix healing has no place at a somatic dig site. Quicker is not always better. Significant, constitutional healing is permanent and takes time. It is valuable to adopt the pace of the Earth; be patient, spacious, and enduring. It is time well spent.

Changes you make become more apparent when the outside world begins to notice them. When peers and family share their observations regarding the shifts you have made, it creates a significant impetus for the continuation of your somatic excavation. The changes you generate become more concrete or tangible when someone else acknowledges them.

After significant digging, and when you see yourself in a new way in your circle, you may find that you have reached a level of healing that is enough for right now. You may not feel the need to continue—you may have dug deep enough for now. This feeling must be honored. You may need to put time into a relationship or your children, you may need to experiment with your new empowerment, you may need to rebuild resources, or you may just need to take a break. When you are ready, you will come back to digging.

Benefits of Digging

If you do decide to dig to the bottom, leaving no stone unturned—whatever that looks like to you—you will be greatly rewarded. You will know yourself very well and hence have self-love; you will have developed the skills necessary to handle daily stress and future events effectively; you will be able to experience joy and pleasure in your body; you will be a better friend, spouse, parent; you will have respect for yourself, others, and the environment; you will be able to speak up and stand up for yourself; you will have the ability to use your creative potential with freedom; and you will be able to recycle your experiences for the good of all.

How do you know when you are done? When you say so. Believe in your ability to heal yourself. Believe that you will succeed. Empowering yourself to thrive, rather than just survive, is the ultimate goal.

> *Often we search for something meaningful to fill the gap between the here and now and destiny. Maybe it is a gift, a reason to grow, a remembering, a symbolic measure of our divinity, a valuable relationship that touches our hearts and stretches our capacity. Because this thing we search for is unfa-*

miliar to us, we do not always recognize it when we stumble across it. How can we be sure that we've found something precious, when we don't have any bearings to determine what it looks or feels like? All I can say is this. God speaks to our strengths, not our weaknesses. Listen carefully to your joy. It will show you the way.

—Ruby Gibson, original poem

5

Aromatherapy for Balancing Brain and Body

"Let thy food be thy medicine and thy medicine be thy food."

—Hippocrates

Aroma is the oldest means of reaching and influencing the deepest human instincts. Fragrances can have a calming, stimulating, elevating, or suppressing action. They enhance brain wave function, relax muscles, increase circulation, release emotions, or stimulate your hormonal system, and work in a synergistic way in order to bring about a beautiful balance to your body, heart, mind, and soul. Through topical application or inhalation, therapeutic essential oils—the most concentrated plant fragrances—provide a relatively quick, convenient, safe, and fragrant means to pain reduction, emotional balance, memory evocation, and health enhancement. In addition, aromatherapy will lubricate your emotional body and brain so that you can access memories with greater ease.

What Are Essential Oils?

Essential oils are the life force of the plant containing vitamins, minerals, enzymes, and hormones. Concentrated essences of various flowers, fruits, herbs, and plants have been used for centuries all over the world and are one of the greatest untapped resources on our planet. Modern scientific research has proven that essential oils are potent, with remarkable healing properties. There has been a growing modern interest in the restorative power of essential oils, and scientists are continually researching new plants for their therapeutic benefits.

Essential oils are chemically very complex in their molecular structure, consisting of hundreds of different chemical compounds. Moreover, they are highly concentrated and far more potent than dried herbs. The distillation process is what makes essential oils so concentrated. It often requires an entire plant or more to produce a single drop of distilled essential oil. (*Essential Oil Desk Reference*, Fourth Edition, 2007)

Essential oils are chemically heterogenic, meaning they are very diverse in their effects and have different actions. This gives them a paradoxical nature, which can be difficult to understand only until we compare them to another paradoxical group—human beings. For example, a person may have many different roles: an accountant, husband, father, church volunteer, scoutmaster, golfer, etc., but he is still one person. And so it is with essential oils. Lavender, for example, is the essential oil of one plant, but it can be used for many conditions: burns, insect bites, headaches, skin conditions, PMS, insomnia, stress, and so forth. This diversity is beneficial when working with healing and recovery, because the complexities inherent in our bodies and the layers developed in our memory systems are difficult to address independent of each other.

The wisdom of the plant world is revealed when we recognize the natural symbiotic relationship we have with the plant world. When we exhale, we exhale carbon dioxide. When a plant inhales, it inhales carbon dioxide. When a plant exhales, it releases oxygen, and when we inhale, we take in oxygen. What the plant no longer needs becomes our lifeline, and what we no longer need becomes the plant's source of nourishment. What a beautiful exchange! Essential oils, as the lifeblood of the plant world, feed us and heal us with oxygen. Oxygen is vital to the healthy functioning of our body. It is the vehicle that delivers nutrients to our cells, fuels all of our systems, fires chemical reactions, eliminates wastes and toxins, and invigorates our will. Pure essential oils provide energetic medicine for balance and enhancement on all levels.

Essential Oils Are Not All the Same

As we begin to understand the power of essential oils in the realm of personal recovery, we will appreciate the necessity for obtaining the purest essential oils possible. No matter how costly pure oils may be, there can be no substitutes. Inferior quality or adulterated oils most likely will not produce therapeutic results and could possibly be toxic. (*Essential Oil Desk Reference*, Fourth Edition, 2007)

There are significant differences between synthetic fragrance oils (made possible by recent advances in chemistry) and pure essential oils. Synthetic fragrance oils may duplicate the smell of the pure botanical, but the complex chemical components of each natural essential oil determine its true therapeutic benefits. While synthetic fragrance oils are not suitable for aromatherapy, they add an approximation of the natural scent to crafts, potpourri, soap, and perfume at a fraction of the cost.

The key to producing a therapeutic-grade essential oil is to preserve as many of the delicate aromatic compounds within the essential oil as possible through organic farming methods and distillation processes. High temperature and pressure easily destroy fragile aromatic chemicals, as does contact with chemically reactive metals such as copper and aluminum. The plant material should also be free of pesticides, herbicides, and other agrichemicals. These can react with the essential oil during distillation to produce toxic compounds. Because many pesticides are oil-soluble, they can also mix into the essential oil. (*Essential Oil Desk Reference*, Fourth Edition, 2007)

Today, 98 percent of the approximately three hundred essential oils distilled or extracted are used in the perfume and cosmetic industry. Only about 2 percent are produced for therapeutic and medicinal applications, so I encourage you to be a wise and savvy consumer when it comes to purchasing quality essential oils.

Currently the United States has no agency responsible for certifying that an essential oil is therapeutic grade. However, in Europe, standards have been established to outline the chemical profile and principal constituents that a quality essential oil should have. Known as AFNOR (*Association française de Normalisation*) and ISO (International Standards Organization), these guidelines help buyers differentiate between a therapeutic-grade essential oil and lower grade oils with similar chemical makeup and fragrance.

Young Living Essential Oils, an international essential oil producer based in Utah, collaborates with government-certified analytical chemists in Europe to ensure that its essential oils meet AFNOR standards. The company also has FDA approval for many of its oils, certifying that many of them safe for human consumption. Young Living is dedicated to uniting ancient traditions and modern science to grow and produce the highest-quality essential oils and oil-enhanced products in the world. (See Appendix for more information on Young Living.)

Use only pure organic essential oils of the highest quality. All of the therapeutic effects of the essential oils listed in this book are based on essential oils that have been graded according to AFNOR standards. Young Living are the essential oils of choice for Somatic Archaeology.

Aromatherapy and the Brain

Research on the impact of therapeutic essential oils and the brain abounds right now, and data is still coming in. According to the *Essential Oil Desk Reference*, researchers have been able to conclude that the fragrance of an essential oil can directly affect everything from emotional states to lifespan.

When a person inhales a fragrance, the odor molecules travel up the nose where they are trapped by olfactory membranes well protected by the lining inside the nose. Each odor molecule fits like a little puzzle piece into specific receptor sites lining a membrane known as the olfactory epithelium. When stimulated by odor molecules, this lining of nerve cells triggers electrical impulses to the olfactory bulb in the brain, which then transmits the impulses to the gustatory center (where the sensation of taste is perceived), the amygdala (where emotional memories are stored), and other parts of the limbic system of the brain. Because the limbic system is directly connected to those parts of the brain that store and release emotional trauma, breathing, memory, and stress levels, essential oils can have profound physiological and psychological effects.

Odor triggers the limbic system to release brain-affecting chemicals known as neurochemicals. Enkephalin reduces pain and creates a feeling of well-being. Endorphins also reduce pain and induce sexual feelings. Serotonin helps relax and calm. The sense of smell is the only one of the five senses directly linked to the limbic lobe of the brain, the emotional content center; anxiety, depression, fear, anger, gratitude, and happiness all emanate from this region. A fragrance can evoke memories and emotions before we are even consciously aware of it. When you sniff something, signals from the odor receptors in your nose reach your amygdala first, producing an immediate, visceral reaction.

"With all of the other senses, you think before you respond, but with scent, your brain responds before you think," says Pam Scholder Ellen, a Georgia State University marketing professor.

A student who participated in an essential oil training I was teaching had an experience that displays the power of aromatherapy and memory. Through kinesiology or muscle testing, we determined that the Young Living essential oil of Idaho balsam fir might be helpful for her. She applied two drops of this oil topically over her heart and lungs. Within thirty seconds of application and repeated inhalation, gentle tears began rolling down her cheeks.

When I asked her what she was noticing, she replied that she suddenly had a memory. She recalled that when she was eighteen years old, both of her parents had passed away six months apart in two separate car accidents. The grief had been overwhelming. Soon after, she developed asthma. Although she had never connected her grief with the asthma, she could now easily feel the trail from the events to her symptoms. She could feel the grief that had been buried in her chest and lungs. Currently in her early thirties, she had been using an inhaler ever since to help manage the asthma. Her emotional release was relatively calm, and despite the intensity of the traumatic event, it lasted for about five minutes, then gradually passed.

Later that day, she shared with me that she had not needed to use her inhaler since applying the Idaho balsam fir oil. In follow-up phone calls over the next few months, she informed me that her asthma symptoms were mostly gone, and when she did begin to feel tightness in her chest, she simply applied more Idaho balsam fir. (Note: although it was effective for her, others with asthma have applied the same fir oil without the same results.)

This was a turning point in my understanding of the healing possibilities available through the use of essential oils. What seemed like a miracle at that time was simply the chemistry of essential oils at work in her brain. "The emotional power of smell-triggered memory has an intensity unequaled by sight—and sound-triggered ones," writes Rachel Herz, a Brown University neuroscientist, in a paper summing up more than a decade of her research.

Let's take a closer look at the brain. James Donahue, author of *The Amazing Brain Music Adventure*, writes, "The three pounds of solid neurocircuitry between every person's ears is the most complex structure we know of in the entire universe. You have more connections in your brain than there are literally grains of sand on all the beaches on Earth. Carl Sagan has pointed out that in every brain, your fantastic one included, there are more combinations of connections than there are protons and neutrons in the universe. Heck, telepathy is nothing for your infinity brain calculator."

Donahue continues, "Studies by behaviorist and researcher T.D.A. Lingo, in his work from 1957 through 1993, have been able to pinpoint this area of the brain which seems to be responsible for releasing enormous levels of untapped intelligence, creativity, and pleasure. Additionally, and remarkably so, stimulating the amygdala frequently turns on such 'hidden' brain functions as precognition, clairvoyance, clairaudience, telepathy, telekinesis, and can even allow the ability for some individuals to communicate with non-ordinary physical and non-physical intelligences and entities.

"In addition to evoking memories and balancing body systems, we now know that stimulating the amygdala with pure unadulterated plant essences can produce intense emotional states known historically throughout world cultures and religions by various names: nirvana, satori, samadhi, peak experience, cosmic consciousness, or one-with-the-universe rapture."

This tells us that suffering and joy sit side by side in our brain. At the same time we are stimulating our amygdala to release traumatic memories, we are also connecting to our source of pleasure. By inhaling essential oils and applying them on the anterior amygdala, we can cause an increase in frontal lobes processes, which instantly create increased and measurable levels of intelligence, creativity, contentment, and, often, various "normal-paranormal" experiences.

Essential Oils and ADHD

Attention Deficit Disorder (ADD) and Attention Deficit/Hyperactivity Disorder (ADHD) are terms that describe a group of chronic neurobiological disorders affecting brain function, and occurring since childhood. A person with ADD/ADHD has problems formulating goals, making plans to reach those goals, and organizing and integrating information. Other common symptoms include mood swings, short temper, talking excessively, impulsivity, inability to control physical activity, and difficulty sustaining attention and concentration.

It is estimated that in the United States, 4 to 7 percent of children and 3 to 5 percent of adults have ADD/ADHD; however, some school classrooms report that as many as 30 percent of the students are being treated for this illness. According to a number of researchers, up to half the people afflicted with this condition are still undiagnosed. Two-thirds of children exhibiting ADD/ADHD will have it as an adult.

In the following study, conducted by Dr. Terry Friedmann, essential oils were used to help children ages six to fourteen who were previously diagnosed as having ADHD. None of them was being treated with medication at the time nor had even taken medication specifically for this disorder. In the study, sixteen controls received no treatment, and eighteen subjects were treated with one of three essential oils.[1]

In the study, Friedmann used real-time electroencephalograph (EEG) to measure electrical impulses in the brain by placing small sensors called electrodes on the scalp to detect the electrical impulses moving through the brain. While the real-time EEG equipment is capable of measuring all the brain waves, only two parameter types were measured, beta and theta waves. The beta brain waves, whose frequency is thirteen to thirty cycles per second, reflect those waves that are being produced by the brain when the subject is alert and/or performing a task. The theta waves, on the other hand, whose frequency is four to eight cycles per second, reflect the brain in the state of sleep or daydreaming but awake.

Friedmann observed that initially there was a difference between the waves of normal children compared to ADHD children. While brain waves from normal children were high in amounts of beta waves and low in the amounts of theta waves during waking hours, the reverse was true in the children diagnosed with ADHD. In other words, ADHD children had higher amounts of theta waves as compared to beta waves.

The first oil administered was cedarwood, chosen because its high concentration of sesquiterpenes, which make up 50 percent of its constituents, improves oxygenation of the cells of the brain. The second oil was vetiver, which calms and balances the nervous system and at the same time stimulates the circulatory system. The third oil was lavender, which has a sedative as well as a stimulating action. It sedates part of the brain and at the same time stimulates the limbic region of the brain. The subjects inhaled the chosen essential oil of choice daily for a period of thirty days, after which they were retested, and the beta-theta ratios were again recorded.

In studies conducted at Vienna and Berlin Universities, researchers found that sesquiterpenes, found in essential oils such as vetiver, patchouli, cedarwood, san-

---

1. Friedmann is an internationally acclaimed author, speaker, and practitioner. For over thirty years, he has helped people discover how essential oils help attain and maintain wellness of body, mind, and spirit. A pioneer in holistic medicine, Friedmann discovered cures for problems for which conventional medicine has no answers. He is the author of several books on natural medicine and essential oils for wellness. (www.DrFriedmannEssentialOils.com).

dalwood, melissa, myrrh, clove, and frankincense increase levels of oxygen in the brain by up to 28 percent (Nasel, 1992). Such an increase in oxygen leads to a heightened level of activity in the hypothalamus and limbic systems, which have dramatic effects on not only emotions, learning and attitude, but also on many physical processes such as immune function, hormone balance, and energy levels. These essential oils—through their fragrance and unique molecular structure—exert a profound effect on mind and body.

According to Friedmann, treatment outcome results reveal that the essential oil vetiver improved the brain activity and reduced the symptoms in subjects diagnosed with ADHD. The improvement was 32 percent. Similar results were found with the essential oil cedarwood, although not as statistically significant. The lavender group showed no apparent improvement after the treatment program.

In addition, parents stated that their children's behavior at home had improved. In several cases, school educators informed them that their child's performance improved in the classroom, and report cards reflected this improvement as well. Based on this study, the use of the essential oils vetiver or cedarwood proved to be the treatment of choice for children diagnosed with ADHD, and may help adults with this diagnosis as well.

If you have difficulty concentrating while doing a somatic excavation, or suffer from ADHD, these particular oils may offer you assistance. Apply the oil at the base of your skull and on your temples. Inhale deeply and repeatedly as needed.

Essential Oils as Energy Medicine

Plants transmute life energy from one form to another by using light in their metabolic process. Called photosynthesis, this process allows green plants to produce simple carbohydrates from carbon dioxide and hydrogen, using energy that chlorophyll absorbs from radiant sources. Plants raise the vibration of molecules by using light. Essential oils, then, are fundamentally light in a bottle.

When we view the body as an energetic blueprint designed by our life experiences, we understand that we can alter our blueprint through shifts in energy. As energy, or light medicine, essential oils create pathways for movement in our blueprint, shining a flashlight on our excavation site and allowing us to release physical congestion and emotional imprints more easily.

Every living thing has a vibration, a wavelength that is measurable and tangible. According to Dr. Royal R. Rife, every disease has a frequency as well. He explains that a substance with a higher frequency will destroy disease with its lower frequency. Measuring in hertz, food has a frequency from 0-15Hz, dry herbs from 15-22Hz, and fresh herbs from 20-27Hz. Essential oils start at 50Hz and go as high as 320Hz, which is the frequency of therapeutic-grade rose oil. A healthy body from head to foot typically has a frequency ranging from 62-78Hz. Disease begins at 58Hz.

Clinical research shows that essential oils have the highest frequency of any substance known to man, creating an environment in which disease, bacteria, virus, fungus, etc., cannot live. This high frequency of essential oils also impacts our emotional state, energetically shifting us from a depressed state to an enlivened feeling. In addition, these higher frequencies can bring enhanced spiritual sensitivity and alignment. (*Essential Oil Desk Reference,* Fourth Edition, 2007)

Aroma Memory

You may inhale a particular fragrance and enjoy it, whereas someone else may find the same aroma distasteful. This difference is based on what I like to call *aroma memory*. Particular aromas are stored alongside the memory of an event. For example, when storykeepers unearth memories of medical or surgical procedures, the aroma of anesthesia may be discharged as they liberate the associated fear, even if it has been years since the actual event. One somatic client released the definitive aroma of her perpetrator's aftershave while unearthing memories of incest. Concurrently, clients who uncover joyful memories buried underneath a traumatic experience can evoke an aroma of something pleasurable, such as the smell of homemade cookies or the aroma of pine trees.

This works the other way around as well. A man who, as a young boy, got stung by a bee while breathing a rose bush had an instant recall of that memory upon inhaling rose oil with great distaste. In another case, one aromatherapy student was repelled by the aroma of juniper and began to feel nauseous. As she breathed into the sensations in her stomach, she remembered that as a young girl, she had to trim the juniper bushes along the walkway of her family home. It was one of her most despised jobs, as the work was hard and the juniper branches scratched her arms. She was able, with the help of the juniper oil, to release the anger and resentment she was holding in her stomach.

Certain essential oils are very calming and sedating to the central nervous system (including both the sympathetic and parasympathetic systems), giving our bodies an outlet for trapped anxiety, allowing it to release instead of build up. Anxiety creates an acidic condition in the body that activates the transcript enzyme, which then transcribes that anxiety on the RNA template and stores it in the DNA. Once transcribed, that emotion becomes predominant from that moment forward, and it can be passed on to future generations, establishing somatic memories and belief patterns. (*Essential Oil Desk Reference,* Fourth Edition, 2007)

Essential oils can also encourage mental clarity and help program the mind with positive beliefs by opening the subconscious mind, allowing the release of emotions and negative stored memories. Essential oils raise our body frequencies, encourage spiritual connection, and amplify our intent. While enhancing intuition, they will deepen your awareness of personal patterns and inspire self-love and self-esteem—plus, they smell great!

Application of Essential Oils

Many therapeutic-grade essential oils are safe to apply topically, but since each person's body is different, first test the oil on a small patch of skin for fifteen minutes. Apply diluted oil to the sensitive skin on the inside of your inner arm. If redness, burning, or irritation occurs, discontinue use, and apply a few more drops of carrier oil to dilute further. Do not use water to dilute; it will increase the action of the oil. If there is no skin reaction, you may continue use.

For dilution, mix 50/50; or dilute one to three drops of essential oil with a half teaspoon of massage oil or a quality organic carrier oil such as grapeseed, olive, wheat germ, apricot seed kernel, jojoba, or sweet almond oil, or a blend of these. Before and after applying oils, wash your hands thoroughly with soap and water.

When starting an essential oil application, it may be helpful to apply the oils to the bottom of your feet first; which can typically be done with an undiluted oil. This allows your body to become acclimated to the oil. Frequency of use depends upon the individual. As a general rule, when applying oils to yourself for the first time, do not apply more than two singles or blends at one time. Rub the oil clockwise into your body and allow it to absorb for two to three minutes before applying another oil. Breathe the fragrance in slowly and deeply three times to stimulate the amygdala.

Safety Tips

Essential oils are very concentrated, so it's important to handle them with care. Treat them as you would any medicine, and be sure to keep them out of the reach of children, with caps tightly closed. Always store essential oils in glass or earthenware containers, as plastic particles can leach into oils when they are stored in plastic bottles. Essential oils are an investment and so you should keep them out of extreme temperatures, especially heat, and out of direct sunlight, so they will last many years. Do not touch the top of the bottles with your fingers, as this will contaminate pure oil; instead turn the bottle at a slight angle and allow the drops to fall into your hand.

Always read and follow all label warnings and cautions on bottles. Keep oils away from eyes, inside of ears, and mucous membranes as they will irritate sensitive areas. It is advisable to double your intake of water when using essential oils to assist in flushing any toxins that may be released.

Angelica and all citrus oils make the skin more sensitive to ultraviolet light. Do not go out into the sun with citrus oils on your skin. Some essential oils should be avoided during pregnancy, or if you have epilepsy, high blood pressure, or cancer. Please check with your physician or health care professional before administering essential oils to yourself.

Application Protocol

Below is a reference list of aromatic single oils and carefully designed Young Living essential oil blends that commonly accompany the Practice of Somatic Archaeology. It is nice, but not at all necessary, to have the oils listed; choose essential oils that align with your personal needs and recovery goals. Apply before beginning or during your somatic excavation.

1. Choose an essential oil; trust your intuition and let your heart guide you. Play with different oils and take time to savor your chosen fragrance.

2. While holding an essential oil in your hands, begin by coming into a state of gratitude for the gifts of the plant world and for the harmony of Mother Earth, being mindful to acknowledge those who helped plant, water, harvest, distill, package, and ship the essential oil, until it arrived in your hands. Send blessings out to all.

3. Place a few drops of the essential oil of choice into your non-dominant hand, then use the pointer finger of your dominant hand to *charge* the oil by mixing or swirling clockwise. To enhance charging, focus your mind on your intent or affirmation. Add the same amount of carrier oil to your hand if you decide to dilute.

4. Apply essential oil in a clockwise motion to the desired area of your body until it is absorbed. If any skin irritation or sensitivity occurs upon applica-

tion, you may dilute again topically with a quality carrier oil on the site of application.

5. Rub your hands together, and with hands cupped over your nose, deeply inhale the essential oil three times, feeling and visualizing the aroma reaching all the cells in your brain, concentrating on both hemispheres—and especially on your frontal lobe, amygdala, hypothalamus, and hippocampus. You can place the palm of your hand over your forehead to encompass your frontal lobe. Visualize that everything under your hand is your frontal lobe.

6. While breathing in the aroma, repeat an affirmation or intent for your healing process. Be sure to use empowering language, such as, "I am in alignment with the universal flow," versus, "I want to be in alignment." Choose words that have positive influence and are not coercive or based on needing, wanting, or trying—affirmations that use these words will amplify need, want, and the ambivalence of trying. Begin affirmations with words such as: I am, I can, I will, I choose, I create, I love, I enjoy.

7. You can also create an aromatic mood enhancer mist by adding a few drops of your chosen essential oil into water in a mister bottle. Spray on clothes, pillows, or into the air to sweeten a space, enhance meditation, or create a relaxing atmosphere.

Aroma-Mood Reference Guide

(Augmented with references from Young Living's *Essential Oil Desk Reference*, and *Releasing Emotional Patterns with Essential Oils* by Dr. Carolyn Mein.)

For Depression, Grief, and Regret

Aroma Life is a trademarked blend of cypress, marjoram, helichrysum, and ylang ylang. It combines the harmonizing effects of ylang ylang with oils good for your heart, circulatory system, and lungs. Pulsing with life, this vibrant blend energizes your life force and helps to ease loneliness and longing. It is best applied over the front and back of your heart chakra and chest.

Geranium helps release negative memories and eases nervous tension. It balances the emotions, lifts the spirits, and fosters peace, well-being, and hope with a wonderfully uplifting, calming, flowery scent. It is excellent for the skin, and its aromatic influence helps release negative memories. Apply over your heart and on hands and feet.

Joy is a sweet blend of bergamot, ylang ylang, geranium, rosewood, lemon, mandarin, jasmine, Roman chamomile, palmarosa, and rose. It enhances self-love and joyfulness, and is excellent for grief and fear of judgment. This trademarked blend creates magnetic energy, and, when worn as cologne or perfume, it exudes an alluring fragrance that inspires romance and togetherness. When diffused, it can be refreshing and uplifting. Apply it over your heart and on the bridge of your nose for grief.

Palo Santo comes from the same botanical family as frankincense, although it is found in South America rather than the Middle East. Like frankincense, Palo Santo is known as a spiritual oil, traditionally used by the Incas to purify and cleanse the spirit from negative energies. Even its Spanish name reflects how highly this oil is regarded: Palo Santo means *holy wood* or *sacred wood*. Apply on the spine or at the base of the skull for meditation and relaxation.

Patchouli has a musky, earthy aroma commonly used to provide general support for health and to help release negative emotions. It is very beneficial for the skin, helping to reduce a wrinkled or chapped appearance. Patchouli is a general tonic that supports the digestive system, releases anxiety in the belly, and is grounding and sedating.

Rose is a beautiful, strong floral fragrance that is intoxicating and highly romantic. It helps bring balance and harmony with stimulating and uplifting properties that create a sense of well-being, self-confidence, and wholeness. It increases self-love and unification of all aspects of self. Apply it around the navel and over your heart.

Ylang Ylang balances the male/female energies, enhances spiritual attunement, and combats anger and low self-esteem. This aroma restores confidence and peace, filtering out negative energy, thoughts, and nervous irritability. It is good for possessiveness and fear of wisdom. Ylang ylang is extremely effective in calming and bringing about a sense of relaxation and romance. Apply on the front of the throat chakra and over your heart.

For Recent Trauma or Shock

Ruta VaLa is a blend of ruta graveolens, valerian root, and lavender. It promotes relaxation of the body and mind while helping to ease tension and relieve stress through the parasympathetic nervous system. Use it to overcome negative feelings while encouraging a positive attitude and comfort. It is also good for insomnia. Apply it topically to the back of neck, on the spine, or on the bottoms of your feet.

Trauma Life is a trademarked blend of frankincense, sandalwood, valerian, lavender, davana, spruce, geranium, helichrysum, citrus hystrix, and rose, formulated to help release buried emotional trauma resulting from accidents, neglect, death of a loved one, assault, or abuse. It purges stress and restlessness, and is excellent for shock. Apply where needed, or on the base of skull for head injuries.

Valor is a copyrighted blend of spruce, rosewood, blue tansy, and frankincense. It works with both the physical and spiritual aspects of the body to foster feelings of strength, courage, and self-esteem in the face of adversity. Renowned for its strengthening qualities, it enhances an individual's internal resources and helps align energy in the body. It is beneficial for those who feel unable to cope with life or current day-to-day stressors. Apply it to the soles of your feet, your hips, and between your shoulder blades.

For Grounding and Encouraging Feelings of Safety

Black pepper has a pungent, crisp aroma that is comforting and energizing. It supports the digestive system and is useful topically for soothing muscle discomfort following exercise. Use this oil for psychic attack, invasive thoughts, or when you feel that you are stuck in a black hole. Breathe it in while applying it on hands and wrists, then sprinkle it into your energy field by flicking your fingers around you.

Gathering is a trademarked blend of lavender, galbanum, frankincense, geranium, ylang ylang, spruce, cinnamon, rose, and sandalwood. It helps overcome chaotic energy that bombards our everyday life and clouds our focus, and helps gather our emotional and spiritual forces so we can achieve greater unity of purpose. It is good for the person who lacks the ability to see stored emotions clearly. Apply it on the crown of the head and the base of the skull.

Grounding is a trademarked blend of white fir, spruce, ylang ylang, pine, cedarwood, angelica, and juniper. Use this oil when memories are so horrific that the recipient is unable to endure them and decides that he/she wants to leave this life physically or mentally. Use it to create a stabilizing influence and to help cope with reality in a positive manner. Apply it to the back of your neck, sternum, and bottoms of feet.

Lavender is the most versatile of all essential oils, always soothing and refreshing. It can assist the body when adapting to stress or imbalances. It is a great aid for relaxing and winding down before bedtime, yet has balancing properties that can also boost stamina and energy. Therapeutic-grade lavender is highly regarded for skin and beauty, and may be used to soothe and cleanse common cuts, bruises, and skin irritations. When applied on the hips it may help with feelings of abandonment. Apply over the heart, on wrists, and on the back of neck before sleep.

Sacred Mountain is a trademarked blend of spruce, ylang ylang, fir, and cedarwood for evoking feelings of sanctity that are typically found in the mountains. It promotes feelings of strength, empowerment, grounding, and protection that are a result of being close to nature. Spiritually aligning, it is good to use before making decisions. Apply it on the solar plexus or over your heart.

Valor is a trademarked blend of spruce, rosewood, blue tansy, and frankincense. It works with both the physical and spiritual aspects of the body to foster feelings of strength, courage, and self-esteem in the face of adversity. Renowned for its strengthening qualities, it enhances an individual's internal resources and helps align energy in the body. It is beneficial for those who feel unable to cope with life or current day-to-day stressors. Apply it to the soles of your feet, your hips, and between your shoulder blades.

White Angelica is a trademarked blend of bergamot, geranium, myrrh, sandalwood, rosewood, ylang ylang, spruce, hyssop, melissa, and rose. It is calming and soothing, and encourages feelings of protection and security. It enhances your body's aura to bring about a sense of strength and endurance. Many people use it as protection against negative energy, and it is excellent for loneliness. Apply it on your shoulders and over your heart and navel.

For Uprooting and Integrating Memories

Acceptance is a trademarked blend of rosewood, geranium, frankincense, blue tansy, sandalwood, and neroli. It stimulates the mind with oils specially blended to promote feelings of acceptance of ourselves and others regardless of perceived barriers. It is useful for those who are unable to get past memory blocks. This blend also helps overcome procrastination and denial. Apply it on the forehead.

Forgiveness is a trademarked blend of melissa, geranium, frankincense, rosewood, sandalwood, angelica, lavender, lemon, jasmine, Roman chamomile, bergamot, ylang ylang, palmarosa, helichrysum, and rose. It enables one to forgive, forget, and move forward. Forgiveness may enhance the ability to release hurtful memories and move beyond emotional barriers. Apply it around the navel.

Inner Child is a trademarked blend of orange, tangerine, jasmine, ylang ylang, spruce, sandalwood, lemongrass, and neroli. Inner Child opens the pathway to connecting with the inner self that may have been damaged through childhood abuse. The sweet fragrance of this blend may stimulate memory response and help reconnect with the authentic self and emotional balance. Apply it around your navel, on your forehead, and under your nose.

Myrrh promotes spiritual awareness and is one of the oldest known essential oils on record. It is helpful for those who have a fear of facing the world. Myrrh is purifying, restorative, revitalizing, and uplifting. It is a helpful aid to meditation, having one of the highest levels of sesquiterpenes (a class of compounds that have a direct effect on the hypothalamus, pituitary, and amygdala, the seat of our emotions). Apply it on your third eye, the base of your skull, or on your feet for grounding.

Present Time is a trademarked blend of neroli, spruce, and ylang ylang. It has an empowering fragrance that heightens the sense of being "in the moment." You can go forward and progress when you focus on the present time; this oil is perfect for a person who is overly focused on the past. It is good for TMJ and jaw tension. Apply it over the thymus or on your mandibular joint on the lower jaw.

Purification is a trademarked blend of citronella, lemongrass, rosemary, melaleuca, lavandin, and myrtle. It is excellent for those who are afraid of being seen; apply it liberally to the base of your skull. It helps to break through negative or erroneous thoughts, and is useful for releasing anger and breaking addictive patterns when massaged over the liver. Apply it on the solar plexus, liver, or at the base of the skull. Purification can be used directly on the skin to cleanse and soothe insect bites, cuts, and scrapes. When diffused, it helps to purify and cleanse the air from environmental impurities including cigarette smoke and other disagreeable odors.

Release is a trademarked blend of ylang ylang, lavandin, geranium, sandalwood, and blue tansy. It combines uplifting and calming oils, which help you to let go of anger and frustration, enabling a sense of peace and emotional well-being. It is good for rebellion and repressed negative emotions that lie at the root of health concerns. It promotes harmony and balance in the mind and body when applied over the liver area, on the throat, and on the crown of your head.

SARA is a trademarked blend of ylang ylang, geranium, lavender, orange, blue tansy, cedarwood, rose, and white lotus, an empowering blend designed to help soothe deep emotional wounds. It may help you release and begin recovery from traumatic memories of sexual or ritual torment and other forms of physical or emotional abuse. SARA is an acronym for Sexual And Ritual Abuse. Apply it to the navel, chest, or second chakra for clearing.

Surrender is a trademarked blend of lavender, Roman chamomile, German chamomile, angelica, mountain savory, lemon, and spruce. This calming, soothing blend is formulated for individuals who feel a need to control. It helps quiet troubled hearts so that negative emotions can be released. Surrender may also help return feelings of equilibrium and inner strength. It is best used with frankincense or conifer oils. Apply it at the hairline on the brow to stimulate the amygdala.

For Stress and Insomnia

Lavender is the most versatile of all essential oils, always soothing and refreshing. It can assist the body when adapting to stress or imbalances. It is a great aid for relaxing and winding down before bedtime, yet has balancing properties that can also boost stamina and energy. Therapeutic-grade lavender is highly regarded for skin and beauty, and may be used to soothe and cleanse common cuts, bruises, and skin irritations. When applied on the hips it may help with feelings of abandonment. Apply over the heart, on wrists, and on the back of neck before sleep.

Palo Santo comes from the same botanical family as frankincense, although it is found in South America rather than the Middle East. Like frankincense, Palo Santo is known as a spiritual oil, traditionally used by the Incas to purify and cleanse the spirit from negative energies. Even its Spanish name reflects how highly this oil is regarded: Palo Santo means *holy wood* or *sacred wood*. Apply on the spine or at the base of the skull for meditation or relaxation.

Peace & Calming is a trademarked blend of tangerine, orange, ylang ylang, patchouli, and blue tansy. It promotes relaxation and a deep sense of peace. This is a gentle, fragrant blend that helps calm tensions and uplift the spirit. When massaged on the bottoms of your feet, it can be a wonderful prelude to a peaceful night's rest. It is especially calming and comforting to young children after an overactive and stressful day. Apply on your shoulders to reduce addictive tendencies, depression, anxiety, stress, and insomnia. Diffuse it at home or work, and apply it at the base of your neck or on your wrists.

Ruta VaLa is a blend of ruta graveolens, valerian root, and lavender. It promotes relaxation of the body and mind while helping to ease tension and relieve stress through the parasympathetic nervous system. Use it to overcome negative feelings while encouraging a positive attitude and comfort. It is also good for insomnia. Apply it topically to the back of neck, on the spine, or on the bottoms of your feet.

Sandalwood enhances deep sleep and may help remove negative programming from the cells. It is good for fear of the unknown when applied to the third eye or sixth chakra. Used traditionally as incense in religious ceremonies and for meditation, it is uplifting and relaxing.

For Mental Balance and Clarity

Brain Power is a trademarked blend of sandalwood, cedarwood, melissa, frankincense, blue cypress, lavender, and helichrysum that give your brain a boost with essential oils that are high in sesquiterpenes. Use it to clarify thought, develop greater focus, and remedy apathy and brain fog. It increases mental potential and clarity and helps to channel physical energy into mental energy. It promotes deep concentration. Apply it on your temples or on the back of your neck.

Cedarwood stimulates the limbic region of the brain. It has been studied as a successful support oil for ADD and ADHD in children. It is noted for its calming, grounding, and purifying properties, and helps recipients deal with conceit. Apply it on temples or the third eye, at the base of your brain, at the base of your spine, or at the first chakra.

Clarity is a trademarked blend of basil, cardamom, rosemary, peppermint, rosewood, geranium, lemon, palmarosa, ylang ylang, bergamot, Roman chamomile, and jasmine. It has been used to promote a clear mind and mental alertness when applied on the back of the neck and temples. Clarity may help keep one awake while driving and also keep one from going into shock during times of trauma. It is excellent when it is applied topically over the ovaries when clearing memories from your female lineage. Dilute it with a carrier oil if sensitivity occurs.

Frankincense increases spiritual awareness and promotes meditation. It is useful for visualizing or improving one's spiritual connection, and it has comforting properties that help focus the mind and overcome stress and despair. It may also help improve attitude and uplift spirits, which helps strengthen the immune system. Apply it over the solar plexus when anger is projected at others, especially when decisions need to be made during crises. It is high in sesquiterpenes, and beneficial when rubbed on your forehead and on your temples.

Envision is a trademarked blend of spruce, geranium, orange, lavender, sage, and rose, which stimulates creative and intuitive abilities in a positive and progressive way. Envision stimulates creativity and resourcefulness, encouraging renewed faith in the future and the ability to maintain the emotional fortitude necessary to achieve goals and dreams. Apply it over your heart and on the crown of your head to awaken and renew internal drives to overcome fear and experience more rewarding dimensions.

Lemon promotes clarity of thought and purpose. Lemon has a strong, purifying, citrus scent that is revitalizing and uplifting. It boosts immunity, consisting of 68 percent D-limonene, a powerful antioxidant. It is delightfully refreshing in water and may be beneficial for the skin. In his book, *The Practice of Aromatherapy*, Jean Valnet writes that lemon is a tonic for supporting the nervous and sympathetic nervous system. Apply it on the front of throat, on lymph glands, or on your wrists.

Peppermint is purifying and stimulating to the conscious mind. It has a strong, clean, fresh aroma, and is one of the most highly regarded herbs for soothing digestion. Peppermint has been studied for its supportive effect on the liver and respiratory systems, and its role in improving taste and smell when inhaled. Dr. Alan Hirsch studied peppermint's ability to affect directly the brain's satiety center, which triggers a sensation of fullness after meals. Apply it on the back of your neck or temples for headaches, or topically on any area that is red, swollen, or inflamed for quick relief. Apply it on your belly for stomachaches or nausea. Keep it away from your eyes and mucous membranes. This powerful essential oil is often diluted before topical application.

Vetiver has a heavy, earthy fragrance similar to patchouli with a touch of lemon. It is psychologically grounding, calming, and stabilizing. One of the oils that is highest in sesquiterpenes, vetiver was studied by Dr. Terry Friedmann for improving ADHD behavior in children. It may help when coping with stress and to recover from emotional trauma and shock. Apply it on the back of your neck, on temples, and on brow. Breathe in fully for best results.

For Balance, Enhancement, and Harmony

Abundance is a trademarked blend of orange, frankincense, patchouli, clove, ginger, myrrh, cinnamon, and spruce essential oils. It enhances the frequency of your luminous body and brings about an abundance of physical and emotional health which can be amplified with the use of positive affirmations while applying it. It creates what is called "the law of attraction," opening up a wealth of possibilities. Apply it topically on your wrists or you're your heart. Because of possible skin sensitivity, dilute it with a carrier oil before using.

Aroma Life is a trademarked blend of cypress, marjoram, helichrysum, and ylang ylang. It combines the harmonizing effects of ylang ylang with oils good for your heart, circulatory system, and lungs. Pulsing with life, this vibrant blend energizes your life force, and helps to ease loneliness and longing. It is best applied over the front and back of your heart chakra and chest.

Awaken is a trademarked combination of several other oil Young Living blends—Joy, Present Time, Forgiveness, Dream Catcher, and Harmony—that help bring about inner knowing and awakening, the first step toward making successful changes and desirable transitions. This blend enhances your highest potential. Apply it on the sacrum for staying grounded while changing, or on your brow to encourage awareness.

Gratitude is a trademarked blend of Idaho balsam fir, frankincense, rosewood, myrrh, galbanum, and ylang ylang. This soothing blend is designed to elevate the spirit, calm emotions, and bring relief to the body while helping to foster a grateful attitude. Use it for spiritual inspiration and affirmation of your blessings. Apply it over your heart, on the crown of your head, or on your feet.

Harmony is a beautiful trademarked blend of lavender, sandalwood, ylang ylang, frankincense, orange, angelica, geranium, hyssop, spruce, Spanish sage, rosewood, lemon, jasmine, Roman chamomile, bergamot, palmarosa, and rose. It promotes physical and emotional well-being by bringing harmonic balance to the energy centers of the body. The liberating, balancing, and calming essential oils in this blend open you to new possibilities while contributing to an overall feeling of harmony. Place a couple of drops on the energy meridians, on chakras, and over your heart.

Hope is a trademarked blend of melissa, myrrh, juniper, and spruce. Hope helps you reconnect with feelings of strength and grounding, restoring hope for tomorrow. This unique blend brings together the benefits of essential oils with the power to uplift and balance the emotions, making you more open to the joys that lie ahead. It may also help you to overcome severe dark thoughts. It restores the vision of goals and dreams, and it may help lift you from feelings of despair. Massage it on the outer edges of your ears and over your heart.

Idaho balsam fir is a conifer oil distilled in northern Idaho. It has a refreshing and uplifting scent. It is soothing for muscle and body discomfort associated with exercise and it creates clarity of mind and harmonious relationships. Rub it on your chest for asthma. Apply it a few inches above the crown of your head to clear your eighth chakra and help you to stay grounded in your body.

Into the Future is a trademarked blend of clary sage, ylang ylang, white fir, Idaho tansy, juniper, jasmine, frankincense, orange, and cedarwood. It was formulated to foster feelings of determination and a pioneering spirit, helping you leave the past behind so that you can move forward with vision and excitement. Apply it on the crown of your head, above your eyes and over your solar plexus.

Thieves is a trademarked blend of clove, lemon, cinnamon, eucalyptus radiata, and rosemary. Thieves was created based on research about four thieves in France who covered themselves with cloves, rosemary, and other aromatics in order to protect themselves from sickness while they were robbing plague victims. This proprietary essential oil blend was university tested for its cleansing abilities. It is highly effective in supporting the immune system and good health. It is also good to use when you are uncertain or unable to focus. Apply it to lymph glands or on your feet. Dilute it for sensitive skin and children. Keep away from the eyes and mucous membranes.

Ylang ylang balances the male/female energies, enhances spiritual attunement, and combats anger and low self-esteem. This aroma restores confidence and peace, filtering out negative energy, thoughts, and nervous irritability. It is good for possessiveness and fear of wisdom. Ylang ylang is extremely effective in calming and bringing about a sense of relaxation and romance. Apply on the front of the throat chakra and over your heart.

The Food and Drug Administration has not evaluated the statements above, and these products are not intended to diagnose, treat, cure, or prevent any disease.

> *Every little cell in my body is happy, every little cell in my body is well.*
> *Every little cell in my body is happy, every little cell in my body is swell.*
> *I can tell, every little cell, every little cell in my body is well*
> *I can tell, every little cell, every little cell in my body is swell.*
>
> —Somatic Archaeology theme song

6

Tools to Excavate Your Story

Australian Aborigines say that the big stories—the stories worth telling and retelling, the ones in which you may find the meaning of your life—are forever stalking the right teller, sniffing and tracking like predators hunting their prey in the bush.

—Robert Moss, *Dreamgates*

There are three archetypes for Somatic Archaeologists to include in their tool belts. The Warrior, the Magician, and the Lover are the three basic earthbound mythological personalities that manifest in our interactions with people and situations. In Carl Jung's psychological framework, archetypes are innate, universal prototypes for ideas that may be used to interpret observations. They are deeply woven into our collective consciousness. Deliberately shifting from one archetypal state of mind to another will allow you to use the excavation tools in this chapter to your best ability. Embody the role you need to approach your somatic excavation with confidence and compassion.

The Warrior

The Warrior is the activist, the part of you that fights for what it wants and needs, reclaiming ownership of your body and story, standing ground and maintaining boundaries. When the battle seems lost, the Warrior rides over the hill and saves the day. Tough and courageous, this archetype evolved from the models of our animal companions. Assuming the stance of a particular animal will ally you with their powers. The Warrior is the part of us that helps set and achieve goals, overcome obstacles, and persist in difficult times. The Warrior speaks the truth and demands clarity, justice, and respect—this is my body, this is my story, and this is my life!

The Magician

The Magician creates the bridge to move from one state of mind to another; it is the part of you that dreams a new story and uses alchemy to convert your losses into gains, turning your suffering into joy. The Magician archetype searches out the fundamental laws of science and metaphysics to understand how to regenerate, transform situations, influence people, and make visions into realities. The Magician aligns with sacred law instead of human law, relying on the stars and cosmos for inspiration and guidance. The Magician can take the beauty from inside of you and build a temple with it in your life.

The Lover

The Lover holds space for it all to happen; it is the part of you unattached to circumstance or outcome, the compassionate and enduring companion of fate. The Lover honors your human process and blesses your body, witnessing the absolute perfection of your story and those who play a part in it. The Lover dances with the plant world, using the power of flowers, trees, and roots to achieve balance and kinship. The Lover archetype governs all kinds of love, from parental love to friendship to spiritual love to romantic love. It helps us experience pleasure, create intimacy, make commitments, and follow our bliss.

Fear of Your Story

Embody these three archetypes as you address the fears and self-doubt that are an integral part of the excavation process. Fear of witnessing or remembering your story can immobilize you and keep you from moving forward or changing. It is important to allow yourself to acknowledge any fears you have *and* continue to excavate. Fear cannot dominate your self-exploration. It is useful to feel your fear to the fullest, smile at it, thank it, and then dig right through it, for you have important things to remember. Become the Warrior to give you strength to look fear in the eyes; become the Magician to transform fear into power; become the Lover to embrace and tenderize fear by singing to it sweetly.

Fear programs you to protect, to cover, to create facades, and to wear masks. If you have to hold yourself together and be stoic, how deeply can you dig? There are times during a somatic excavation when you just can't wear a suit and tie. You must leave behind your starched white shirt and jump into the muck. Don't hold back. Have courage, take heart, and remind yourself that you are revealing your story in order to find your future. The goal is to meet yourself in the shadows with your eyes wide open.

Talk about your fears and how they make you feel; notice where they originate in your body. Breathe into them and expose them, make sense of them, address them, and find accommodations for them. They are the deep scars of your humanity, your trapped aspirations, your failures, and the shadow side of your dreams. Touch them, witness them, and honor your vulnerability. You cannot think your way out of fear, but you can feel your way out.

Somatic Excavation Techniques

1) Somatic Breathwork, or *Stirring the Dirt*

Somatic breathwork is done by consciously breathing into specific areas of your body. Your breath is the vehicle of your awareness. Where your breath goes, your awareness goes. When you use your breath to connect to your soma, it keeps you present and instigates release of emotional patterns. Pay attention to the places your breath avoids; this is the best indicator of where charged emotional holding patterns are buried. Somatic breathwork develops awareness of tension patterns and aids in relaxation; it helps you to pay attention to your body. The energy in your body naturally flows from left to right, from top to bottom, and from back to front. Navigate with your breath and encourage these natural flows for balancing and pain release. This is the work of the Lover Archetype, holding space for all. Use this technique daily and regularly as a centering tool and for stress reduction. This technique is beneficial for anyone, regardless of his or her goals, and is the primary therapeutic tool in Somatic Archaeology. See chapter 7 for detailed somatic breathing exercises.

2) Sound Work, or *Shaking Out the Grit*

Deliberately exhaling with an accompanying sound assists in the release of somatically trapped words, thoughts, or messages. It helps you regain your voice. Verbal expression aids in exposing your story, allowing your body to articulate its struggles. Sounding creates energetic vibrations for breakthrough experiences that support your body in releasing tension, stress, memories, and somatic blockages. Singing, chanting, yelling, sighing, and howling all help to establish a reconnection with your instinctual self, which forms the basis for empowerment. Keep your voice on a low or deep note as opposed to higher notes that may damage your vocal cords. If you are fearful of making noise or do not want to disturb others, you can do a silent scream, opening your mouth and letting an imaginary noise come out, while exhaling the pent-up emotional energy. Bring in the Warrior Archetype to fight for change. Notice any area of your body that may be triggered as you release this energy, and breathe into it for a more complete surrender. Sound work may be done sitting or lying, in the shower or in the car, during a somatic excavation or as a singular approach. Make some noise!

3) Body Mapping, or *Designing a Dig Site*

This technique allows you to draw on what you feel internally to externalize it onto a full-size body map. Employ it when you are seeking body awareness, when you have little awareness of sensation in your body, or if you are apprehensive about beginning a somatic excavation. This technique is also wonderful for children. It can lead to ownership of body parts and helps to objectify pain. It is especially useful for those who are visually or artistically oriented. My favorite way to do body mapping is to invest in some colorful markers and a large roll of paper at least three feet wide. Roll the paper out on the floor and cut a piece that is a little longer than the length of your body. Then lie on your back on the paper with your arms and legs spread out. You will need someone to trace the outline of your body with a marker. Stay in your outline while doing somatic breathwork or meditation to relax. As you breathe into your body, become curious about where your joy lives, where your pain lives, where your power lives, where your story lives, etc. Choose one at a time. Imagine the quality of the sensation, its shape, color or symbol, and how it moves or is restricted inside you. This process may take ten to thirty minutes. Make a mental image of the sensation, then get up and draw, or map out, on the paper what you felt in your body. This technique is always very revealing. Write or place emotional words, images, statements, symbols, etc., on your body map. This can become a plan for your archaeological dig.

Decide where you wish to start excavating, identify the places you want to explore, and determine areas that are off limit for now.

4) Somatic Exploration, or *Digging It Up*

This technique assists you to experience your body somatically from the inside out. It is a very simple technique, yet it requires that you have the ability to direct your breath throughout your body and bring your concentration to specific areas. Somatic exploration is most effective if you have your eyes closed, so that you can keep your focus inside and be curious about what your body is holding and how it is feeling. Concentration is the vehicle that gets you there, and breath is what powers the movement. Bring your combined breath, awareness, and concentration to an area of pain or discomfort. Balloon your breath into the sensation to explore and release stories trapped within the soma. Stay with it and be curious. It may take some time to connect with your body. Imagine that your memories rise to the surface as you expand your breath into them and make room. This encourages somatic unwinding, so be prepared to feel memories you did not know you were holding. This technique can often bring about an emotional release or increased awareness. Somatic exploring is best done lying down or sitting with your spine straight. If it feels unsafe to explore your body or you are unable to stay present, another person can act as a somatic guide to facilitate the excavation and help monitor your process. Gently move your attention in and out of the sensation until it feels comfortable to stay with it.

Note: If you are unable to notice anything, this means that you are attempting to access your body from your mind. Be careful not to *think* about how it feels, but rather *feel* it directly. It may take some time to refine your somatic awareness skills. The more you practice, the better you will get. Your sixth sense is like a muscle that needs to be flexed and exercised often.

5) Moving Energy, or *Playing With The Matrix*

Altering your energy patterns is fundamental in Somatic Archaeology. Any somatic investigation will begin to shift established patterns, although the skills here will give you tools to create deliberate movement of stuck energy through your breath and visualization. Learn to manage your energy body in response to daily needs and experiences. This is an empowering tool to establish somatic ownership and proactive self-care. The Magician Archetype helps you to transform your holding patterns. Here are four ways to play with your personal energetic matrix.

Contract: Use this technique when you feel too expansive or out of control. It will help to establish boundaries and draw you back to center when you feel fearful, exposed, vulnerable, or in danger. While breathing into the centerline of your body, imagine a tight clockwise spin pulling you inward, much like tightening the lid on a jar. Visualize this tight spin from the base of your body to the crown of your head. Imagine that you take up as little space as possible, contracting your breath as you feel yourself shrinking in to center. This technique will draw you together when needed, but is not necessarily a good way to stay indefinitely. Use it to center, establish safety, reorganize after shock or emotional upheaval, or before going into public places.

Expand: This technique can be helpful when you feel stuck, are holding back, or impeding movement. While breathing into the centerline of your body, imagine a corkscrew motion unwinding, increasing in scope and dimension from the base of your body upward. Widen the core of your body, expanding in all directions, much like loosening the lid on a jar. Take up as much room as possible. Make room for yourself and your memories with deep cleansing breaths. Surrender, let go, and soften with each exhalation. Expand when you are meditating, connecting with loved ones, dreaming, healing, and communing with nature. When appropriate, remember to contract, or draw yourself back in slightly before ending the exercise.

Ground: This technique is for those who feel spacey, overwhelmed, anxious, or too mental. Use this following shock, trauma, or accidents. Take a deep breath into the core of your body and exhale downward into the Earth through the base of your spine. Imagine that you are like a lightning rod, draining excess energy out through your first chakra to anchor and stabilize in the Earth. Continue this grounding breath visualization as long as necessary to maintain a continuous link. If you feel angry, have been exposed to too much fire energy or to electromagnetic fields such as cell phones or computers, visualize a blue/silver colored energy channeling through the lightning rod. Give away what no longer serves you to Mother Earth.

Spiral: This technique creates movement either in or out of an area. Use this exercise to release congested energy or emotion from organs, chakras, or joints. All energy generally moves in a corkscrew motion, so you are supporting a natural flow with your breath and imagination when practicing this technique. North of the equator, a clockwise spiral will spin to the right and will draw energy in. A counter-clockwise spiral will spin to the left and will draw energy out. If you are south of the equator, reverse these directions. When drawing energy in, imagine that the spiral decreases in size as it comes into your center. When extending energy out, imagine that the spiral increases in size. You can also use these spirals to generate movement of chronic pain or energy from the back of your body to the front, from above to below, or below to above, or from left to right. Focus on your visualization of the spiral, and spin it with your breath.

6) Somatic Tracking, or *Keeping Your Ear To The Ground*

This technique tracks your somatic responses and instinctive movement through the neurological avenues of your body as you perform your somatic exploration. Tracking primarily means being exquisitely aware of every little thing; it is the ability to hone in and become sensitive to all somatic clues—visual, oral, auditory, spiritual, psychic, and energetic. Somatic responses that you will be tracking include subtle or overt breath changes (notice if your breath is rapid, slow, shallow, or deep); muscular twitches; desire to shift or stretch your body; temperature changes (sweating or goose bumps); the need to voice a noise, word, or sound; eye movement (blinking, unfocused, tearing up); tightness in your chest, throat, or belly; repetitious swallowing; jaw clenching; fist clenching; repeated yawning; or any nervous habit. Pay attention and use your breath to make room for what you notice. Become curious about these responses—they will eventually lead you to an excavation site or memory. Breathe expansively into your entire spinal column to assist in relaxing, moving from a sympathetic to a parasympathetic state. This helps unwind tension or nervous energy so that you can go deeper into the sensations you are tracking. The more you practice tracking, the more you will notice.

7) Somatic Dialoguing, or *Language Of The Heart*

Body dialogue is an important part of a somatic exploration. Breathe deeply to come into contact with a sensation, and imagine that you can have a dialogue with your tissues and the stories buried there. Ask your body if it has anything it needs to say, or ask an area what it needs to relax or find relief, or ask anything that you are curious about! Just as in any dialogue, you must ask and then be prepared to listen. The information will come from your body, not from your mind, and this could take a few moments. The answer may come immediately, or you may need to wait. In your somatic exploration, you may come across an image of a person with whom you will develop a dialogue. If this happens, you could receive quite a lot of information. Developing communication and rapport with your body sensations is a valuable way to get to know your story on a subconscious level. Soundwork may erupt from the dialogue, exposing an inner need to yell or communicate a profound stored feeling. This helps even if you are afraid to make noise or to be seen. Remember, you bring it up to let it go.

8) Somatic Journaling, or *Documenting Your Excavation*

Journaling your story from a body perspective is effective for those who are writers, poets, and visionaries, or are deeply emotional. Develop a personal archive of your somatic excavations to honor your story and to recognize your healing progress. Somatic journaling is best done immediately following an excavation when thoughts, impressions, and insights are fresh. I encourage you to let your body speak through your hands, documenting your hopes, resistance, defeats, successes, completion of goals, and setbacks. Journal your dreams; your subconscious releases fragments of your story while you are sleeping that can give incredible insight into your healing. The process of writing down your feelings gives validity to your changes and helps you make sense of chaos. This is the Lover Archetype in action. Journaling can be daily, weekly, or when needed, and should primarily honor the creative process. It is a powerful tool when used for the writing of affirmations, for the exploration of personal potential and the expression of spiritual or inspired visions.

9) Somatic Emotional Release, or *Getting Your Hands Dirty*

The release of emotional patterns reflects a significant shift in the excavation process. When tracking, be sure to notice your breath and be attentive to somatic clues. A significant holding of breath and rigidity of breath patterns reflects fear and keeps your emotions at bay. Fluidity of breath patterns signals emotional freedom. Deeper breathing will assist in releasing trapped emotions along with the somatic tension that has been holding them. All the watery systems of your body—urine, blood, sweat, and lymph—are adversely affected by emotional repression, emotional avoidance, or emotional vacancy. Your musculature adapts to emotional stress by restricting movement, causing physical discomfort, lack of coordination, insomnia, decreased blood flow, armoring, weight gain, poor posture, and body splits (left/right or above/below). When you release your emotions, you find relief of physical pain. The difference between a typical emotional release and a somatic emotional release is that you stay connected to your body during the process of somatic emoting, and you release it completely with your breath. You bring it up to let it go. Do not hold onto it, analyze it, or agonize over it. Feel the emotion cleansing you as you make room for it to exit. Find an exit for the emotion, typically through your mouth, the top of your head, or through a chakra, relying on the natural flows of energy in your body to support the release. The more extreme or intense your breath pattern is, the more forceful the emotional release. The spiral breathing technique above is perfect for emotional release. Deep breathing is the simplest, most effective way to create an emotional release. If you sense that an emotion is coming up too fast, normalize your breath to slow down the rise of emotions. Sometimes emotions are so ready to move that you will not be able to hold them back. Use the skills below to manage your movement.

10) Stopping an Emotional Release, or *Wrapping It Up For The Day*

The fastest and simplest way to stop an emotional release is to slow your breath rate down. That is primary. Drop your jaw and exhale through a wide-open mouth. Breathe slowly, establishing a momentum for your inhalations. Keep doing this until you feel centered and the wave of emotion has passed. If you have difficulty staying present, or find yourself dissociating, look for something to anchor yourself—a drink of water, a short walk, eye contact with a trusted friend, or prayer will all help. Ground yourself. Do these things until you feel safe. It can be common for those with childhood abuse histories to regress to the age of wounding during an emotional release. If this happens, be patient, gentle, and deliberate with yourself. Create links from the traumatic arousal inside to the real world outside. In the event that new traumatic memories are uprooted during the release, take time to honor your sadness, anger, shame, or fear. Stay with your body experience and notice what has changed. Move around and stretch, feel your feet on the ground, and drink some water. Use Breathing Exercise 1 in chapter 7 to help ground yourself. You may be fragile following an intense emotional release. If this happens regularly, I highly recommend finding a somatic therapist to work with to support your excavations. Be sure to take time to journal or write down your experience.

11) Tools for Healing Anger, or *Breathing Out The Fire*

Anger is referred to as red energy and is related to fire. It is a powerful force that is usually associated with violence or destruction. Consequently, most of us are afraid of anger. When you have witnessed someone expressing anger in a violent manner, or have been violated or assaulted, you will tend to avoid confrontations that include anger—including your own. This creates a repression or backlog of anger that builds up over time. When you can no longer hold it in, it explodes. This explosion may be harmful to you and your body, or to those around you.

If your anger is subdued, your power will be subdued. If it is left untended or unexpressed it can be detrimental to your system. You've heard the phrases "my blood was boiling," or "I am so furious, I could explode," or "I am hot under the collar." These statements reflect a fire energy that does not have a channel for expression and creates heat and tension in your body. Withheld fire energy may be reflected in physical symptoms such as high blood pressure, hypertension, hives, fever, infection, inflammation/swelling, shingles, boils, ulcers, blisters, and digestive difficulties, as well as addictive tendencies. Giving an outlet for your anger and maintaining fire equilibrium in your body supports weight loss, controls inflammatory tendencies, and diminishes your desire for substance abuse and cigarette smoking.

We have few models in our society for expressing anger in a healthy manner. This is unfortunate, because anger has many positive attributes. Fear can immobilize you. Anger, on the other hand, is a motivator; it puts a fire under your fear and forces movement. Your anger encourages you to change, to create justice where there is injustice, and to protect yourself. This is where the Warrior Archetype is best embodied. When well directed and properly expressed, anger can be utilized to your benefit. Many ways of releasing your anger are not dangerous to yourself or to others. To create a container for the somatic release of anger, you must remind yourself that you now have the ability to choose how you express your anger. You can do it differently.

Always begin any excavation of anger by creating a grounding cord, which will act as a lightning rod for the fire. Instructions are found in Breathing Exercise 1 in chapter 7. Based upon individual need, possible options could include:

a) Explore where your anger is stored somatically and breathe it out. You may notice a sensation of heat, redness, or swelling; or you may feel anger while exploring a certain area of your body. With visualization, imagine that you breathe and expand into this area, and with your exhalation, push the red energy or fire out with your breath. Give yourself time to develop a natural outlet. If angry emotions begin to surface, be tenacious and continually choose to release your anger through your breath. Stay with it until the fire dissipates. I call this exercise the "fire-breathing dragon." (See Somatic Breathing Exercise 3 in chapter 7 for more detailed instruction.) It is an excellent way to release pent-up red energy, and is an especially good exercise for hyper, unmanageable, or traumatized children. Do it together with them and it will help both of you.

b) A similar way to release the anger is through dance. This is for the person who actively feels the need to punch or physically demonstrate his/her feelings. Play some sharp, staccato type of music with a strong rhythm. Allow your body to respond to the music, releasing the red energy through movement, foot stomping, air punching, or twirling; many times spinning in a counterclockwise direction unleashes anger. Incorporate full deep breathing into your dance. Be attentive to levels of intensity. If you get extremely heated, you could pass out, dissociate, or go into an emotional release. It is important not to traumatize your body while releasing anger. Go slowly; you don't have to release it all at once!

c) Expressing anger through sound is effective for those who feel they have not been heard. This may be incorporated into the fire-breathing dragon exercise or dance release. Upon exploring anger in your body, give yourself permission to express your feelings through a sound, a yell, a word, or a statement. Direct the force at a pillow or inanimate object. It is important to stay with your body sensations while doing this, pulling the sound from the area of holding and moving it outward. Keep your breathing focused, your voice pitch down, and maintain awareness of any change in sensation. It is helpful to articulate simple statements such as "Yes!" or "No!" or to give your body a voice to express stories that it has been holding.

d) Acknowledge that the anger is present. Ask yourself, "What am I really angry about?" or "What is it that I need?" Stay out of your head, and continue bringing yourself back to your body. Do some fire-breathing dragon breaths (usually a dozen will do), while staying with the awareness of your anger. Expand into the fire and make room for the emotion to move. If there is resistance, play with what feels good or different. Soften around it. Tighten around it. Ground it like a lightning rod. Unwind it by visualizing that the energy spins counterclockwise and upward. Be creative and listen to your instincts. Usually when your anger is released, you will find that underneath the protective sheath of anger is a more vulnerable feeling or story. Stay with the process until you get through the many layers of stored emotion.

12) Somatic and Cognitive Intuition, or *Trusting Your Gut*

Intuition is your sixth sense, and it can be a very dynamic tool. Intuition—finely tuned awareness—is effective when you know yourself well enough to tell the difference between when something is imagined or when it is intuited. Cognitive intuition is when you receive thoughts or impressions. Trusting and encouraging these impressions adds insight. There is also somatic intuition. These impressions are received on a physical level as a gut feeling. You may suddenly feel drawn to a certain area of your body; feel a heaviness or pressure; begin to cry for no obvious reason; or your facial features may change. This is your body's way of telling you something that your mind cannot understand. This physical knowing must be acknowledged as an important aspect of somatic communication and, when used, can bring dramatic awareness of your story. The role that you allow your intuition to play is based on trust. As your body and mind become receptive to intuitive information, you will know more clearly what your body is remembering. This is a great empowerment tool for somatic excavation.

13) Breaking Somatic Contracts, or *Changing the Grid*

If you find it difficult to break through repetitive patterns of behavior, or if you feel "stuck," or if you can't break out of unhealthy relationships or addictions, it might be necessary to break a somatic contract. Contracts made in the unseen world are typically fear-based. Thought patterns or statements (verbal or non-verbal) such as, "I will never do that again!" or, "I will never let you go!" or, "I will hate you forever!" actually lock you into an agreement with yourself or others that perpetuate the dynamic. Sometimes an intense event will bind you to someone, as in Rey's story about the dead hitchhiker. When you agree to comply with someone in order to stay safe, or you bypass your integrity to survive, or you lie to get your way, you set up an energetic pattern that infiltrates your body and plays out the promise or pact. These covenants can even take the form of spells or family curses that were placed in the past. Bargaining in order to conform will always have a backlash. Fortunately, somaticized contracts can be broken. This is an advanced tool, and I recommend you practice somatic meditation and breathing techniques before you initiate this process.

Here is the step-by-step procedure, but keep in mind the following before you begin: breaking contracts requires that you pay attention to detail, that you stay connected to your body and stay present during the process, and that you bring together all the energies that created the contract. The contract will be felt by all those involved; may need to be broken more than once to address varied issues and multiple participants; and breaking it will always release the emotional backlog or story that has been bound up in it, so be sure to take care of yourself afterward. Witness the Warrior in you taking action, and setting boundaries.

Step 1: Begin by creating a very good grounding cord or roots into the Earth. Do this by dropping your energy or awareness downward in your lower pelvis or first chakra. Imagine that roots extend from the base of your body down into the soil and rocks. Exhale into these roots and expand your awareness into the natural world. This helps to ground out any energy that is released from the contract.

Step 2: Notice where in your body the contract is held. You will be able to sense the location because the energy or blockage will be very stubborn, unwilling to release even with repeated breathwork and visualization.

Step 3: Sense how you hold the blockage in your body and how the rest of your system responds to it. Can you move it or soften it? Get a sense of any cords of energy that are coming out of it or into it. Follow those cords to see who or what they are attached to. Really take time to play with the energy block and notice what or whom it reminds you of. If it seems appropriate, you can visualize cutting the cords with imaginary scissors.

Step 4: Notice your emotions. What are you feeling? Make room for your feelings. Most contracts have a strong emotional element, so you will want to stir the energy up as much as possible to bring the contract to the surface.

Step 5: Breathe fully and deeply into the area of holding. Expand into the grid and all around it. You will want to have a felt sense of what you are holding, but do not need to understand it at this point. You may go to the next step if you have a fairly good idea of what the contract is about or what it relates to. You will also want to feel safe enough to break it and move on. If you do not feel confident, repeat Steps 1-3.

Step 6: Imagine in your mind's eye a legal document. See that it says *Contract* at the top. Imagine that the words on this contract reflect what you are feeling and what you are locked into. Visualize specific language relating exactly to what you are experiencing physically, emotionally, mentally, and spiritually. Write it out in detail in your mind and take your time to get it right. There may be fine print. It could be something such as, "I agree to stay in relationship with this person according to these rules …" or, "I agree to hold myself back in order to …" or, "I am bound by …" Honestly finish the sentences or feel into the content of your contract. Include the reasons that the contract serves you. Every contract has some purpose or outcome. If you can clearly define this reason and imagine it written on the contract, you can then move to the next step. If not, take time to get all the details—and remember, they will not come from mentally analyzing the situation. You will feel the intent of the contract in your body and articulate it from there.

Step 7: See your name signed at the bottom of the page, as well as the names of all the people who agreed to this contract, benefited from it, or in any way contributed to it. These may be people from the past or the present or the future. If you do not know their names, imagine their energy signatures there.

Step 8: Imagine that this contract is like a magnet, drawing to itself all people, events, energies, words, or actions that make it binding. It may take you a few minutes to gather all the energy.

Step 9: When you feel it is complete, collected, and intact, take a deep breath into your body and feel the connection between the physical blockage or sensation and the visualized contract. Make sure you have all the fine print on the contract and all the names.

Step 10: Now imagine that you have a stamp in your right hand that says *Void* or *Cancel*. Take a deep breath into your feet and exhale all the way out your right hand, imagining that you are stamping the contract *Void/Cancel* in big letters. Use your will and your intent to give power to the stamping. Do this step three times—three breaths and three stamps.

Step 11: Rip the contract into pieces. Tear it up.

Step 12: Burn the pieces over a purple or violet flame. Watch them burn and transform to ash. Let the contract go.

Step 13: Take a deep breath into the area that once held the blockage or contract and notice how it feels now. Let yourself emote whatever comes to the surface. Feel the space or openness that has been created. What is different? Imagine that you can fill that space with an image that emboldens you, enlivens you, and makes you feel safe and secure. Visualize a new story in this area of your body that honors your highest potential. Be sure to include colors that heal and revitalize your cells.

14) Somatic Affirmations, or *Sweeping Away The Debris*

Your manner of communication is an important part of creating a healthy relationship with your body. It is beneficial for your self-talk to incorporate choice, flexibility, and sensitivity. Use language that is empowering and choose words that reflect a commitment to your well-being. Sweep away buried belittling beliefs by quickly extinguishing repetitive thoughts or derogatory statements about yourself as they surface, replacing them with tolerant and open-minded affirmations.

This is where the Lover Archetype can meander into your excavation. Be gentle and compassionate with your body and embrace what you are holding. Your heart and body have done the best job they could do to get you to this moment in time. Take the time to develop intimacy with yourself and feel into all the subtle, underground pathways of emotion and experience that design your thoughts and feelings. Send love and acceptance to even the most remote or undesirable parts of your body and being.

Be sure to use words that establish ownership of your body, such as "*my* shoulder" vs. "*this* shoulder," and avoid using words that limit your ability to find wholeness, such as "I never, I always, or I am trying." In addition, be cautious about allowing your diagnosis or symptoms to define you. You are not your disease or your pain; you are much more. Identify with your highest potential and employ affirmations that engage your mind with a fresh and vital belief that supports this possibility. Affirmations can be used for a variety of reasons.

1) *To establish and verbalize intentions:* Intentions are simply your higher self declaring its will. Take time to clarify what needs to be facilitated for the benefit of your whole being. Affirmations can be extremely specific when focusing on changing a particular behavior or when negotiating with your internal critic. Use words that amplify your intent, repeat them three times, and then anchor them into your body with your breath.

2) *To unwind areas of resistance or holding:* Decide upon a specific objective, such as "I am safe and secure" or "I am willing to change," and repeat it to yourself three times, either out loud or silently, and notice what happens in your body as you voice your affirmation. Typically, the areas where you experience resistance or discomfort when speaking your affirmation are coupled with the old story you are changing. Continue the affirmation daily until you no longer have resistance to the statement. Then, go deeper. What is under that? Explore and expand your affirmation to address the next layer you are excavating.

3) *To support shifts that happened during a somatic excavation:* Many times the end of a somatic excavation reveals an understanding of your true story. Once your core needs are recognized, you can create an affirmation that supports the continued process. An affirmation repeated many times daily will cultivate personal evolution and dream work. Doing this establishes responsibility in your healing cycles and prevents relapse into old patterns of thought/behavior.

15) Somatic Dreamscape, or *Bridging Time and Space*

Your dreams can be an active part of your Somatic Archaeology practice. As you explore your internal landscape, you expose your subconscious and bring it into your waking mind or consciousness. Revealing your subconscious layers of memory gives room for buried stories to surface in your dreams. Dreams are ever-present instigators of long-term memory, both personally relevant and collectively founded, and no two dreams are identical.

Freud began to analyze dreams in order to understand aspects of personality as they relate to pathology. He believed that nothing we do occurs by chance; every action and thought is motivated by our unconscious at some level. We tend to hold back our urges and repress our impulses based on our social and familial conditioning. However, these urges and impulses must be released in some way, and we call those dreams.[1] Call in the Magician Archetype to connect the bridge between awareness and lucid dreaming.

Although they are unique to each individual, dreams carry strong cultural imprints. Dreams have played a central and determinative role in the formation of the spiritual worlds of most Native American groups. Most Native Americans consider dreams the most valid means for communicating with spiritual powers, and dreams were actively sought, both in regular sleep and in special fasting. The songs and powers given through them became an intrinsic feature of the social and religious life of the dreamer.[2]

Among the Cherokees, dream interpreters would seek out the "seat of pain" for those who were ill by asking them extensive questions about their dreams ranging back over months and sometimes over a period of years. Dream typologies were developed by means of which particular types of animals, actions, or various other dream images were used diagnostically to predict future events or indicate cures that would bring the dreamer back into harmony with the dream spirits.[3]

Here are some ideas to enhance your somatic dreamscape.

1. Slow your pace down and wake up slowly. It is hard to dream or remember your dreams when you are constantly busy or wake up quickly by an alarm. For a brief time, we drift between worlds, not quite asleep and not quite awake, and this is when the dreamscape is most accessible. Treasure this time and guard it carefully. Stay with it as long as you possibly can. You are receiving and integrating your internal wisdom and the messages of your dreamscape.

2. Let your dreams become allies or friends. Give yourself permission to remember your dreams and create a receptive space within to draw them forward. Invite them into your waking state. Keep a dream journal by your bed to write important insights immediately following the dream, such as symbols, feelings, characters, and sensations.

3. When you wake up from a dream, particularly if there is a strong emotional content, pay close attention to the area of your body that resonates with the

---

1. Barbara Tedlock, *Dreaming: Anthropological and Psychological Interpretations* (Cambridge: Cambridge University Press, 1987).
2. Lee Irwin, *The Dream-Seekers: Native American Visionary Traditions of the Great Plains* (Norman, Okla.: University of Oklahoma Press, 1994).
3. Lee Irwin, *Cherokee Healing: Myth, Dreams, and Medicine* (*American Indian Quarterly*, Vol. 16, No. 2, Spring, 1992)

feeling. The dream is stirring your soma, and you can follow it up by encouraging additional unwinding in a somatic excavation in this specific area when you awake.

4. Symbols are the language of dreams, and they can give great insight when you carefully look at the representation or origin of the symbol. Many wonderful books about dream symbolism can help you decipher deeper meaning and illuminate the mystery.

5. Look for patterns in your dreams. Repetitive dreams indicate a deeply buried or unresolved story that you may need to reveal to your conscious mind. Cyclical events and anniversaries of traumatic experiences can instigate dreams or nightmares. Action in the waking world that resolves the dynamic is advisable, or you can release a conflict through somatic breathwork and further excavation.

6. Dreams that are prophetic emerge from the wavelength of your higher, wise self, while emotionally charged dreams erupt from unresolved historical experiences. Use your breath to expand into the timeline, forward or backward. You are now bridging time and space in your consciousness, allowing the mosaic of life to establish its synchronistic beauty in your dreamscape.

Valerie Wolf, or Little Mother Dreaming Bear, shared with me her advice for dreamers. "The main thing is to learn to understand our dreams again. Remember, they are in the language of the spirits. Recognize that everything in the dream is a spirit. If you dream of the water, you are not dreaming of a place; there is a water spirit that has work with you, that has a message, teaching, or healing for you. You have to develop a relationship with your dreams. When the spirits come to us in dreams, many times we run away from them. If bear comes to you in your dream and you run away—as we so often do in our dreams because we think we are in this world and not the spirit world—and then you wake up and realize that you have run away from the bear, you have to say, 'Please let me go back to sleep so that I can turn around and greet the bear.' I ran from the bear for years. It was my path and my destiny trying to find me. I was afraid of it, but when I stopped running, when I learned to stop and say, 'I am really sorry, let me go back to the bear,' then the bear came to me and embraced me in the dream and my life turned upside down—in the best possible way."

Hibernation ceases today. I unfurl my claws and nails, I mark the spot of my ascent, I push off firm from this world's soil, its dirt no longer binds my heart, I am the keeper of the slave and I release my sentiment, release the pain, the frail, the aged; release the ugly, the father rage.

—Ruby Gibson, original poem

The Practice

7

Somatic Breathing Techniques

With my breath I find myself now.
Under the rubble of yesterday surfaces the memory
of eloquence, the uncertain hum of holiness,
the exquisite space that knows no bounds.
I recover my capacity and remember my gifts,
recognizing as a long lost friend
the grace of my soul.

—Ruby Gibson, original poem

A healthy mind has an easy breath. A fearful mind has a controlled breath. A healthy body has a tranquil breath. An overwhelmed body has a labored breath. Your breath is a direct reflection of your state of mind and body, and vice versa. You can use your breath to quiet your mind, and you can use your mind to slow down your breath pattern, hence relaxing your body.

Your body is very responsive to your breathing patterns. The simplest way to stay present in your body is to take a deep breath. Breathe in your power; breathe out your fear. Stay conscious of your breath patterns throughout the day, monitoring the times when you hold your breath and the times when you breathe fluidly. These are good indicators of whether you feel safe or not, and altering your breath patterns at these times helps to deactivate neurological patterns of stress and activation.

The act of breathing is living. Oxygen is elemental for life, and our bodies are dependent upon it for health and vitality. Oxygen is the carrier of nutrients to your cells, and, as well, the carrier of inspiration to your heart.

> *You know that our breathing is the inhaling and exhaling of air. The organ that serves for this are the lungs that lie round the heart, so that the air passing through them thereby envelops the heart. Thus breathing is a natural way to the heart. And so, having collected your mind within you, lead it into the channel of breathing through which air reaches the heart and, together with this inhaled air, force your mind to descend into the heart and to remain there.*
>
> —Nicephorus the Solitary

Breath Assessment

Take some time to develop a relationship with your breath. Begin by noticing if you regularly breathe deeply or if you have light, surface breaths. Notice how your breath differs when driving, working, relating to others, or when you are going to sleep. Do you breathe consciously or automatically? Do you pay attention to your breath patterns? Does your breath seem to flow freely or is it controlled?

Play with altering your breath so that you breathe fully and consciously as often as possible, and notice where your breath avoids expanding in your body. Your breath is the vehicle of your awareness: where your breath goes, your consciousness goes. Be purposeful. The more comfortable you get with conscious breathing, the easier these exercises will be.

Start directing your breath to different areas of your body. As you breathe, can you determine where in your body your breath/awareness is or is not going? Does it seem to stop at your throat or does it come all the way down into your lungs? How noticeable is the movement of your diaphragm? Does it barely rise, or does it fill up all the way? Unless you can effectively use your breath to move through your body, healing will be restricted.

Determine if you can breathe into your belly. This means that you breathe down through your diaphragm and extend your abdomen with each breath. This important skill is necessary for you to be effective with your somatic excavation.

Finally, can you consciously direct your breath to different areas of your body? It is helpful to have the ability to bring your breath/awareness into your foot, knee, or arm, for example, to assist in somatic unwinding and the release of discomfort. This is done primarily through your imagination and your will, with your breath as the medium. Once you recognize an area of congestion, you can create accelerated movement by breathing through, or by breathing out, the tension, pain, or somatic sensation.

Dr. Andrew Weil said, "If I had to limit my advice on healthier living to just one tip, it would be simply to learn how to breathe correctly." Establishing new breath patterns is a learned behavior that can take time. I recommend incorporating conscious breathing into your daily schedule, developing awareness of your breath patterns throughout the day.

Once you have developed competence with the belly breath, begin with one of the following breathing exercises designed to initiate somatic awareness and to flex your sixth sense muscles. These are primary exercises upon which the Somatic Archaeology Breathing Exercises can be built. For each of these, you will want to create a quiet and sacred space in which you can relax and lay down or sit comfortably.

For all of the breathing exercises, breathe in through your nose and out through your mouth. Relax your jaw and tongue, exhaling through a wide-open mouth, as if you are fogging up a mirror. Use an "*ahhhhh*" sound with the exhalation that comes from the back of your throat. Exhaling with pursed lips or a tight jaw controls the release and will limit the possibilities for full somatic unwinding. Let go of the need to control your breath. Maintain an out breath that is the same length as the in breath. Find balance and rhythm to your breathing pattern.

Four Basic Soma-Breaths

Cleansing Breath

This can be done before an excavation or at the end. It is also good for stress relief throughout the day. The main thought to keep in mind is that you are surrendering stress and built-up energy. Breathe in fully, expanding your belly and lungs, and hold the breath for a count of seven. Then release your breath with a *whoosh-*

ing sound, until all the oxygen is released—another count of seven. Do this at least four times. Upon exhalation, release any tension, thoughts, or worries that you are holding onto, cleansing your body, mind, and heart so that you are open to receive divine guidance. Practicing this breath in the shower is a good extension of this exercise. Each time you exhale, repeat the affirmation, "All the stress and all the strain, all the tension and all the pain, down the drain." Visualize heaviness or tension washing away as you practice your cleansing breaths. Lavender essential oil is the perfect companion for this exercise.

Full Circle Balancing Breath

This breath helps to balance the two sides of your body, and exposes where holding patterns exist. I recommend doing it with your eyes closed to assist in visualization. Breathe in through the left side of your body, and out through the right side. Imagine drawing breath up from the Earth, in through your left foot and leg, in through your left hand and arm, filling up your torso with breath and energy. Allow your breath to pass over the centerline of your body (the imaginary line that runs from the base of your body to the top of your head). Exhale from your torso, down your right arm and out through your right hand, down your right leg and out through your right foot, giving away your breath to the Earth. Imagine that your breath gets recycled in Mother Earth, and returns back to you as you breathe in again. Feel the rhythmic pulse of breath as it flows through your body, left to right. Receive and give in one balanced movement—indicative of the heartbeat of Mother Earth—and align yourself with this natural flow to achieve balance. Continue this circular breathing, in through the left and out through the right, giving yourself permission to release anything that is in the way of your joy and your divine well-being. You are encouraging a natural flow of creation, and it will balance and set your energy at ease, allowing you to access your creative and artistic currents. Visualize any color that comes to mind. Take a few moments to notice as your breath crosses the centerline of your body. Where does it flow easily and unrestricted? Where does your breath get stuck, or where is there a barrier to movement? Feel from the inside out. The stuck places are generally indicative of where your body is holding subconscious patterns or memories of fear and disease. Allow your breath to illuminate your excavation site. When you find a congested area, notice which chakra it is near, as this will give you insight into what you may possibly be holding onto. Use the spiral visualization, or any other proactive imagery, to shift the manner in which you are holding. Any image that helps to loosen, soften, relax, or expand is helpful. This creates the perfect awareness with which to begin the Five Steps of Somatic Archaeology in chapter 8. For this exercise, you can use ylang ylang over your heart as a balancing oil, along with the essential oils of lavender, patchouli, lemon, or rose.

Heaven and Earth Breath

This breath bridges heaven and Earth, or above and below in your body. Use it to release stress, especially power, control or rage issues, and to eliminate nervous energy in your belly. Sitting upright, breathe in from below, drawing Earth energies up through the root of your torso (your first chakra) up to your solar plexus (third chakra). Simultaneously draw heaven or etheric energies down from above through the top of your head (crown chakra) and into your solar plexus. Visualize connecting above and below, heaven and Earth, simultaneously in the center of your body. Gather both energies in your belly, then exhale forward through your solar plexus, opening an imaginary door to release tension and stress from your stomach, liver, diaphragm, and mid-section. It may take you several practice breaths. Do this as often as you need to until you feel at ease and connected above and below. It will become a natural breath pattern for easing bound up energy, allowing you to stand in balanced power. As you exhale, affirm, "I come from my strength." This breathing exercise is excellent in times of duress, emotional crisis, or for shock. It also serves to relax hyperactive children or to diffuse anger and frustration. Apply frankincense, Sacred Mountain and Purification oils topically to the solar plexus during this breathing exercise.

Chakra Clearing Breath

This breath serves to unwind congested chakras and to release core energies or subconscious patterns that are twisted or bound up in your luminous body. Breathe into your root chakra at the base of your body and imagine that your breath rises upward in a counterclockwise spiral, moving through each chakra, out through the crown of your head. Do this several times until you feel an unhindered flow. Affirm, "I am one in body, mind, and spirt." Take your time to breathe consciously and slowly, moving your consciousness from below to above, opening, unwinding, and connecting to spiritual body. Once there is movement and expansion in your center core, you can balance your chakras by breathing expansively into the wheel of each chakra, visualizing the corresponding color flooding it, and applying an essential oil to that part of your body. (See chapter 3 for chakra descriptions and associated colors/oils.)

Somatic Archaeology Breathing Exercises

The following breathing exercises are for remedying specific acute conditions, for establishing an awareness of chronic patterns in your body, and for encouraging the unearthing of your story. As you breathe consciously and deliberately, allow yourself to slow down and drop into the tissues and neurological pathways of your body. When this happens, you can access your subconscious and stored memories for movement and healing.

Please take time to be responsive to your own body wisdom. If your body has a natural inclination to breathe or exhale in a specific manner, by all means, follow that tendency. Be careful, though, not to hyperventilate—slow, deep breathing is best. These exercises, although specifically for certain conditions, are generic in nature. Above all, trust your body and modify these exercises to encourage your natural flows. Be creative and let your body show you where it is holding and how it wants to release. Each body is unique and complex, requiring individualized avenues of expression.

All energy flows in a spiral pattern. When encouraging energy with your breath, you can visualize a spiral movement to enhance unwinding. A clockwise movement (to the right) will bring energy in, or tighten energy fields, encouraging boundaries. A counterclockwise movement (to the left) will open, or release energy flows, expand boundaries, and unwind holding patterns. Be mindful of your ability to alter energy with your breath according to your wisdom and needs. It is empowering simply to recognize that you have a choice to make it different. (See Somatic Excavation Technique 5 in chapter 6.)

I have recommended specific essential oils for use with the breathwork. They are optional. Essential oils amplify your intent and enhance breathwork. They also encourage movement of emotion by influencing the amygdala, the emotional storage center in the frontal lobe of your brain. If you use essential oils, breathe each one in deeply three times to get the full affect. Essential oils can also be applied to your body for physical support and detoxification. Be sure to use only therapeutic-grade essential oils for inhalation and topical application. Cosmetic grade oils are toxic to inhale and will be counterproductive. (See chapter 5 for more detailed use and description of essential oils.)

One more thought: I encourage you to breathe without thought of limitation. Breathe as if you are surrendering to yourself. Breathe without fear. Your body is capable of remedying all pain, all disease, and all suffering as long as you are in flux. Stagnancy is where energy pools and gets trapped. Notice where you are stagnant and break it up with your breath, releasing it from your form. When the energetic patterns no longer exist, the physical symptoms can no longer exist. Keep that concept of simplicity in mind when breathing.

I recommend becoming proficient with Breathing Exercise 1 before moving to other exercises. This will center you in your body and provide a baseline of safety and skills. Do not hurry; take your time and enjoy the oxygen.

1. **For those who have difficulty staying grounded and centered in their body, are working with anger, or experience fixated fear**: Begin by inhaling into your belly and exhaling downward through the base of your body—from your first or second chakras—into the Earth. Imagine that you extend roots down into the soil, through the loamy layers of Earth, through the granite and rocks, through the deep underground waters, through the crystals and gems, all the way into the center of Mother Earth—the fiery and fluid molten magma at her core. Give away any tension in your body to the structure of the Earth and visualize yourself rooted and disposed downward. When rooted, inhale upward from the Earth, drawing nourishment back up through the roots to replenish your body. Create a circular breath, exhaling while sending tension or stress downward, and inhaling while drawing refreshed energy upward. Repeat throughout the day or during times when you feel overwhelmed or spacey. Give thanks to Mother Earth. Black pepper, Grounding, Gathering, and Valor essential oils enhance grounding when you apply them to your feet and at the base of your skull, and then inhale them deeply.

2. **For those who have pain from inflammation, or are prone to anger, rage, or addictions**: This is an exercise called the *fire-breathing dragon breath*. You will want to breathe into the area(s) in your body that are hot, fiery, or inflamed, expanding into the fire or tension as if you are making room for what you are holding. Then exhale through a wide-open mouth, imagining that your breath is bright red and hot, exhaling the fire in your body like a dragon. Use an *"ahhh"* exhalation rather than pushing your breath out through pursed lips. Relax your jaw. For this exercise to succeed, it is important that you exhale from your belly, not from your throat. Otherwise, you can aggravate symptoms or emotions without full release. This is great for children during temper-tantrums—be sure to breathe with them. Use this breath when you have trouble making clear choices because of anger built up inside. Repeat the fire-breathing dragon breath at least ten times before action. This allows you to diffuse anger and will clear your head. It can be beneficial to do this breathing exercise in front of a mirror, maintaining eye contact with yourself. Pay attention to any sound, word, or noise that wants

to be expressed along with your breath, giving yourself permission to voice or communicate the sound while exhaling. Keep going until all the fiery or pent-up energy is released—you can tell because your body will begin to relax and your symptoms will dissipate. Apply essential oils of frankincense, Purification or Sacred Mountain over your liver and stomach or on any inflamed area to aid in balancing the liver, releasing anger, and promoting forgiveness.

3. **For those with a predisposition to, or diagnosis of, breast cancer**: Breathe into your chest, fully expanding into your lungs and breasts, and then exhale out through your nipples, releasing any trapped energy in your breasts. Visualize your nipples opening and the energy moving outward, giving away the withheld toxins and emotions. You can also visualize the expulsion of tumors or cysts as you exhale a warm color. Breathe from back to front, feeling the opening of your heart. Anoint your breasts with therapeutic-grade essential oils such as frankincense, lavender, Joy, cypress and grapefruit before you begin.

4. **For those who have asthma, heartache, depression, grief, or chest pain**: If the pain or congestion is in the back of your body, or is historical in nature, lie flat on your back and breathe expansively behind your heart. Imagine a door opening in the back of your body. As it opens, exhale out the door, allowing any burdens or tension to drop like a heavy load out of your body. Give yourself permission to exhale fully and surrender what you are holding. If the emotion is current or is in the front of your body, breathe into your lungs or into the center of your chest and exhale forward, opening a door or pathway to the future. Give away any congestion, grief, or sorrow, accepting what has occurred. Breathe into your heart and make room for it by imaging that it expands and relaxes. Repeated breathing will be necessary to fully release layers that have been stored. Pay attention to emotions that arise and let them flow. If it feels hot or fiery, use the fire-breathing dragon breath in Breathing Exercise 3. When done, fill and infuse the area with a sunny yellow color. Apply and inhale essential oils of Aroma Life, Forgiveness, Harmony, Joy, and rose to encourage self-love.

5. **For those who have TMJ, throat constriction, difficulty communicating or expressing vocally**: Breathe fully into your belly, especially your hips and low back (second chakra) filling your womb or pelvis with energy. Take repeated breaths to deepen the connection. Then exhale upward through the center or core of your body, imagining your breath passing through your throat and neck, exhaling through a wide-open mouth. Keep your jaw relaxed and stretch the

muscles while exhaling, opening your mouth wide as you exhale. The colors blue or yellow will enhance movement. Play with it and repeat this several times for relief, especially when experiencing tension, pain, or withholding. Inhale lemon, Present Time, Release, and ylang ylang essential oils and apply them topically to your jaw and throat.

6. **For those who have experienced visual trauma or witnessed violence**: Breathe expansively into your heart and exhale out your eyes, breathing through your eyeballs and lenses, releasing tension and images, allowing your eyes to relax and unwind. Do this several times. Feel the wind of your breath cleansing your eyeballs and releasing associated memories. Relax your eyes and brow. This exercise can also ease eyestrain or headaches that are centered around your eyes or temples. Apply essential oils of cedarwood, sandalwood, peppermint, Ruta VaLa, or Trauma Life to support this clearing, being sure to apply oils on your temples and scalp, but never near your eyes.

7. **For those with fibromyalgia, MS, neurological issues, or spinal injury**: Get as comfortable as possible and breathe into your spine. Breath from below to above, drawing your breath into the base of your spine and exhaling out through the top of your head. Visualize a counterclockwise spiral of energy moving upward and encourage its movement with your breath, spinning the pain or energy in an upward motion, particularly focusing on the areas where you are experiencing discomfort. Imagine expanding into your spine or tissues, thus releasing any energy you are holding into the spiral for exhaling upward. Release it all the way through the crown of your head to harmonize your neurological system. It is beneficial to visualize this spiral of energy as a bright silvery-blue electric color. Apply frankincense, Gathering, Grounding, Ruta VaLa, or Valor essential oils on the bottom of your feet, on your tailbone, and at the base of your skull for enhancement.

8. **For those with reproductive concerns, endometriosis, ovarian/uterine/ prostate cancer, unhealthy or abusive sexual experiences, or who are carrying unwanted ancestral patterns from their mother's lineage**: Breathe into your low back, sacrum, or behind your second chakra. Fill this area full of breath and then exhale forward through the front of your womb or lower abdomen in a counterclockwise motion. Clearing these energies could take many breaths with repeated attempts, as information in this area of the body is layered and can be dense. Just begin where you feel the most congestion and stay dedicated to move-

ment. Imagine an exit or door opening in the front of your belly, and give away whatever energy is suppressed in a counterclockwise spiral. Visualize orange or red to support letting go, encouraging memories and buried emotions to loosen. It is helpful to have an anatomical chart to understand where specific organs are so that you can concentrate your breath into those areas that need support or healing. Inhale essential oils of black pepper, Clarity, rose, SARA, and ylang ylang; apply them topically on the front of your lower belly or near your navel to encourage forward movement.

9. **For those with migraines, headaches or mental confusion**: Breathe into the injured or painful area, fully expanding your breath into the tissues. Exhale forward through your third eye or sixth chakra, imaging a door opening in the front of your head, and releasing the pain or congestion forward in a counterclockwise motion. Create a deliberate spiral flow and keep it going all day by encouraging it with your breath at hourly intervals. This may initially increase the discomfort, but will quickly eliminate the pain if you stay with it. Use a blue or purple color such as indigo to aid in movement and soothe your brain tissues. You may want to extend your expansion in-breath all the way down into your neck and shoulders, exhaling upward and out from there. Tension in the neck and shoulders can contribute to headache pain. The essential oil peppermint is a wonderful anti-inflammatory. Apply it topically to back of your neck and the base of your skull to reduce pain quickly. You can apply it directly on the headache site, but be sure to keep it away from your eyes. Breathe Brain Power, Purification or Ruta VaLa essential oil blends deeply for added relief, and apply them on the base of your skull.

10. **For those with head or brain injuries:** This specific breathing technique will help to heal your brain, and it is useful for the insomnia or restlessness that accompanies head or brain injuries. It is useful for those who have difficulty getting out of their heads and into their bodies. For this brain integration exercise, imagine both hemispheres of your brain, one at a time, and notice how they feel in your head, paying attention to any differences in sensation. Become aware of patterns of tension, discomfort, or numbness. Begin by breathing into the right side of your brain. Notice how it feels—if it is shrunken or expanded, hard or soft, etc. Take a few moments to make room for it with your breath. Now breathe into the left side of your brain and notice how it feels. Is it similar to the right side? Make room for it. Now imagine that the right side of your brain begins to melt and soften into the left side, and that the left side of your brain

begins to blend into the right. Allow the hemispheres of your brain to merge, paying attention to the areas that resist blending. This may take some time. Continue to encourage relaxation and softening with your breath, and visualize the cells and neurons flowing together in harmony. Do this when lying down to rest to aid in a good night's sleep. The colors blue or indigo enhance the blending. Apply the essential oils of lavender, Ruta VaLa, or Trauma Life to your forehead and the back of your neck and skull, and inhale deeply three times before you begin.

11. **For those with depression, anxiety, or panic disorders**: These types of diagnoses are based on the suppression of energy and life force, and typically can have a lot of fear associated with them. This suppression can live anywhere in your body, so pay attention to the areas in your body that carry sensations of constriction or nervous energy. Breathing into the heavy or jittery energy in your body is helpful, but go slowly. It may be easy to dissociate or disconnect while breathing into these areas. Take your time and give attention to staying focused and present. Exhale the internalized energy slowly and consciously—it typically will look like a muddy brown or yellow color. If emotions arise while exhaling, give way to them, allowing yourself to cry gently, softening your thoughts and exercising compassion for yourself. Sounds may naturally accompany your exhalation and should be encouraged. If anger arises, change your breath pattern to exhale out bright red fire breaths. (See description above in Breathing Exercise 3.) The use of therapeutic grade essential oils such as Aroma Life, geranium, Idaho balsam fir, Joy, lavender, rose or White Angelica for soothing your heart will assist you to stay present and gentle with yourself.

12. **For those with insomnia or sleep disorders or to encourage deep dreaming**: While lying down in a comfortable position, expand your breath into your entire body as if you are ballooning into your luminous body or energy field. Exhale any obvious tension while pulling your energy body close into you. Then inhale again, expanding out, and exhaling tension while pulling in. Do this a few times to get settled and organized. Feel the rhythm of expansion/contraction, in-breath/out-breath. Next, when you inhale and expand, feel into your day and remember the sequence of events beginning with the moment when you woke up. Bring the first memory into your awareness, remember the details, and then exhale it. Repeat this technique while slowly making your way through your day, remembering each encounter or event, exhaling them one by one. Make your way to the end of the day where you are now, lying in bed, and exhale out this

final image. Bring your energy inward, feeling into the present moment, and relax into the bed, allowing your body to be supported and at ease. Once you have unwound the day, you can then go to sleep with a clear mind. Lavender, Peace & Calming, and Ruta VaLa essential oils are good natural sedatives that will aid you in relaxing.

13. **For those preparing to meditate or pray, or to release obsessive thought patterns**: Find a comfortable upright position where your spine is straight. Take three deep breaths into your belly and relax with the exhalations, bringing yourself to center. Clear your mind by imagining that inside your head is a room with four walls. Then imagine that inside this room are all your thoughts. Imagine that your thoughts take the form of birds and witness how many birds are circling the room. Imagine opening all four windows, allowing the birds to take flight one by one. When the birds have all gone, close the windows and relax into the emptiness of your head. Notice the peace and quiet when your thoughts are gone. Take three more deep breaths into the spaciousness of your head, relax, and fill the space with the color purple. Now set your intent and drop into your meditation or prayers. Clarity, Idaho balsam fir, lavender, Peace & and Calming, palo santo, and sandalwood essential oils assist to relieve worries and tensions.

14. **For those wishing to ease conflict in intimate relationships or for internal harmony**: Breathe into the midline or centerline of your body—the line that separates the right side of your body from the left side. Expand your awareness into it. Notice if the right side feels different from the left side. Notice if they are balanced, or if one is tighter, stronger, weaker, larger, smaller, etc., than the other. Pay attention to how the two sides influence each other. The left side of your body is your feminine or receptive aspect, and the right side of your body is your masculine or expressive aspect. Notice how they blend or detach from each other. Take as much time to explore as necessary. When ready, breathe into your left side and imagine that it softens and melts into your right side. Then breathe into your right side and imagine that it softens and melts into your left side. Use your breath to encourage the melding of left and right, softening your midline and blending both sides of yourself. If there are areas that are resistant to merging, they reflect somatic holding patterns and it would be beneficial to explore these areas more in depth. Noticing near which chakra they are aids in deciphering the content of the resistance. Continue to encourage somatic blending with the essential oils of Harmony, rose or ylang ylang.

15. **For those experiencing psychic attack, hypervigilance, or invasive thoughts**: Sit upright in a safe, quiet place with your spine straight. As you inhale, imagine that you expand into your energy field or luminous body. It will look like an egg-shaped light body. Feel beyond your skin into your field and give yourself permission to take up as much space as possible. Breathe fully into the back of your body, the front of your body, above and below. Feel where there may be any constrictions, heaviness, or holes. Now imagine that your luminous body is the texture of a woman's billowy skirt. Imagine that you shake out this skirt, dusting off anything that may have become attached or is hanging on it. Pop off any debris, much like a dog shakes off water, exhaling fully while doing so. This will eliminate any energetic cling-ons that influence your thoughts or harbor historical agendas in your energy field. Fill your field with radiant light. Repeat several times during the day, or following difficult encounters, dependent upon your situation. The more you practice, the more awareness you will acquire as you learn to pay attention to what you are carrying in your luminous body. This is a good exercise for therapists or caregivers to do at the end of their workday. Black pepper, Gathering, Joy, Purification and Sacred Mountain essential oils aid in psychic clearing when inhaled, diffused, or applied around you.

16. **For those who have a conflict with another person(s)**: This exercise is effective for conflicts you may have with one person, with a family, or with a group. Find a comfortable place to sit or lie down. Take in a few breaths to ground yourself and become centered. Let go of any thoughts of the day, worries, or concerns. Allow your breath and awareness to bring you into present time. Begin by imagining a simple room where you will meet the other person(s). I call this the Dialogue Room. Visualize yourself sitting in the room, and then bring an image of the person(s) that you are experiencing conflict with into the room with you. If there is fear or danger, you can visualize a clear or Plexiglas barrier between the other person and yourself for safety. Make eye contact with the person. What do you notice in your body? Feel into any emotion or tension that ensues. Translate the emotion into words and, as clearly as possible, tell the other person what is on your mind and in your heart. Do not hold anything back and be careful not to judge yourself. Just speak your piece honestly while staying connected to the area of your body that feels charged with emotion or sensation. Imagine that the other person simply sits and listens to you without interruption. Keep talking until you have said everything that is on your mind. Pause for a moment, and then take some time to feel if there is anything else that needs to be communicated. When you feel complete, take three deep cleansing breaths and

bring your awareness back into your body. Release the image of the other person(s) from the room, step out, and close the door of the Dialogue Room. Check in with your body and notice what is different. The next time you meet or talk to this person(s), you should experience a noticeable difference, for the conflicted energy inside you will have been released. Essential oils of Acceptance, Harmony, lemon, Idaho balsam fir, Peace & and Calming, rose, and ylang ylang will enhance this breathing technique.

> *I move through love and forgiveness as if they are the true companions of my heart. Envy tempts me, anger seduces me, deceit, the greatest illusion. I maintain a stronghold of compassion, for her rhythm envelopes my weakness. I sit, gracefully breathing, in the absence of fear.*
>
> —Ruby Gibson, original poem

8

The Five Steps of Somatic Archaeology

The way the night knows itself with the moon, be that with me.

—Rumi

This chapter outlines Somatic Archaeology's step-by-step method of creating a healing relationship with your body and your stories. Do not be deceived by the simplicity. These steps emerged from thousands of healing sessions in which this pattern played out again and again, regardless of the person's storyline or history. Each step leads organically into the other as you focus your attention on the sensations occurring in your body.

What is most important in this process is that you engage with yourself. In many healing modalities, we allow others to heal us, to take our pain away, to figure us out, to become an expert on our individual bodies. The goal here is different. *You* must become the expert on your *own* body. *You* must become the expert on your *own* story. You are the authority. Otherwise, you will continually be looking outside of yourself for cure.

It may take you some time to adapt to this type of empowered healing as you become accustomed to the idea that you have the capacity to pay attention and create shifts, to become your own hero, and to rescue yourself. Yet when you witness your stories face to face, the truth of your past and the potential for your future are undeniable. No one can do this for you. It is important for you to remember, to touch down, feel in, and get to know yourself. As you do this, you source your own creation. This is the way out (or the way in), the key to spiritual awakening, and the path of the mystic or sage.

No one else can teach you about you. Your stories are built upon your experiences, designed by your unique mix, and amplified by your attitude. Someone else can look at your personal story and attempt to understand it, but they will be looking through the lens of their own myths and, consequently, they will modify it to fit their reality. Someone else can teach you to meditate, cleanse your energy field, open your meridians, massage your tissues, give you a pill, hold you close, and help you manage your fears, but at the end of the day it is you sitting in you. Only you can release yourself from suffering.

Every healing technique, traditional and alternative, establishes either suppression or expression of your energy in order to alter or manage symptoms, and this may assist you to feel temporary relief. Reach out when you need support to recognize a pattern or when you feel stuck, but don't forget to make friends with your own inner self. When all is said and done, what rises to the top is your capacity to acknowledge and embrace the fear and the love that loom within you.

Somatic healing is extremely personal. The puzzle of your existence is put together from the pieces of your past—genetic and spiritual lineages—and you become an active participant in the co-creation of your future when you assume an empowered stance. If you feel as if you don't know who you are or what you are passionate about, or how to find meaning in your life, unearthing your story will direct you to the significance of all that has led you to this moment.

The Five Steps

These are the steps to excavate, heal, and embody your personal, familial, and cultural stories. They are described in detail below.

1. *I notice.*

2. *I sense.*

3. *I feel.*

4. *I interpret.*

5. *I reconcile.*

    The steps are described in detail below. Each step leads into the next, designed to gradually immerse you into the silent dialogue of physical sensation. Follow this flow for significant awareness of your excavation site to occur. Do not bypass any step. If you jump from noticing to interpreting, you may have more information, but nothing will change. Transformation comes about when you sense and feel. Do your best not to analyze a symptom before experiencing it—this may shortcut the process with little result. When you add your body's wisdom and your emotional movement to your mental understanding, you illuminate your spirit. Gather information from all aspects of yourself to create the unwinding movement necessary for change.

1. ***I notice:*** Tune into the overall state of your body. What do you notice? Scan for particular areas where you feel congested or where you have chronic pain. Notice where you house repetitive injuries or symptoms. Pay attention to the favored parts of your body, as well as to the places you avoid or dislike. Notice any patterns that are similar to those of your siblings, aunts, uncles, parents, or grandparents. Your body is constantly communicating to you, sending up flares and hoping you will notice your symptoms. Pay attention.

    If you are using pain medications, sleeping pills, SSRI-type drugs, or self-medicating with addictive products, this step can be more difficult. (But that does not mean it's impossible!) Your ability to notice what is happening in your body will most likely be diminished by the numbing effect or suppressing action of certain medications. Most medicines are derived from the plant world, because the plant world is designed to help us give away energy. Used in a natural state and with consciousness, the plant world is a great ally for balancing the emotional body and relieving physical symptoms. Used in a synthetic state, with unhealthy repetition, the plant world becomes a crutch and creates a dependency that does not allow us to be accountable for our experiences.

If you have trouble staying focused, notice areas of pain or discomfort that grab your attention. Take multiple deep breaths to help stay present. Let your analytical mind take a rest. If you lack motivation, ask a trusted friend or loved one to assist you by offering feedback on what they notice. Document your dietary habits, sleeping patterns, and pain cycles alongside your medication schedule to create awareness. Designate the times when you are most alert and use these times to determine the places that you are experiencing pain, confusion, or disorientation. This place will generally feel contracted, like tension or a tight ball of energy. Body Mapping is a good tool to use during Step 1 to encourage body awareness.

When you are able to determine a holding pattern, contracted or repetitive sensation, or area of discomfort, you have found a place to begin exploring. If you have many places in your body all calling to you at once, simply choose one to start with. Ultimately, they are all connected—each point of entry into your somatic matrix will lead you to the others, as energy trails from one destination to another. Over time, generational stories become interwoven with recent memories, compromising and adjusting to your agenda and patterns of suppression, so as you investigate one area it may trigger or influence a sensation in another area. *I notice* is all about being mindful of what your body is experiencing, expressing, and holding in the present moment.

2. ***I sense:*** Drop into your sensory perceptions. This requires that you decelerate to the pace of your body, to the rhythm of the Earth. Bring your awareness out of your head, and take three deep breaths into your body, connecting yourself from head to toe. Slow down. Take time to create a connection with your body. Do not *think* about how it feels to be in your body, but rather *feel* it.

Your sixth sense has a powerful intelligence that every person has. It is body wisdom, somatic intuition, and cellular insight. Unlike our other five senses—seeing, hearing, feeling, touching, and tasting—the sixth sense is not commonly discussed or taught, perhaps because it is not as tangible as the others, or perhaps because it defies reason. Your sixth sense is the voice of your soul, or your higher self, manifest in your body. To hear this voice, you must listen with the ears of a cat, smell with the nose of a wolf, touch with the wings of a butterfly, and see with the eyes of an eagle. The animal world teaches us with instinctual insight that supersedes intellect and allows us to receive information from non-ordinary sources.

If you have trouble paying attention to your body, or have distracting thoughts, I recommend that you establish a grounding cord. (See Somatic Breathing Exercise 1 in chapter 7.) Imagine a thick root extending down from your feet or from the base of your torso into the Earth. Anchor your cord in the soil and rocks. Give away any tension in your body to the structure of the Earth, and feel yourself rooted and disposed downward.

Now, take at least seven deep cleansing breaths into your chosen area to investigate sensations. Breathe in slowly through your nose and out through your mouth, exhaling fully and completely through a wide-open mouth, as if you are fogging up a mirror. Expand into the area of tension, pain, or anxiety, breathing above it, beneath it, and all around it. Explore the perimeters of this region of your body, allowing your breath to be the vehicle of your awareness. (Refer to the Basic Soma-Breaths in chapter 7.)

Notice how it feels to pay attention to this place. If you find yourself distracted or unable to hold attention there, ask your body what it needs in order to feel safe enough to stay present. Let your body answer, not your mind, and then visualize what you need to establish safety. Sometimes the content of a somaticized memory is still very emotionally charged, and it can be difficult to stay present with it. If this happens, continue bringing your breath and your awareness into it and then away from it, titrating in and out. Much as you would get into a bath of hot water, enter slowly as you let your body adjust to the memory.

Once you are able to stay present with the area, become curious about the sensation(s). Based on what you are noticing, allow your questions to gravitate around your curiosity. What grabs your attention? In your inner dialogue with yourself, describe what you feel and follow the questions below to deepen awareness of your excavation site, digging with consciousness while encouraging full breaths to expand into the area.

How much space does the sensation take up?
What shape defines it? Is it round, square, rectangular, flat, swollen?
Is it hard, soft, flexible, dense, fluid, or rigid?
Can I access it, or is it well protected?
Does the sensation move around, or is it anchored in one spot?
How does the rest of my body respond to it?

Again, it is important to let your body answer, even if it takes a while to get a response. You will know the response is accurate, because it will deepen your connection to the sensation and offers insights. Trust your body and be curious, asking any additional pertinent questions. Gravitate your questions around *how, when,* or *what* rather than *why. Why* questions will put you in your head in order to analyze the information. This will take you in a much different direction—generally away from your body.

When you have examined the perimeters of your excavation site and you feel engaged with the sensation, allow your inquiry to become more focused. Continue connecting with your breath and feel into the age of the sensation or memory.

Does it feel old or new?
Does it feel familiar?
What does it remind me of?
Do I remember a time when this sensation wasn't there?
At what age did I first notice this feeling?

The answers to these questions will give you valuable information designed to evoke memory. Pay attention to any referrals, or other areas of your body that get triggered or become activated by your inquiry. Connect the sensations with your breathing. Stay present. This should elicit recognition or expose a trail of memory. Follow it energetically and continue your inquiry for deeper understanding. You may begin feeling emotions arising as your query brings forth memories. This is optimal, and a natural response to somatic excavation. If this happens you can proceed to Step 3, or if manageable, continue to dig further.

The answers to your questions are important, but the true value of this investigation is in making contact with the repressed energy, belief, or memories that the sensation harbors. Let your body tell you a story. Invariably, when you touch into sensation and holding patterns in your body, movement erupts that releases the content.

How does it serve me to hold this here in my body?
What is its job?
Does it keep something in? Keep something out? Is it protective?
Is this something I put here, or is it someone else's energy?
Who or what is it connected to?

Make room for the answers to surface as you delicately dust off the treasure and recognize where it originated and if it is still beneficial for you to keep it buried. Maybe it is time to let it release with a sound or emotion? Maybe it is necessary to maintain the pattern? Check in with your body further. Often, a historical pattern is laced with ancestral agenda, or imprinted with an inherited obligation to carry a burden or belief.

If I had a choice, would I hold onto it or let it go?
What would happen if it were no longer here?
What would I need in order to feel safe enough to let it go?

Stay present, without judgment, as you receive information. It may be helpful to place your hands on the area you are exploring to give a stronger connection. Reinforce your grounding cord if you find your mind distracted or racing. Keep your breath moving through the sensation and around it. Be curious. Expand into the sensation with your breath, ballooning into it, amplifying it and softening it. Play around with your breath, challenging structure and inviting movement. If it feels safe enough to let it go, use breath, sound, and movement to shake it from your soma, bringing in one of the somatic breathing exercises to assist. Remember—*you* created this sensation, and, consequently, *you* can change it. Follow the sensation as needed, trusting your body and responding to its ability to unwind. Let go of the need to control the outcome of your excavation. Stay with it until you evoke an emotional response, gather somatic information, or draw forth a memory. *I sense* is the chief archaeological tool as it holds the key to unlock historical imprints stored in your body.

3. *I feel:* Express your emotions. E-motion is energy in motion. You are looking for movement of some kind. It may be as simple as a deep exhalation or a shudder down your spine. It may feel like heat rising. As emotions express, you may feel anger, grief, embarrassment, shame, resentment, or regret, or, possibly, relief, joy, gratitude, bewilderment, shock, and astonishment. Depending upon how ready or safe you feel to let go, movement can resemble a trickle of energy, or feel similar to an explosion.

   Articulation of emotion can also take the form of physical movement, such as tears, laughter, shaking, trembling, kicking, yelling, sobbing, tingling, or numbing. All are to be expected and honored. If your emotions feel stuck, encourage physical movement by amplifying or exaggerating the expression, such as persuading a jittery feeling in your leg to fully express as a kick. If you are fearful of moving emotion, imagine that you let a little out at a time, much like letting steam out of kettle slowly. The goal is not necessarily an intense cathartic release, but rather a gentle purging that can be easily integrated—a substantial rumble versus an earthquake. If an earthquake does happen, change is imminent, so allow time after you complete the Five Steps for integration and to regain your footing.

This stage can be both exhausting and liberating. Don't force the movement, but don't hold it back. Become fluid like water and follow the path of least resistance. Allow unwinding by imagining a counterclockwise spin drawing pain up and out of your body, or breathe forward through your body from back to front. Use your breath to support and encourage the movement of your tears or your anger. Unlock your jaw, wiggle your toes, shake out your fists, drop your shoulders, and declare your truth.

Remember, you bring it up to let it go. Be careful not to go into self-pity or keep your emotions cycling agonizingly through your body. Exhale out what no longer serves you and trust the innate ability of your body to release the charged energy. Imagine that your tears are cleansing your heart and purifying your bitterness. Rototill those old hurts that have become a burden to your life. Give yourself permission to lighten your load, transforming your body into a carefree, weightless, buoyant form filled with light. Let the feelings flow. *I feel* is reconnecting to the natural stream of life energy and personal power.

4. ***I interpret:*** Make sense of the information gathered. Now that your body has unearthed memories and emotions have been uprooted, new knowledge is available to your mind. You have effectively brought subconscious patterns to your conscious mind. You have brought your shadow into the light of day. You are ready to offer sagacity and significance to the memories and myths that are illuminating.

Take several minutes to fully bring any memories or insights to the present moment. Continue to breathe into them and encourage full expression. Allow all the pieces of the puzzle to come together until it makes sense to you. This 'light bulb' moment lasts until the excavated details are fully exposed. Notice how any recovered memories are playing out in your life right now. Create a bridge from the past to the present as memory timelines open and establish lucidity in your life patterns.

Whether you had a little awakening or a profound shift, the newfound realizations create a foundation for empowerment and hope upon which you can take further steps. Each step is important, even the baby steps. As you grow and practice, the process will become easier and more succinct. Stay present with your body and return often to continue the excavation of your soma, and the sifting of rubble.

Do not analyze the details too much too soon. It will generally take seven days for the released energy to make its way through all the layers of your luminous body. Let things digest and integrate. Be kind and gentle to yourself and continually create safety in your world. Practice self-care. Journal your thoughts, pay attention to your dreams, play with your animals, and get nurtured. Take yourself to the woods, beach, desert, or mountains to absorb the harmony of nature, as you have created new space in your energetic body that is ready for nature to imprint. Establish a new paradigm that allows your personal story to replicate the innate goodness and synchronicity of Mother Earth. *I interpret* is where we rationalize and derive meaning from what we have excavated so that we can create a new myth and storyline for the future.

5. ***I reconcile***: Accept your experiences, reframe the dynamics, and envision a new way of being in life. Reconciliation is simply an act of empowerment that creates compatibility and acquiescence. It moves us from victim consciousness to accountability of experience, hence establishing the mindset that shift dynamics to something new. Releasing long-standing memories from your luminous field allow for the regeneration of life enhancing inner wisdom that has been buried underneath the rubble of fear-based experience.

    Reconciliation is freedom from karma. Removing imprints opens higher consciousness for the opportunity to remember who you are and what your personal destiny is. As each of us re-defines our relationship to our past, this gives us free will to come into alignment with our collective fate as well. We can call this original wisdom, or unification with our higher self.

    Redesigning your myth requires that you remove the limitations of fear-based thoughts, augmenting them with spiritual principles and values. Be wary of religious doctrines that chain you to hierarchal systems. Instead, center your spiritual goals and visions around principles that allow you have a direct relationship with the divine.

    Your mind and spirit have the ability to form ideas and images of things that have never been seen or experienced. This freshness, combined with the wisdom earned from your current and historical experiences, could be the recipe for innovative change and empowered living. This happens one baby step at a time, as each new awareness leads to another and eventually your scope of life becomes broader and clearer.

In order to complete the Five Steps, imagine that you create resolution in the form of protection and empowerment, along with the infusion of love and tenderness. Imagine getting what you needed, then and now; implant it into your memory fields and into every cell in your body. Take some time to dream or visualize a new state of being, and breathe deeply into it. Notice whom you are with, what you are doing, what you are wearing, and how it feels to be in your body. Infuse the image with love and gratitude. It all comes down to being able to take love in and to give it out. When you are able to do that without restriction, you will generate a new myth that will feed your soul and heal generations of suffering.

Now envision a new collective story. This requires outside-the-box thinking. You must think big. You must think inclusively. You must think with compassion. Responsible and affirmative action will change the world. Imagine that you are dedicated to the preservation and care of our beautiful planet, respecting all life that inhabits her terrain. *I reconcile* is empowered action that heals and comes when you recognize you have a choice to live in a different way—with contentment, acceptance for all that has transpired, and peace in your heart.

Somatic Archaeology Protocol

Let's review the Five Steps again, this time breaking them down into a protocol so that you can follow a more detailed description.

I. Set Intent and Container

> First of all, you will want to be free of any recreational drug use or alcohol consumption for at least twenty-four hours prior to an excavation. Longer is preferable for clarity. Burn some incense, sage, cedar, or diffuse essential oils if desired. Turn off phones, pagers, music, or any potentially disruptive noise, put pets in another room, and create a warm, safe space. Focus for a few minutes on your excavation intent and imagine the possibilities. Bring any recent experiences, memories, or triggers to the surface by playing out the scenarios in your mind to evoke recall of feelings and dynamics. Repeat any affirmations or positive thought statements that encourage your goals. Your initial intent may be to focus on one of these following goals, or you may create your own:
>
> To investigate areas of chronic pain, physical ailments, or disease;
>
> To discharge suppressed emotion, depression, anxiety, grief, or guilt;
>
> To integrate current experiences or historical memories;

To stabilize and center, or to ground chaotic or manic energy;
To reorganize memories of excavated events and catalogue details;
To evoke memories that reveal spiritual symbols or ancestral lineage;
To develop skills for somatic exploration which instigate curiosity;
To clear and balance your chakra system.

II. Breathe and Center

Get in a comfortable position—lie down on your back or sit with your spine straight—and close your eyes. Let go of thoughts, needs, agendas, or worries about the day, and bring your awareness into your body. Center yourself with deep belly breaths that connect your entire body, breathing in through your nose and out through your mouth, exhaling with your jaw relaxed. You can use a specific breathing exercise from chapter 7. Take your time, be patient, slow down to the rhythm of your body, and become present.

III. Explore Sensations

How does it feel to be in your body today? What do you notice? Scan your body and pay attention from head to toe. Follow patterns of pain or discomfort, go under the surface of them, and feel from the inside out. Navigate through your body with your breath—feel left/right, above/below, and inside/outside. Notice where there is movement and where there is congestion. Let your body lead you to a sensation, holding pattern, or block. If there is more than one, just choose one to begin with. Define sensation—notice size, placement, density, color, texture, and temperature—and be curious. Play with different questions, but stay away from *why* questions—instead go with *where* or *when* or *how*. Expand into the sensation with focused breaths to deepen your connection. Let the tissues in the area soften as you make room for what you are holding. Pay attention to any symbols or archaic communication that may erupt from past life or spiritual memories.

IV. Create Movement

Track for physical movement/tremors, neurological deactivation, or resistance, and encourage movement with your breath. Move slowly in and out of charged areas or sensations that evoke fear or strong emotions. Keep your mind focused on your intent and stay present. Be sure to stay with how it *feels*, and not how you *think* it feels. Ask this part of your body what it would say if it had a voice. Encourage sound work or vocal expression of withheld words or sounds to awaken deep-seated memories. Ask your body how it serves you to hold this here. Is it protecting, shielding, keeping energy in, or keeping energy out? What would happen if this sensation or blockage were gone? What would you need to feel safe enough to let it go? When ready, visualize movement happening through the dissolving of a structure; with a certain color; by softening hard spots; by unwinding with counterclockwise spirals that move energy up or out; or by encouraging any change that shifts the energy. Allow somatic intuition to guide you.

V. Maintain Safety

Continue to remind yourself that it is safe to dig. Be curious about what you need to be able to trust your ability to manage what is revealed and to take care of yourself. There are no limits to your imagination—if the sensation is dark, find a flashlight; if you are scared, bring in a protector or strong animal totem; if an area feels frozen, melt it; if it is locked, find the key; if it is evil, by all means, call in some angels! You created this sensation/structure, and therefore you can recreate it. Stay empowered!

VI. Emote

Allow emotions to come to the surface and surrender to them. This can take the form of tears, laughter, resistance, yelling, vomiting, etc. Use your breath to encourage movement of your feelings. Keep your jaw relaxed. Continue making room for what you are holding until all related emotion releases. If the feelings are stuck, exhale sound or words through a wide-open mouth and avoid holding your breath. If you have anger or sensations of heat, use the fire-breathing dragon exercise in chapter 7. Allow energy to move through your muscles, facial expressions, and neurological pathways to find an exit, or the pathway of least resistance. Shake, kick, tremble, stretch, contract, expand—give your body a voice without hurting or injuring yourself.

VII. Reestablish Safety

Let your body tell you when the release is over. Slow your breath down, and take a few minutes to reestablish safety by centering and anchoring into the Earth with the grounding breath. Or expand into the natural world, feeling the trees, sun, wind, and rocks to gain stability. Check in with your body and notice any changes. How does the area feel now? What feels different? Track for any further sensations or related pain, and if there is another layer of emotion, repeat the above process. When it feels complete and the sensation or blockage in your body is relieved, move on to the next step.

VIII. Integrate

Normalize your breath pattern and allow your mind to integrate any new information or memories that you have uncovered. Do this by absorbing the knowledge rather than analyzing it. Begin to visualize or dream into your original goal/intent and allow the pieces of your story to come together. Fill any emptiness you may now feel with the image of your dream, or with any feeling or sensation that brings empowerment, resolution, joy, or expansion to your body. Allow yourself to imagine that you get what you need, that you now have a choice, that you are protected, that you are honored, that you are forgiven, or that you forgive—whatever brings peace to your heart, resolves the conflict, or mends the fear. Imagine that every cell in your body resonates with your new dream or story. Give it power by infusing it with three deep full cleansing breaths. Create spaciousness as you relax.

IX. Close the Excavation

Come back to present time and feel your body in the room. Notice what shifts when you open your eyes and come back to an upright position. Do not intellectualize or minimize the experience. Affirm any changes and journal or draw pictures of the excavation or new story line. Make note of anything else that you would like to excavate in the future, and pay attention to your dreams tonight.

X. Gratitude Attitude

Take some time to ground—drink a glass of water, take a slow thoughtful walk, relax in a warm aromatic bath, allow your spirit to rest. Practice self care. Give thanks to your body for all that it has endured, to your heart for its willingness to heal, to your mind for keeping you organized, and to your spirit for inspiration and the faith to remember who you are when you are free. Pat yourself on the back and acknowledge your courage. Smile.

The mighty oak shakes her leaves to the ground
and yet I can't shake you.
Day turns to night and darkness falls
but I remain unchanged
I touch the sky, I touch the Earth
I shimmy in between
And yet your heart beats inside mine

and gratitude makes way.
The moon comes full and beckons love
From where your dream holds me.
I seek the strength to meet you
where the shoreline meets the sea.

—Ruby Gibson, original poem

9

Self-Care for the Somatic Archaeologist

*If stories come to you, care for them.
And learn to give them away where they are needed.
Sometimes a person needs a story more than food to stay alive.*

—Barry Lopez, *Crow and Weasel*

Self-care is essentially personal guardianship. It means diligently attending to your self-assessed needs and developing responsibility for your effectiveness. It is finding the capacity to worship yourself and your body, nourishing it with right actions, right living, and right thinking. You initiate self-care when you believe that you deserve it and when you love yourself enough to administer it. The presence of daily, positive, thoughtful self-care is a clear reflection of your holiness; the lack of it represents an internal disregard for your being. Self-care is the recognition of not only what is necessary to maintain yourself, but also what is vital to fully inhabit your body. It is a preventative measure, as well as a celebratory declaration of your story.

You may think that you take care of yourself by eating regularly, exercising frequently, playing, laughing, and socializing. Yet when you are unearthing your story, you may find that your system of self-care needs improvement or upgrading. It may become apparent that you need more rest, more solitude, more community, more support, more affection, more bodywork, more spirituality, more playful times, more creative outlets, more dancing, more crying, more laughing, and more dreaming. Your body may demand that you continually reassess your personal requirements in order to be effectual.

During your somatic excavations, you will want to be sure to be prepared. Your self-care suitcase should be well packed and versatile. I believe that the following items are indispensable. Include whatever else is useful.

Self-Care Suitcase

Meditation is the key to self-understanding. There are various forms and techniques, some with a religious orientation, some with an exploratory aspect; others use breathwork as a focus. The type of meditation employed is not nearly as important as is the frequency and the dedication to it as a spiritual practice. It is adaptable to any religious or spiritual belief system, primarily requiring that you transcend your ego state of mind in order to find truth or the center of your being. Determining which type of meditative practice to include in your self-care regime is a very individual choice.

It is advantageous to incorporate a meditative practice on a daily basis. This helps you to recognize personal shifts in your growth, moods, cycles, and awareness. It strengthens your ability to concentrate and learn mindful breathing techniques. Meditation deepens your connection to your storyline, and when done out of doors, to the Earth.

Daily meditation aligns you with a calm and peaceful center within that, once obtained, can be easily accessed. It is valuable during times of stress or being overwhelmed—with a few deep breaths you can bring yourself back to center where you can make clearer decisions, becoming responsive rather than reactive.

Meditation engenders respect for self. It enhances awareness and objectivity, developing sensitivity to life's struggles. It supports you in appreciating and honoring creative urges, establishing balance in projects and relationships. Whether visualizing dreams, affirming abundance, clearing your mind, or praying for salvation, meditation is an essential tool in the self-care suitcase.

Journaling offers a creative means for self-expression of your story. Somehow, the process of taking thoughts, feelings, or ideas and giving them written expression makes them more tangible. Journaling gives validity to an otherwise abstract notion. Writing is empowering; it helps you to get to know yourself.

Journaling is the process of tapping into a vein of creative thought. Following a train of thought unravels your story, revealing memories that you never thought existed. The creative process begets fertility. The more you write, the more you expose. Create a documentary of your healing story.

Journal hourly, daily, weekly, or monthly—whenever the mood strikes. Keep a pen and paper handy for momentary bursts of original expression. Allow your passion, whims, defiance, and gratitude to flow from your mind, down your arms, through your fingers, into the pen, and onto the paper. Explore your more aesthetic qualities. Scribble a poem. Form an opinion. Tell a story. Speak your truth. Unfold a new myth.

Give writing a free form. Too much structure sometimes deters the creative process. Journaling assists in moving stagnant thoughts or fears, freeing up airspace in your mind for higher pursuits. It can offer a fresh mental breeze. If you find it difficult to express your thoughts, emotions, or beliefs on a spontaneous basis, create a certain time every day for it. Just sit with pen on paper and wait. It may take time to get the juices flowing, yet with enough dedication, you will find that a small insignificant trickle may turn into a wild river of expression. Be mindful of your resistance and write about *it*. Explore your distractions and give them some written dimension. Self reflection allows you to recognize how you hold back and it promotes self-awareness.

Playing is an outlet for self-enjoyment. It rekindles childhood stories and liveliness by giving you permission to frolic in the moment. Playing is essentially taking pleasure in something for no other purpose than that. Its motivation is pure gratification. Play with children, play with animals, play with toys, play with yourself—just play for the sake of playing. It overcomes rigidity, encourages freedom, lightens your spirit, and gives balance to your work schedule.

I recommend playing at least once a day: a game of cards, hide and seek, checkers, flashlight tag after dark, Scrabble with a friend, jump on a trampoline, go to the playground, do a crossword puzzle, play your guitar, read a good book, draw a picture, or whatever brings you pleasure. And then, *really* play at least once a week: fly a kite, go sailing, go to the mall, knit an afghan, go four-wheeling, watch the sunrise, design a sandcastle, shoot a model rocket, bake a cake, take a kid to the zoo, go to a concert, plant a garden—the possibilities are endless.

Play also encourages you to display empowerment. It subverts suffering and dissuades victimization through the recognition that you have choices in how you play—that you control how you bring pleasure into life. By noticing what activities bring you enjoyment, you can better understand yourself.

Are you a receptive, active, or solitary player? Change your approach and see what happens. How is this reflective of your story? Do you get your kicks through dangerous stunts, bungee jumping, or thrill seeking? Recognize what your goals are; is it possible that you are traumatizing yourself by keeping your nervous system activated? Do you choose playful activities that commonly include food or eating? Explore how your need for nourishment may be connected to your freedom or playfulness. It is valuable to become cognizant of the recreational choices you make, for then you have the opportunity to change and take even better care of your self.

Exercising encourages self-discipline and positive body image. After a nice long walk, swim, bicycle ride, or gym workout, you simply feel better. The workout releases pent-up emotional energy and muscular tension. Exercising clears the mind, assists in relaxation and improvement of sleep patterns, increases appetite, and generally helps you to feel more alive and connected to others. It brings you to the here and now.

Devise an exercise program that you can realistically meet on a daily basis. Yoga in the morning, a walk after work, a softball game on weekends, a bike ride once a week—set up a system that works for *you* and then stick to it. Aerobic exercise supports breathwork and emotional balance. It gives you permission to breathe.

Keep your spine flexible, your abdominals poised, your posture dignified, your weight balanced, and your coordination active. Exercise is somatic maintenance, health prevention, and gratefulness for having a body that works well. Experience the miracle of your physicality and enhance your somatic excavations at the same time!

Receiving is essential for self-acceptance. You may be more comfortable giving than receiving. When you give—touch, love, gifts, or favors—you are in control. When you receive, you are vulnerable. In order to remain effective and compassionate, it is important that you receive on a regular basis. Gift yourself. Receive for the sake of receiving.

It seems that most people are more comfortable being in an active state if giving in our fast-paced, competitive, goal-oriented culture. Therefore, it is important to examine your beliefs about receiving. Establishing a balance between giving and receiving allows for equilibrium of your soul. By nurturing both your demonstrative and your receptive qualities, you can develop internal harmony.

It is best to give by receiving. Trusting yourself to take in nourishment in many forms is a delineation of your growth. Focus on receiving and your reservoir of personal energy will then overflow, and it will not feel like a burden to give. Examine your storyline and ancestral beliefs about scarcity—a perceived shortage of love, money, health, goodness, food, water, and spiritual manna is an invitation to bring in abundance and prosperity from a higher level.

It is possible for your body to have leftover residual emotional content or somatic holding tendencies from your excavations. If you feel heavy, weighted, or disoriented when done, establish rituals of cleansing. Take a brisk walk afterward, or a hot shower or bath with Epsom salts; journal, pray, or smudge yourself; go to a park and lie on the grass while continuing deep breathing; or do anything else that helps you receive energy and alter or purify your energy field. Give away by exhaling out through the right side of your body and creating an exit for the residual energies.

Ascertain what your fundamental requirements are, not only for the survival of your healing story, but also for the maintenance of your well-being—continuing to thrive. You are responsible for getting what you need. You deserve to be buoyant and glowing. Receive from yourself by determining the steps that are vital to enhance your life and maintain your effectiveness. Accept your vulnerability as a condition of being human and honor your need to take in support.

Dancing enhances your recognition of self-celebration. It is the experience of embodying joy through movement. Free-form movement helps you develop responsiveness to the rhythms of music and of life, allowing creative expression. Structured movement, such as ballet or folk dancing, helps you to meet physical challenges and goals to build confidence, coordination, and grace. Dance is a fine place to find balance between being active and receptive.

Dance can help you discern where you are not fluid in your body. Notice in your body where you tend to hold back; notice where the movement flows easily; notice what types of music are more comfortable to move to; notice how you breathe when you move; notice if you are self-conscious when you dance. Experiment with different rhythms and beats and challenge yourself to experiment with new dance steps and movement styles.

A quick dance can be a pick-me-up on a difficult day or helpful as a replacement to a coffee break. When you have a dilemma to work through, turn on some music and dance before making any decisions. It will clear your mind and bring you present in your body—a more centered place to be decisive.

Dance can also be used as a therapeutic tool during Somatic Archaeology excavations. It reminds you to lighten up. When you have reached an impasse or gotten too serious, dance. Shake out the resistance. Dance is a means to self-awareness and offers enhancement to any relationship—especially the relationship to self.

Humor is an important way to access and vent your joy. It comes at odd times during the unearthing of your story. It may be the last thing you think would help, and yet it erupts to ease your tension. Humor can be used remedially to give relief to a difficult issue or topic, or it can be incorporated as part of an emotional release. You may alternate between outbursts of laughing and crying, with no obvious reason for it. Laughter is spontaneous and healing, sending positive vibrations throughout your body. Laughter is emotional release.

Encourage a sense of lightheartedness. Wear life loosely. Storytelling can be a serious matter, yet it can at times enslave you to sadness and remorse. Storytelling littered with humor and laughter can be empowering, offering an outlet for the many varied ways you have compensated for your dilemmas. The ability to laugh is advantageous because it objectifies pain. Use humor to keep a balance between work and play, and to keep from getting depressed when you've had a bad day. Humor can bond and bring you together with others, offering commonality in predicaments and perspectives in healing.

Eating is the primary form of self-nourishment. Food is physically, emotionally, and spiritually nutritious. It sustains your will, alleviates cravings, and feeds your soul. The types of food that you choose to eat are a reflection of self-respect. Some foods nourish and enhance, while others deplete and are toxic. Notice what you ingest and how that serves your needs. Foods consumed due to historical influence are usually rich in emotional content and must be observed closely. Also watch your intake of foods that activate your nervous system and create stress: caffeine, chocolate, alcohol, and sugar.

Eating close to the bottom of the food chain is beneficial for longevity and prevention of disease. Foods of vegetable and plant origin offer the best nutrients, are easily digested, have vibrant energy, and are the least toxic. Always go organic if possible. Foods of animal origin are heavy, high in fat and cholesterol, are harder to digest, and carry unnecessary chemicals and synthetic hormones.

Water is a source of physical nourishment, lubrication, and cleansing. Plenty of fresh water is essential when excavating. Use it in abundance, doubling your intake before, during, and after excavations. Its importance cannot be underestimated. It assists in metabolism and keeps you grounded, fluid, and energetically stabilized. Use purified or spring water when possible.

Symbolic systems are the path to self-preservation. They are personalized methods of relating to unique signs that represent your need for order and stability. Use positive, inspirational, and culturally familiar symbols that make sense to your individual story and spiritual beliefs.

Symbolic systems may include, but are certainly not limited to, gardening or the planting of seeds; prayer or worship; listening to or playing music; methods of divination; use of symbolic or spiritual fetishes; ceremony or ritual; religious studies; traveling, playing, or working with animals; star gazing; rock climbing or hiking; rafting; camping; or any earth-centered activity.

Amidst the chaos of unearthing tragic stories, Mother Earth can offer a predictable regulated system of operation that meets our fundamental need for a normal or expected sequence of events. It helps to keep connected to rhythmic external cycles, such as watching the sun rise or set, or aligning to lunar phases or astrological trends in order to preserve a sense of hopefulness.

Your symbolic necessities are unique to your own lifestyle. Having a ritual of watching the same television show at the same time every day may meet your need for order. You may choose to be attentive to symbolic details, such as a hawk or eagle flying overhead, or a shooting star, and view these as omens or signs of universal communion. You may pray once a day, routinely keep your house in order, have power objects that you connect with, trees that you hug, altars that you construct, special places that you visit, etc.

Symbols may be abstract, such as personal visions, chanting, or basking in the moon glow; or they may be concrete, such as a bible, a picture, a teddy bear, or a statue. Many times they will be based on your religious or cultural orientation. Use of a symbolic system that assists you in feeling secure and recognizes your inherent need to believe in grace and miracles is beneficial. It helps repair any disconnection that you have with the Divine. Healing your story is a miraculous experience and leads you to those things that you have learned to respect.

Examine what self-preserving systems you already have in place. Do they meet your needs? Were you aware that you had them? Do they need to be enhanced or altered? What feels centering and calming to you? What gives you faith in divine order? What helps you to feel spiritually abundant? What or who do you call on for your strength?

Answering these questions will assist you in recognizing your personal symbolic systems. However small or large, significant or insignificant, your self-care suitcase can accommodate these symbolic gifts you bestow on your self.

Self-Sabotage

Identify the ceiling of contentment that you have in your life. Is it based on inherited stories, cultural expectations, your upbringing, and your physical environment? What do you expect from life? Have you identified and determined a certain level of success and pleasure for your life and when you reach it, are you satisfied to stop there? Are you proud that you have at least done better than your predecessors? Is this all there is?

As you heal your story, your ceiling of contentment may become more pronounced and obvious, and you may progressively feel less comfortable with it. Like a plant that has outgrown its pot, your ceiling can feel cramped or restrictive. These inherited standards may be recognizable through language—notice when you use restrictive, disempowering, or demeaning language in reference to your self and lifestyle. Or through action—notice when you make choices that are detrimental to your healing process, such as drinking, smoking, or drug use, overeating or purging, self-mutilation, or reengagement with abusive relationships. Or through physical maladies—such as injuries that keep you from moving forward in your healing process at crucial stages.

These limitations undermine your recovery, and are an expression of the internal struggle for empowerment. As a form of self-sabotage, many of us create crises to diffuse our focus or avoid confrontation, or when uncomfortable feelings may be coming too close to the surface, or change is eminent. If you don't feel deserving of healing or success, it is easy to deter or disrupt your healing journey.

Because self-sabotage patterns are learned and modeled early in life, they are deeply buried in our excavation sites. Do not give up on yourself if you become frustrated. Keep digging. Explore the resistance in your body, not your mind. You cannot think your way out of fear, but you can feel your way out. Allow your body to teach you about the origins of your defiance. Challenge your apathy. Explore where and when you gave up on yourself. Be willing to *feel* it. Break whatever contracts you made with yourself or others to struggle through this life. Who told you that you couldn't succeed? Forgive the past, lighten your heart, and use the fire of your anger to generate movement.

It all comes down to power. Do you squander your energy tending to things that don't produce results? Are you still holding resentment about the one who broke your heart? Or remorseful about the schoolyard criticism that you dished out? Are you punishing yourself for the dreams that you squashed? Or for the abortion you had, or the job you lost, or the mistake you made? Whatever has a grip on your heart, whatever you obsess about and choose not to forgive—no matter how harsh or horrific—becomes a black hole that sucks your power right into it.

Black Holes

Celestially, a black hole is a swirling object in space thought to contain such a strong gravitational pull that no matter or energy can escape from it. Somatically, a black hole is a dark energetic place in your luminous body into which memories or feelings disappear, never to be seen again. Such black holes are established during times of great grief, loss, trauma, or pain, when there is no foreseeable remedy or hope for change. Some are big, some are small, some are inherited, some are self-created, but the common denominator is that they are established as a storage unit for irreconcilable emotional experiences birthed from a loss of spiritual power.

Out of sight, out of mind is the paradigm. Out of body is not the result. These whirlpools of collapsed energy stagnate life force in your body, and, consequently, toxins also pool in these areas. Many chronic diseases manifest as a result of black holes and exhibit in the corresponding organ or body part. Once a figurative place of emptiness and isolation, black holes become visible in our symptoms, addictions, and repetitive emotional patterns. They are difficult to self-recognize, and do not discriminate between what energy they absorb. Light itself becomes trapped, and the content becomes invisible.

Healing black holes is possible and necessary for growth and advancement on all levels. They can be confusing to explore somatically because the force of a black hole mutilates energetic structures, symbols, and memories, so that what originally went into the black hole will look much different when it comes out. Do not focus on the need to figure out what happened, but rather give your attention to expressing the tapered and constricted energy.

Initially you can use your anger or frustration about self-sabotage circumstances to fuel the motivation to confront a black hole and let go of what binds you to it. Internal accountability is the first step to remedy a hole; blaming others exaggerates a black hole. The second step is to forgive yourself, others, and especially to forgive God, the Great Spirit, for your state of affairs. Speak to the Divine in your heart, saying, "I'm sorry, please forgive me, I love you." Allow these words to cleanse your soul of harshness, while using somatic fire-breathing to release related anger, burning energetic cords that bind you to others in regret. Do this as many times as necessary for you to feel relief and a growing sense of peace in your heart. Bless those who have been your obvious teachers, as well as the unlikely people in your life that I refer to as *gurus in drag*—implausible teachers who provide lessons in an unconventional manner.

When you are prepared to release and heal the content of a black hole, here is the next step. Locate and visualize the black hole in your luminous body. It will most likely be situated near an area of disease, pain, anxiety, or constriction. Breathe into it to establish an awareness and connection. It may feel cold or numb. Feel the direction of its spin. Now imagine that you can energetically extend your arm to make it longer, and reach into the black hole all the way to the bottom. (There is a bottom!) Imagine that you grab the bottom, and then pull it out, much like you would turn a sock inside out, to release the stored memories and energy. Do this a few times until your concentration and visualization skills improve, while remembering to exhale fully with a cleansing breath. Take care of yourself for a couple of days afterward, being gentle and compassionate with feelings that come forward, affirming forgiveness, and paying attention to your dreams.

Is there anything else you need to address to feel safe enough to continue your excavation in a progressive manner? Find out and make it so. Stay confident in your abilities and the techniques, even if you experience doubt. Believe in yourself, practice self-care, and align with the internal query, "What would I do if I was free?" The answer to this question will help you avoid future traps of self-sabotage and black holes.

Your Touch Story

Self-sabotage and self-care models are generally established when we are children, mimicking the behavior and habits of our families, communities, or caretakers. The quality and amount of touch you received as a child also influences your expectations of life, your quota of happiness, and what you believe you deserve.

Touch is simply about coming into relationship. Touch defines who you are and is the channel for coming into contact with another person. Without touch, you cannot survive. Your story is predetermined by touch, for it instills the ability to relate, to be intimate, to receive nurturing, and to take in support. Your touch story delineates boundaries and mirrors your sense of personal respect.

Touch overlaps somatic sensors and seeps into emotional, spiritual, and cognitive fields. Whether cuddling an infant, shaking hands with a friend, stroking a lover, hugging a family member, or brushing up against a stranger, thought, emotion, and intention are immediately apparent through contact. You may contract, relax, or soften dependent upon what you sense or feel when being touched. When you are touched in a healthy, caring manner, touch is interpreted as trusting, and consequently acceptance and bonding occur, and your body feels safe.

We inherit the ways in which our caretakers make contact with us. Violent and abusive touch can create fear, shyness, and hesitancy. There is an implied collective responsibility to touch our children lovingly and with respect, yet abusive and violent touch is commonly misdirected toward children. As we grow, each contact we make can remind us of our touch story. Hence, there are times when we reject the very thing that could ease our pain.

Loving touch and physical nurturing that are abundant with caring and gentleness and that contain the important ingredients of love and acceptance will feed your soul and establish a foundation of self-perception from which you will grow into adulthood. Loving touch tells your soul that it is wanted, notifies your mind that it is safe to be here, creates a fertile environment for the maturation of the emotional state, and supports your body in its unhindered growth and health. Loving touch is inherited from affectionate and caring relatives, but it can also be deliberately learned to change family patterning. Loving touch is unconditional and gentle, with clear boundaries and intent.

Vacant touch may appear kind and gentle, but it may be sterile. This type of empty touch may be given by a young parent who holds her baby, yet dreams of being somewhere else, or it may be engendered with the thought, "I am holding you, but I resent every minute of it." The caregiver may not even be aware of the inconsistency of his or her touch, for she is busy attending to her own needs or concerns. Vacant touch signals your body to retract, your mind to question the conflicting messages, your emotions to parch, and your soul to play hide and seek. Vacant touch usually goes undiagnosed, and we cannot pinpoint why we feel empty inside. Adults who received vacant touch as children feel unfulfilled and typically look for nourishment in other ways. This type of touch story predisposes you to eating disorders, addictions, self-injury, and most commonly, to depression.

Violent touch is riddled with intense emotions and verbal slandering. Hitting, slapping, pinching, spanking, aggressive tickling, and physical torture not only carry physical pain, but with it the onslaught of the internalized feelings of the aggressor. It transfers emotional and mental havoc inwardly, and can predispose you to heightened fear and numbing of sensation. Violent touch is passed through generations. It mirrors to us the storyline that it is not okay for my parent to be here, so it is not okay for me to be here; somatically you sense that your parent hurts physically so that means that you must hurt. You know that emotions are outbursts that seem to only cause pain, so you'd better keep yours in. Your soul not only questions its ability to be here, it knows that it is not safe to be here. With this touch story, you lose hope and resign on many levels to minimize your existence. Your dreams, ambitions, and compassion are smothered because the fuel of excitement for passion about life is gone.

Sexualized touch creates blame, confusion, and mistrust. When caregivers or adults use touch in a sexually suggestive or exploitive manner, they are taking advantage of the innocent nature of children to meet their own needs. All inappropriate sexualized touch contains the elements of guilt, shame, dominance, and humiliation. Touch that is provocative in nature can imprint many confusing stories. Generally sexualized touch received as a child teaches you physically that your body is not your own and thus you grow to abuse it; emotionally you decipher that you are worthless; cognitively you learn how to manipulate; and your soul seeks invisibility. The same outcome is apparent in adults who are raped or sexually abused.

Heal Your Sexual Story

If you experienced unhealthy or inappropriate sexualized touch as a child, or have been sexually exploited by others, it is common to feel shame or extreme modesty regarding your body and its functions. This type of violation ruptures a healthy sense of boundaries and self-worth, establishing a disconnection from wholesomeness. The innocence you once knew can get buried under the emotional burdens of sexual abuse. These scars can last a lifetime, or more, as it breaches intimacy, inflicts invisible wounds, generates self-doubt, and shatters trust in God or the Divine, a force that you expected to protect you. Fortunately, Somatic Archaeology excavations can help you to recover the sacredness of your body.

Sexual violation can occur with touch or without touch. Sexual shame is prevalent in our society and in our religious institutions; therefore, it is commonplace to become sexually manipulative, sexually frigid, sexually incompetent, or sexually covert. Early exposure to sexualized scenes, provocative television or advertising, pornography, Internet sites, and peer pressure at school establish a concept that sexuality is mysterious and off limits, rather than loving and candid. Sexual dysfunction is merely a reflection of our cultural fears and deviations. Rape and incest are not crimes of passion, but rather crimes of control and dominance.

With secure boundaries in place, you may feel safe enough to excavate your sexual story. Sexual inhibitions and addictions and patterns of incest are repetitive cycles that are passed on through generations and, therefore, they may not be your own issues, or may have gotten aggravated in your story. Unresolved sexual abuse stories, sexual infidelity, and sexual vulnerabilities are commonly passed forward from mother to daughter, or grandmother to granddaughter; and from father to son, or grandfather to grandson. The stories are also handed down from father to daughter or son, and mother to daughter or son during incestual exchanges. As you explore your own sexuality, you can unearth imprints that predisposed you to present-day experiences.

You can address these imprints through breathwork and somatic excavation. Begin by setting an intent to expose or release the memories and recognize any familial patterns that exist. Pay attention to subtle behavioral tendencies in your family, and take responsibility for how you hold sexual energy in your body. Blame does not serve healing at this point, and will only be disempowering, short-circuiting your progress. The blurry line between victim and perpetrator exists in many family systems, due to the fact that many perpetrators were once victims themselves. We must step out of self-imposed or culturally imposed roles that fuse our identity to sexual shame and the notion that we are forever flawed when we act out of sexual integrity. All people have the right to heal.

Typically, sexual imprints are buried and will take some digging to expose. Secrets and lies run rampant around sexual issues and therefore many of us develop amnesia with certain memories, or disconnect from our bodies in an attempt to keep the patterns concealed. When excavating sexual patterns, focus on the memories you do have, and specifically ask your body to reveal to you where the roots of your sexual story exist. Breathe into your belly, womb, or genitals, and look for areas of darkness or congestion. When you locate them, breathe them forward, from the back of your body to the front, with a counterclockwise spiral movement. (See Somatic Breathing Exercise 9 in chapter 7.) By opening up your Pandora's Box of sexual memories, you will bring into the daylight many hidden memories and stories that lie camouflaged or may have been censored. Take your time and be gentle with yourself. If you are afraid to excavate this area alone, it would be prudent to consult with a somatic therapist or psychotherapist who can help facilitate your process.

You may also find lost remnants of your sexual power or innocence have been hidden along with the secrets. Take your time to sift through what was obscured, for the roots may be deep. When you find your way back to the origin and bring it into consciousness, release any accompanying emotions or anger. You can effectively clear inherited patterns and recover your sacred sexuality by imagining golden light blessing your reproductive organs. Let pure energy in, sending it through your entire endocrine system. This is good for menstrual complaints and cramping or infertility issues, while benefiting your children and future generations by unburdening them from having to carry forward this unfortunate inheritance.

During somatic excavations, it is possible to uncouple the sensation of sexual abuse or inhibition from your current sexual experiences so that you can have a fulfilling marriage or partnership unhindered by old sexual roles and dynamics. This is a realistic goal which frequently includes the desire to have an unrestricted orgasm, and it can be approached in the same way as you would approach the unwinding of any area of somatic holding. Utilize the Five Steps of Somatic Archaeology to expose emotional attachments. Awareness and honesty of your sexual cycles, needs, and boundaries is essential, along with a loving and considerate partner.

Because sexual memories are highly charged, you will want to titrate in and out of the sensations, releasing the feelings a little at a time. Somatic titration refers to the ability to measure and adjust the balance of a somatic response. To titrate, gradually bring your breath and awareness into a somatic location that holds a memory. If you get triggered or have trouble staying present or paying attention, back off to regulate activation or dissociation. Then, when ready, come back to the emotionally charged sensation and continue somatic breathing and unwinding techniques. Go back and forth, deepening with each re-entry into the memory, until it feels comfortable and safe enough to stay present and engaged. Give it time; you may not be able to do this in one somatic excavation. Return as often as needed to gently complete the Five Steps of Somatic Archaeology.

Sexual stimulation brings forth sensations that accompany the memory, and it is common to develop somatic filters to avoid feeling the energy of the experience. It is therefore important to stay present, to continue active breathing, and always to keep in mind that you bring it up to let it go. Each time you feel the sensation, remembering a little more and emoting a little more, you are effectively and slowly uncoupling the memories lodged in your second chakra. With each release, your cells purge and your neurology decompresses, establishing additional feelings of trust and safety for further excavation. You will know it is all released when loving sexual exchanges no longer feel violating, but rather feel enjoyable and ecstatic.

Be sensitive to shame issues as you disengage feelings of humiliation and embarrassment that accompany sexual arousal. Shame is toxic and encourages alienation from physical pleasure. Usually, it is found buried in conjunction with anger. Identify where shame is seated in your body and explore its story, being careful to stay with sensations and away from analyzing feelings of degradation. Focus on your sexual energy flowing free and in alignment with spiritual principles.

Many subtle dynamics and projections may come to the surface when unearthing sexual stories. The goal is to create healthy boundaries and a comfortable sense of your own sexuality and procreative energies. It all boils down to intimacy, with others and yourself. Develop authenticity to understand and manage your personal needs. Challenge behaviors or activities that follow unhealthy sexual stories.

Maintain Healthy Boundaries

Boundaries are the borders of your personal space. It is where you stop and another begins. Development of healthy boundaries is created in childhood through parental modeling which honors the inherent need we each have for control over when and how our bodies will be touched. Having a body gives you power. The more you demonstrate ownership of your body, the more power you have.

Boundary violations may be physical, such as medical procedures, violence, sexual assault, auto accidents, war experiences, environmental disasters, torture, etc. They may also be mental and emotional such as threats, coercive or manipulative language, demeaning or vengeful statements, and authoritarian demands. They may be sexual, such as voyeurism, pornography, witnessing sexual acts, incest, and sexually explicit behavior or language; or they may be spiritual, such as forced religious orientation, religious manipulation, and cult or ritual abuse.

Traumatic events and stories disrupt the natural development of healthy boundaries. The result is usually two forms of boundary adaptation. The first is the development of a rigid boundary system that becomes extremely inflexible and overly defined due to repeated violation. With a rigid system, any connection seems threatening and intimacy is difficult. It may be immediately apparent or well disguised, yet your system will arm itself at any potential threat.

The second is the development of an undefined boundary system that exhibits an inability to protect yourself, encouraging vulnerability and helplessness along with a loss of desire to change. Enmeshment is common; akin to a sponge, you take on the impressions, feelings, and attitudes of those surrounding you because you have not had the opportunity to develop a significant sense of self. The lack of boundaries allows you to merge with the void and become invisible.

The common denominator of both systems is the fear of being violated again. It is the result of having no control. It is helpful to reflect honestly on the development of your boundary system and the struggles inherent in the process. Working toward healthy personal borders is a continual process that happens as you excavate your story.

A healthy personal boundary system is one that is well defined, yet flexible. This means that you are capable of allowing others into your personal, physical space without feeling threatened, or equally comfortable demanding that they back off. Emotionally, you can differentiate between your needs or feelings and another's, and intimacy is enriching rather than suffocating. Underlying a healthy sense of boundaries is autonomy—responsibility and ownership of your body, emotions, and story.

A good boundary exercise is to sit on the floor across from another person, make eye contact, take a deep breath, and notice if it feels comfortable to be in relationship. Dependent upon what you notice, shift your body closer or away from them to find a secure distance. Then ask your partner to draw an imaginary line around his or her body to delineate his personal space. You do the same. Then take turns entering each other's space with permission and without permission, and notice the difference. Take your time, being sure to pay attention to somatic safety clues—breath patterns, eye contact, body temperature, anxiety levels—and play with the dynamic. This is a safe way to learn to sense and define your boundaries.

Because somatic excavation exposes boundary and safety issues, I invite you to create healthy boundaries by either gently challenging yourself to experience vulnerability that is non-threatening, or to build structure and define borders where there is vacancy. Be respectful, demand respect for yourself, and always attempt to be congruent; that is, be willing to express on the outside what you feel on the inside.

Responding versus Reacting

Self-care is a choice. The development of a healthy boundary system is a choice. Unearthing your story is a choice. When you accept responsibility for what has happened to you and what is happening to you now, ownership of your body and mind develops along with the power to dictate your future.

You also have a choice in how you act in response to any given situation. The difference is between reacting and responding. Typically, when we *respond* to a situation, we take time to think through the consequences of our actions, we consider the inclination of our story, and we are able to base our choices on common sense and loving exchanges. It is a patient and mindful response that enhances or mends the situation. When we *react* to a situation, it is generally a fast and unconscious behavior that comes from a historical fear-based story. It is impulsive and irrational, generating repetitive patterns of fear and anger.

This reactive stance, although helpful to mobilize us in dangerous circumstances, can be damaging to relationships, especially when dealing with young children in our care, or with partners who receive the brunt of past hurts. If you are inclined to reactive impulses, use somatic awareness skills to notice where the impulse originates in your body, and then take a few moments to exhale out the fear or anger. Calm down before acting or speaking. Somatic fire-breathing is very effective for reactive persons, particularly those who are prone to violence or aggression. When confronted with a choice in any given situation, always ask yourself, "What would I do right now if I loved myself?" That is the greatest resource you have.

Choose how you heal by educating yourself about your past and giving your body an active voice in your daily life. Develop awareness of when you hold your breath, and give yourself permission to cry and to laugh. Choose relationships that fulfill your needs. Explore your limitations and your potential for movement, and believe in your capacity to heal yourself. Honor the inherent wisdom in your body and your story, and make choices for your own reasons and not by coercion from others. Dream into who you are when you are free—this is the essence of self-care for the storykeeper.

> *The delightful taste of blackberry sage tea warms me as I gaze out the window. Aspen leaves twirl like tiny helicopters in a steady wind whose job it is to make way for winter. The grass, just dried and bent like an old woman, accepts the cascade of yellow and orange thankfully, resting securely at last under a blanket of leaves. I wonder if the tree has trouble letting go, shedding*

her blessed decoration, releasing the little offspring she has nurtured for a season, becoming naked—exposed to the other trees. The wind must console her as it strips her down, howling. Resistance is futile. Time to let go. Stretch down into your roots and release your small, round dreams to the world. You must die to be reborn. Remember, the rhythm is found underground. "All that I can give you up here is chaosssssss," cries the wind's wailing voice as it wraps around her trunk, helping her to surrender her gifts to the grass.

—Ruby Gibson, original poem

The Way of Life

10

The Circle of Life

*When people run around and around in circles, we say they are crazy.
When planets do it, we say they are orbiting.
Clouds just keep circling the Earth around and around.
And around. There is not much else to do.*

—Author unknown

The circle has always been a symbol for change in our lives. Whether a wheel, the cycle of seasons or the roundness of the sun and moon as they choreograph our day, the shape of change is a circle. Somatic Archaeology draws on the revolutionary power of the circle to initiate a process that ends where it began and always repeats itself. Based on ancient models of problem solving, we can utilize the circle to alter our attitudes, shift our perspectives, and find peaceful resolution to the many problems that we face in our communities and our world. We can all find our place and speak our truth while remembering the mosaic of life.

The Sacred Medicine Wheel

The Medicine Wheel is an ancient symbol of life, movement, harmony, and evolution. It is considered a major symbol of peaceful interaction among all living beings on Earth, and its principles are primary in the oldest teachings of First Nations people.

The Medicine Wheel represents all aspects of life—human, animal, mineral, and plant—and is symbolic of Mother Earth, holding the container for every experience. The four cardinal directions of the wheel depict not only north, east, south, and west, but the seasons (winter, spring, summer, autumn), the elements (air, fire, water, earth), the four hills of life (elder, infant, youth, adult), and the four colors or races of man (white, yellow, red, and black).

Truth can be experienced when we are aligned with each direction, including the center of the wheel, allowing us to feel and understand many perspectives and aspects of life. The teachings found on the Medicine Wheel present a sensible and all-inclusive model for human behavior and interaction, and its wisdom offers a model for walking the Earth in a harmonious and good way. It has been used to view self, society, relationships, and the balance of nature. A Medicine Wheel can best be described as a teacher or a mirror in which everything about the human condition is reflected back.

Students of the Medicine Wheel, the sacred hoop of life, find that many life experiences will force or propel you to different positions on the wheel, or you can choose consciously to place yourself around the center in a deliberate action to instigate self-awareness and spiritual growth. It is only from all viewpoints that one can truly experience the fullness of life.

The cyclical dance of the wheel guides us to recognize that balancing the four aspects of self—mental, spiritual, emotional, and physical—creates a dynamic thrust for personal accountability and constitutional healing. With a holistic spin of the wheel, all energy encounters an alchemical exchange and equilibrium.

A Personal Medicine Wheel

Aligning our personal energy according to the following Medicine Wheel principles helps us achieve equilibrium. We will always come into balance with our individual Medicine Wheel by determining a course of action based on our spiritual principles. Because suffering, traumatic events, and violence incite fear and suppression, they freeze us into automatic reactions that inhibit our spiritual connection. When this happens, we learn to determine based on our emotional needs, physical cravings, or mental thoughts. Making life decisions from cravings or needs typically places us in jeopardy, and causes us to repeat historical patterns.

Choosing to make life decisions according to spiritual principles and guidance allows you to sit in relationship to your wheel in a balanced way, regulating all other directions. Your spiritual self is a natural determiner of energy, your mental self is a receiver of energy, your emotional self is a giver of energy, and your physical self is the holder of energy. When you apply these principles to self-expression, you establish harmonious action.

If you find yourself disconnected from spiritual knowledge or driven by nostalgic longings, the Medicine Wheel presents the perfect remedy. Movement is again the key; stagnancy locks us into one position on the wheel, but movement focuses our attention on progressive cures. As you read about the Wheel of Healing below, apply your personal experiences and inner motivations to designing a circular healing path for yourself. The medicine of the hoop of life is an offering from our ancestors for choreographing the elements that can restore your heart and life.

Please remember that there are ancestral guardians for each direction, keepers of wisdom and memory for the totality of existence. Honor the complexity of the wheel as well as its simplicity. The same is true within you. The guardians of your knowledge are your ancestors. At each turn, they are teachers you hear when you quiet yourself and search inside the center of your being for truth.

164   My Body, My Earth

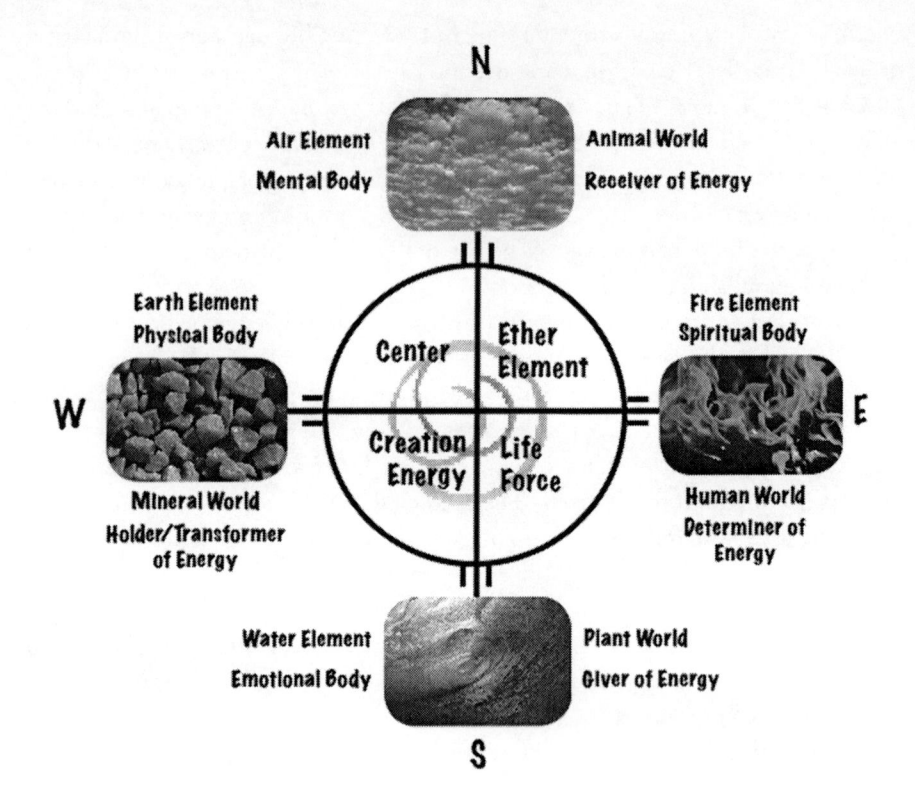

N

Air Element
Mental Body

Animal World
Receiver of Energy

Earth Element
Physical Body

Center | Ether Element

Creation Energy | Life Force

Fire Element
Spiritual Body

W

Mineral World
Holder/Transformer
of Energy

Human World
Determiner of Energy

E

Water Element
Emotional Body

Plant World
Giver of Energy

S

The Alchemy of Healing

Elements of Life	Human Parallel	Position on Wheel	World Parallel
Ether	Life Force	Center	Creator
Air	Mental	North	Animal World
Fire	Spiritual	East	Human World
Water	Emotional	South	Plant World
Earth	Physical	West	Mineral World

Note: The placement of these attributes on a medicine wheel may differ from tribe to tribe, based on cultural traditions and environmental differences.

This elemental model is based on shamanic principles, Earth-based wisdom, indigenous traditions, and polarity concepts. This design is helpful because it simplifies the healing process. It gives you a unique perspective into the macrocosm of life, relating the human experience to the whole of nature's symphony. When you step out of the human viewpoint and see things from other directions, you gain a perspective into healing that offers solutions to benefit every living plant, animal, mineral, and human on the Earth.

The Earth has four elements—air, fire, water, and earth—that coincide and work together. When they are balanced, there is harmony. You can see it when observing nature. A gentle breeze, a warm shining sun, flowing rivers, blooming flowers, falling leaves—in these things you witness harmony of the elements in the cycles of the Earth. The equivalent elements—spiritual, mental, emotional, and physical—are harmonious as well, when they move together with ease in alignment with your natural cycles.

> *What is the Earth's Kundalini? It probably would best be explained from a human perspective, because the Earth and the human body are almost identical energetically. Not only is the Earth's Kundalini energy very similar to a human being's, but also even such massive energy fields as the Mer-Ka-Ba field of the planet and the human Light Body are exactly the same except for*

proportional size. Every electromagnetic geometrical field within the Mer-Ka-Ba field of the Earth is exactly identical to every human being on Earth.

—Drunvalo Melchizedek, *Serpent of Light*

For somatic healing or transformation, it is important to begin by recognizing your body as the holder or container of your energy and memory. Therefore, adapt to the pace of your body by synchronizing with its natural rhythms. Your body does not move as quickly as your mind. Your body moves like the Earth. It enjoys permanence, structure, and predictability. It is an organic compilation of systems, all interdependent on each other, so your body must move slowly to ensure that digestion, absorption, and integration occur.

Your mind, on the other hand, is the most common element of connection in our fast paced world. It moves like air, thoughts floating and fleeting, coming and going quickly like the wind. In his book *Ageless Body, Timeless Mind*, Deepak Chopra states "The average mind thinks sixty thousand thoughts a day, 90 percent of those thoughts being the same thoughts as the day before. Our tormentor today is ourselves left over from yesterday."

That's a lot of thinking. Your mind is very busy figuring things out, analyzing your body and your life. The information you are looking for while excavating is much deeper than you can mentally evaluate. Of course, once you have retrieved somatic information, your mental body can come in quite handy to figure it all out.

Changing physical symptoms occurs in your body much like they do in the Earth. What is a natural mover of Earth? Water: the element of your emotions. Water can change Earth gradually, shifting Earth progressively over years by eating away at rocks, canyons, and beaches, slowly and continuously, taking the path of least resistance. Or water can change Earth quite dramatically through floods, tsunamis, and hurricanes. (Keep this in mind as you consider the importance of gentle emotional release.) Water moves Earth; therefore, emotion moves our physical forms. By thawing, expressing, and unleashing your emotions, you allow your tears (water) to flow, and then your body (Earth) can change. It is therefore essential when seeking body changes to address your emotions, for they are dependent upon each other.

When your emotion (water) is repressed, similar to a stagnant pool of water, it breeds bacteria and microorganisms and begins to sour. Because your body contains and holds water, often you will develop disease or illness in the areas where your emotions (water) are not moving. In all healthy environments, free-flowing water is crucial to overall health. If you feel that it is not safe to express your feelings, a pattern of holding back emotional expression could be the single most influential element in your lack of physical well-being. All the watery systems of your body—urine, blood, sweat, and lymph—are adversely affected by emotional repression, emotional avoidance, or emotional vacancy.

So what moves water? Any sailor will tell you that it is air; just watch the wind on the water. Air moves water; consequently, mind moves emotion. Encouraging positive thinking, releasing mental fears, eliminating obsessive thoughts, opening your mind to new ideas, and breathing deeply all encourage the movement of air. What does air also feed? Fire, of course. Moving your emotions (water) and tending to your spirit (fire) happen simultaneously as you change your thoughts and inhale full breaths of air. In order to shift our Earth (body), we must move our water (emotions), and in order to move our water, we must move our air (breath and mind). Can you begin to see the connections in this elemental theory and why balance is so important?

Too much withheld emotion (water) can also extinguish your spirit (fire). When you are emotionally overwhelmed, you have little energy for life or spiritual pursuits. Aerobic exercise, affirmations, chanting, and focused breathwork will feed your fire and can help to influence emotional imbalance. Learning, reading, philosophical discussions, and creative pursuits are akin to opening windows in your mind, allowing the wind to clear cobwebs and create movement for a healthy mental state.

Spiritual (fire) imbalances affect your body's heat systems—heart, temperature, digestion, and inflammatory conditions. You can keep your fire balanced with the demonstration of your willpower, the healthy expression of your anger, and by living in alignment with your spiritual values. When your anger is suppressed, it is akin to having a pressure cooker inside your gut. Explosive outbursts can come at inappropriate times as your fire seeks movement. You have probably heard the phrases *burning mad, hot under my collar, fuming with rage, incensed,* etc. These are reflective of a spirit (a fire) that needs to burn. *Burning* equates with change on some level. To help expedite the shifts you seek and to ease the heat in your body, use your breath (air) to expand into your fire while exhaling bright red energy with fire breaths.

There is a saying, "Never play with fire, because it can burn." This is true with healing as well; cautiously releasing a little at a time is better than burning down the house! Water can also freeze. So remember, many emotional patterns can thaw as your heat increases, and you will want to do it gradually. Releasing water with emotional cleansing will also create physical detoxification, so be sure to nourish yourself well during these times.

Another important aspect to this theory is that Earth holds water. Your body will swell and grow if you are holding back emotionally to contain the reservoirs of water. The easiest way to lose weight (Earth) is to move your emotions (water). On the contrary, if your body is too lean, it is representative of an overactive fire, which movement of water can quench as well.

When the elements of nature seek to rebalance, Mother Earth creates earthquakes, volcanic explosions, rainstorms, blizzards, fires, etc., to establish cycles and to cleanse her body. It is similar in your body. To find balance, your body creates colds, sneezes, coughing, tears, fevers, pimples, boils, headaches, etc. to cleanse and maintain cycles. Encouraging your physical and emotional detoxification, instead of suppressing these cleansing symptoms, is of great benefit to your entire system. When you suppress symptoms or do not cleanse regularly, you force your body to seek balance in stronger, more active ways, such as heart attacks, kidney stones, strokes, migraines, infections, asthma, etc., that are more dangerous to your health.

> *Those who've come before us tell us: By changing your body, you will be able to accommodate the changes of the Earth, because ultimately our bodies are made of the same stuff as the Earth. Whatever happens to the Earth, happens to our bodies. The magnetics that affect the elements of the Earth affect the elements of our bodies in the same way.*
>
> —Gregg Braden, as quoted in the movie, *2012 The Odyssey*

The fifth element, ether, is the life force that feeds and organizes all the other elements into a functional system. Ether has no boundaries or limits and, although indicative of all creation, ether is represented uniquely, symbolically, and mythologically in each person. Your distinctive design is influenced by ancestral memories that create a semblance of order and compliance. As you spiritually evolve, you alter your blueprint and invite change from a higher level, giving movement to creative and mystical patterns. This center of the wheel is where you reframe your karma and step into your destiny.

I invite you to draw some comparisons between the natural world and your somatic world. Look out the window. How the elements interact on the Earth is the same way they interact within your body. This is a generous clue to finding your elemental recipe for well-being.

Balancing the Four Worlds

The plant world, mineral world, animal world, and human world make up the hoop of life. They are four aspects of one creation, and are interdependent upon each other for survival. What happens to one world affects the other through their intrinsic design.

The Human World

Action: Determiner of energy
Counterpart: Spiritual attributes
Element: Fire
Direction: East
Systems: Digestion, neurological, inflammatory, heart, sexual/reproduction

The human world sits in the east of the wheel, the place of illumination and clarity. This is the direction of your spiritual self and correlates to the fire element. The human world is the determiner of energy, exhibiting great power and, therefore, the need for mindful action. In order to determine how to use energy, you must have a baseline of spiritual principles that take into consideration the good of all. It is an enormous responsibility.

Humans are the inventors, philosophers, pioneers, and dreamers of life, as well as the builders and destroyers. They are ingenious and deliberate, having been created in the unique position to formulate ideas and reason cognitively. Although they thrive on problem-solving, care must be taken to seek solutions that are not based on greed, superiority, or domination. Technological advances and complicated social and environmental concerns test the responsibility of being a determiner of energy. Creative and inspired conflict resolution removes the limitations of historical racism, bigotry, and hate-based interactions.

The four races of man exist in order to balance each other and measure compatibility. Social and cultural interaction fuels the fire of progress and competition, aiding in the evolution of our species. Arts, music, sports, literature, and fashion have become the backdrop for getting to know *you*. Learning happens initially through modeling and secondly through practicing what you have learned. Active demonstration of creativity is how maturity is achieved.

The east defines power and the transformation of energy. Religious models, healing techniques, altruism, and collaborative social ventures define the vast compassion at the heart of the human world. Love is that which transforms fear and suffering, the ultimate adventure of human dynamics. Engaging in sympathetic community service offers passages for reflection and personal mastery, and establishes gentle power—power that comes from awareness of the whole, and not from the need for control.

A power imbalance is a fire imbalance. Power differentials and control mechanisms in any scenario are a reflection of a disconnection from spiritual principles, where ego-based needs rule and untended anger flares. Anger is simply a fire that is seeking change and movement. Fire is balanced through the movement of air and the movement of water, and is honored as a force that warms the heart for companionship. Our passion and sexual desire urge us to connect, as the seed of creation ignites from the interplay of male and female, the flickering of shadow and light.

Humans sit in balance when they determine from spirit. Determinations made from emotional, physical, or mental aspects of self can lead to lusts, cravings, fear-based action, and repetitious cycles of behavior. Although spiritual principles and values may differ, there are sacred laws that supersede manmade laws. Spiritual devotion, contemplation, prayer, meditation, and ritual bring you into alignment with sacred law and common truths. You are invited to walk with consciousness. Every person has a valuable gift to contribute to the circle.

The Plant World

Action: Giver of energy
Counterpart: Emotional attributes
Element: Water
Direction: South
Systems: Elimination, sweat, circulatory, lymphatic, urinary, joints

In the south of the wheel sits the plant world. This is the place of innocence and trust. It has a direct correlation to your emotional body. In a balanced wheel your emotional body is the giver of energy. The same attribute applies to the plant world—it is a giver of energy to all worlds—as you can clearly observe from the above exchange. The plant world helps you to give away what no longer serves you. It is most closely associated with the water element, and can be soothing, nourishing, activating, and cleansing to your emotional body.

Herbs, tinctures, salves, teas, poultices, essential oils, flower essences, incense, and smudging are all healthy uses of the plant world to assist you in cleansing and releasing toxic emotional energy from your body. Drug, alcohol, food, and tobacco addictions are plants used in excess to numb your emotional body, or to give away surface emotions without reconciling them. This causes you to continue repeating unhealthy patterns of emotional avoidance, and hence entrenches suffering deeper in your body and psyche.

The waters are the bloodline of Mother Earth. Their flow represents the beating of her heart, as the tides rhythmically pulse the aliveness and motion of existence in response to the moon and stars. Water nourishes, lubricates, balances, and dances the other elements. Water is your tears, your blood, and the carrier of oxygen to your cells. It makes up 75 percent of your body weight, and 75 percent of the Earth as well. Water, both internal and external, is impacted by your thoughts. It can be frozen by your fear, evaporated by your anger, and harmonized by your prayers. We are all caretakers of the water element.

The plant world is your food, your clothing, your shelter, and your warmth. It gives to you every day and is a blessed companion on your life's journey. The plant world is a giver to the animal world, feeding, nourishing, and housing all species, which in turn fertilize and transport the plants. As an architect of the intricate cycles of our seasons, the plant world is the seed of subsistence. It complements and thrives on the mineral world and gives beauty through its flowers, trees, bushes, grasses, and astonishing landscapes. Respect the gifts of the plant world as it supports, enhances, and balances the sacred hoop of life. Use it wisely in your healing journey.

The Mineral World

Action: Holder/transformer of energy
Counterpart: Physical attributes
Element: Earth
Direction: West
Systems: Skeletal, muscular, tissue, weight distribution, body mass

The mineral world sits at the west of the Medicine Wheel. It correlates to the Earth element and the physical body. It is a natural holder and transformer of energy. This is reflected in how your physical body takes in food, holding and then transforming this nourishment to give you energy for the day. It is the place of introspection and strength.

The mineral world is the structure or bones of Mother Earth. It is the soil, sand, rocks, and molten lava. The crystals and gems are the brains of Mother Earth, and are the greatest transformers and magnifiers of energy. The mineral world is the mountains, valleys, riverbeds, deserts, jungles, and forests. It filters and holds water, gives a barrier to air, and gives ground for fire to transform. It is an absorbent, magnetic container. The mineral world feeds the plant world, houses the animal world, and offers permanency to the human world. It is the playground of all existence.

The Earth is similar to your physical body in many respects. The Earth stores information in layers much like your body does, recording history in its bones and cells, preserving past cultures. It responds to the moon, the sun, and the planets, and its cycles thrive on their revolutions and magnetism, much like your body does. It has a heartbeat, a rhythm, and many colors, voices, faces, and personalities. The Earth can take many forms—bumpy, smooth, hard, soft, or full of curves. The Earth is enduring and without prejudice or bias.

The mineral world is a great ally in the healing of suffering. It can teach you to be enduring and resilient. It offers predictability in a world that is full of change and chaos. Stones and rocks are used to create boundaries, walls, homes, and structures. Crystals can be used in the healing process to amplify a clearing, to protect during vulnerability, and to establish a spiritual connection.

Group or tribal Medicine Wheels are built of stones and are used to track time, design ceremonies, ground energy, honor ancestors, fulfill visions, and teach community balance. The mineral world is the gathering place of both the seen and the unseen, and holds the treasures of the ancients. Full of wisdom, love and patience, our body, our Earth, is an amazing tribute to where we have been and where we are going. Walk softly, with gratitude and with reverence.

The Animal World

Action: Receiver of energy
Counterpart: Mental attributes
Element: Air
Direction: North
Systems: Psychic, respiratory, absorption, thoughts/beliefs

In the north of the wheel sits the animal world. The animal world is the receiver of energy and correlates to the air element and to the mental body. The north is the place of wisdom, of cleansing, and of purity. Animals represent the symbols and abstract thoughts that speak to your higher minds. In your dreams, animals communicate archaic knowledge and transform you in your fantasies.

Animals are your traveling companions on this Earth walk. They offer unconditional love and hope, evoke strength, give you vision, and demonstrate collective purpose. You readily receive their gifts and become their caretakers. Innocent and generous in nature, animals encourage you toward selfless action. They accept you totally, no matter how you look, walk, or talk.

The stress of your mental body can be alleviated when you align yourself with animal medicine. This world teaches you to receive knowledge, instead of having to "know it all." Animals instruct you how to respond appropriately to the elements around you, and to indulge in group thought without ego or self-consciousness. Dolphins and whales are the humble record-keepers for the planet, and we come to them for help in solving our greatest problems. They hold the models for respectful, cooperative interactions.

Animals represent the warriors of the Earth and teach you when to fight is the right thing, epitomizing traits of fierceness, pride, courage, determination, and ingenuity. We use their names and images for clans, sports teams, clubs, schools, clothing, and even for cars, to instill fear and admiration. Animal symbols characterize our most powerful principles and define government and cultural differences. They teach you how and when to roar, purr, howl, bark, cluck, squeak, and moan.

Come to the north of the wheel for healing when you need to receive inspiration and clarity. The air element is infused and balanced through deep, conscious breathing and meditation. Deeply mythological and prophetic, animals are the messengers of the spirit world. They instruct you about the passages and phases of life, linking you to past cultures and giving you vision for the future. Their survival instincts are renowned, and you would do well to observe and interact with them honorably, with deep appreciation and continued wonder.

The Center

Action: Life Force
Counterpart: Creator
Element: Ether
Direction: Center
Systems: Creative, love, joy, unification

The essence of the Creator creator symbolizes the center of the wheel, manifesting love and truth. Your etheric life force erupts from the center, as well as your procreative and creative energies. When you arrive at the center of the wheel you are able to see and experience all four directions at once, not as separate functions, but as one moving whole. Many traditions refer to those who have achieved enlightenment or transcended the need for personal gain as the zero chief—the one who sits at the center of the wheel—for they know themselves in all ways and instinctively surrender to the force generated for the good of the whole.

In the center, there is no separateness. It represents all phases and dimensions of life blended into one movement. Unification can be represented as an individual process of recognizing wholeness within through alignment of the chakra system, of a collaborative venture as an alliance works together for one goal, or as a joining of all energies with universal significance.

The center of the wheel is the Great Mystery. The sweetness and the magic of creation cannot be solved or understood. We are absorbed into it as we unite our power with love for the heart of the world. In the center there is humility, integrity, grace, and total acceptance of the rhythms of life. It is the symbol of the yin/yang or balanced path of the feminine and masculine aspects of self, represented by the light and shadow of spirit.

> *We've learned from Mayan timekeepers that around the Winter Solstice 2012, the Earth lines up in a certain angle to the Pleiades constellation, creating a snakelike universal birth canal through the Milky Way all the way to planet Earth. This canal allows us to change the vibration in which our Earth exists, birthing a new experience on this planet. The end-of-the-world concept is simply a moment in time when we come full circle—when we can dissociate from our earthly identity and remember who we are as larger beings. In order to participate in this shift, we must be willing to remember, to advance, to progress, and, essentially, to heal our historical wounds.*
>
> —Ruby Gibson

11

Mend the Circle

Everything the Power of the World does is done in a circle.
The sky is round and I have heard that
The Earth is round like a ball and so are all the stars.
The wind, in its greatest power, whirls.
Birds make their nests in circles,
For theirs is the same religion as ours.
The sun comes forth and goes down again in a circle.
The moon does the same and both are round.
Even the seasons form a great circle in their changing
And always come back again to where they were.
The life of man is a circle from childhood to childhood.
And so it is in everything where power moves.

—Black Elk

As you excavate your body in a circular fashion, you will adjust and respond to the information revealed. Your stories will weave together into all aspects of your self, and, as well, they will bridge you to the greater circle of life and community.

Witness the changes and allow the movement to infiltrate into a beautiful mending of self on all levels. Feel the synchronicity of living on the wheel of creation.

Jim's Story

"When I first began Somatic Archaeology sessions, amazing things happened. Once, as I began to clear a memory, a thunderhead formed over the building we were in; it built as I released and then slowly moved east after I completed my session. It was the 'life of its own' thing I experienced for the first time. I realized then that I was a part of something bigger than just myself. I am part of a circle—a circle that allows me to give as I receive, and vice versa.

"During that session, I was able to explore feelings and memories that were stored in my soma and then release them. The release freed me from the burden of not knowing why I was feeling the way I did. After running the cycle of emotions, my anxiety dissipated. I converted the pain of 'holding on' into the freedom of 'letting go'. The tightness, cramping, and discomfort in my body gave way to the looseness of deep relaxation as my muscles were given permission and a sense of safety to release on their own accord, in their own timeframe.

"I have revisited my somatic excavation sites many times over, but each time I go back, I pass through another layer I never knew was there. Sometimes it is just a fleeting vision and then a deep understanding of something that my mind never fully grasped. My heart awakens and gives life to me once again—another healing, another change in perspective, another reason to live.

"My life is often filled with times that keep me distant from myself and the true reality that I am a part of. It is nice to know that I can always get myself back again whenever I see the need. I have learned that I will never be healed once and for all; it is the continual healing journey that allows my soul to grow and evolve. For that, I give thanks. I also give thanks for Somatic Archaeology. It has given me the tools to live my life one healing at a time; each session gives a fresh perspective and a new chance at that which is life."

Somatic Archaeology Wheel of Suffering

The following diagram displays how the Wheel of Suffering becomes somatically fixated. It helps to keep this visual in mind, because it offers methodology and objectivity in a world where chaos reigns. Examining the holographic view allows you to emotionally remove yourself for a moment from the drama of the trauma, so that you can look down on yourself, so to speak, and recognize that this vantage point is not only important while discovering how suffering has become imbedded, but also in recognizing how the Wheel of Suffering unwinds.

This Medicine Wheel is designed to portray the continuum of the human experience of suffering. It helps to recognize the patterns that somatically entrench suffering and reinforce dysfunctional patterns. It is also a wheel of learning. Each direction and element is choreographed to bring awareness of fear based patterns and limitations.

The Wheel of Suffering begins with a primary origin, which is defined as a loss of self-love and a separation from spirit. This fragmentation is the result of any series of traumatic events, generational, historical or current, where one finds his or herself in danger, or in a potentially threatening situation where there is a power imbalance. The origin of the Wheel of Suffering is epitomized by the loss of ability to choose, to have a voice, or to respond in a favorable, self-protective manner.

The severity or mildness of any traumatic experience is not reflected in this diagram. A baseline of suffering is used as a model to explain how traumatic experiences impact one's life and legacy. Therefore, these are generalizations. Please make accommodations for your individual experiences and backgrounds. As a rule, a history of severe trauma would require repeated rounds of unwinding to heal all aspects of the self, while a history of mild trauma would require fewer revolutions around the wheel.

My Body, My Earth

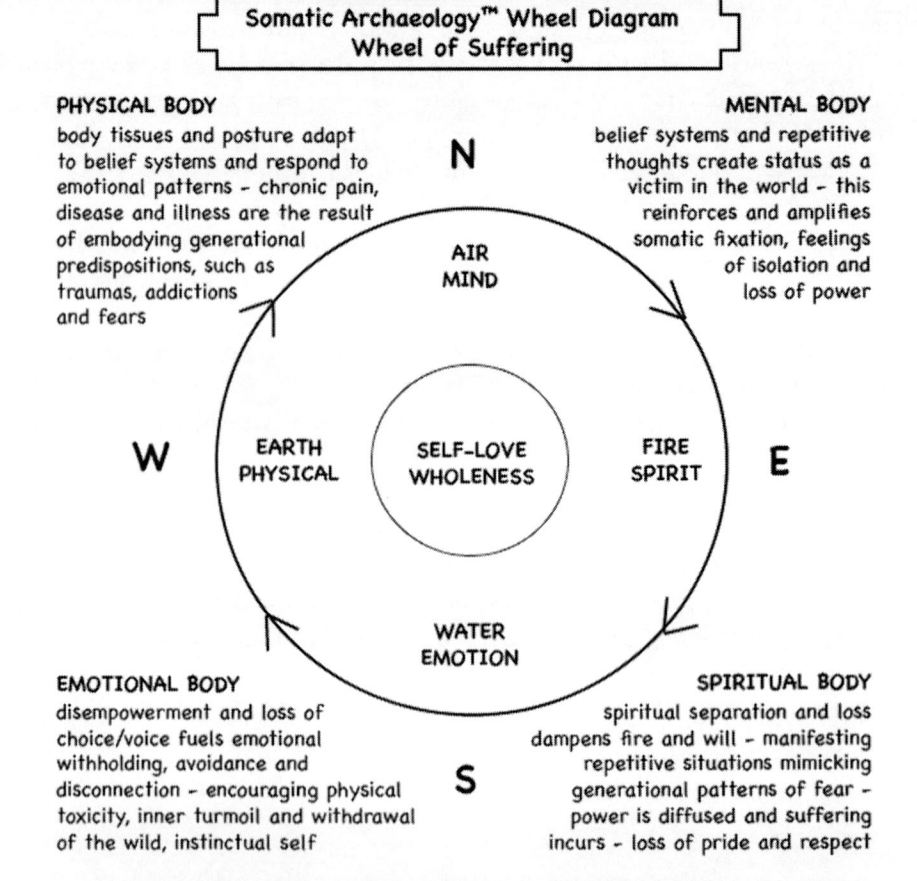

Somatic Archaeology™ Wheel Diagram
Wheel of Suffering

N — AIR / MIND

W — EARTH / PHYSICAL

E — FIRE / SPIRIT

S — WATER / EMOTION

Center: **SELF-LOVE / WHOLENESS**

PHYSICAL BODY
body tissues and posture adapt to belief systems and respond to emotional patterns - chronic pain, disease and illness are the result of embodying generational predispositions, such as traumas, addictions and fears

MENTAL BODY
belief systems and repetitive thoughts create status as a victim in the world - this reinforces and amplifies somatic fixation, feelings of isolation and loss of power

EMOTIONAL BODY
disempowerment and loss of choice/voice fuels emotional withholding, avoidance and disconnection - encouraging physical toxicity, inner turmoil and withdrawal of the wild, instinctual self

SPIRITUAL BODY
spiritual separation and loss dampens fire and will - manifesting repetitive situations mimicking generational patterns of fear - power is diffused and suffering incurs - loss of pride and respect

The origin of the Wheel of Suffering generally begins at the center with a loss of self-love, detachment from wholeness and the onset of fear due to a feeling of separation. Trauma to any of the four aspects of self can induce a felt sense of suffering and establish patterns of somatic holding. A loss of accountablity for ones actions, as well as historical amnesia, keep this wheel spiraling inward. This is displayed in a clockwise motion reflecting a pervasive and repetitive cycle of entrapment and a loss of joy in all the aspects of self.

Overview of the Wheel of Suffering

Our innate reaction to traumatic events is to attempt to fight, flee, faint, freeze, or talk our way out of it. When we are incapable of successfully doing something that removes us from danger or loss, a state of helplessness results. It is within this state when you lack power or resources that suffering sets in and fear incubates.

Post-traumatic stress (PTSD) is the subsequent aftereffect that many people have in response to a traumatic event. Symptoms can be long-term or short-term. They can include nightmares, night sweats, hyper-vigilance, anxiety, phobias, loss of boundaries, hallucinations, aggressive behavior, addictions, confusion, disorientation, profound emotional outbursts, dissociation, numbness, loss of identity, chronic pain patterns, suicidal tendencies, and more.

The origin or starting point on the Wheel of Suffering may be known or unknown. It is not necessarily important, in a therapeutic context, to recognize what a primary scenario consisted of. You may feel as if you have no clear memory of original event(s), or you may clearly remember what happened, but bury the emotions that accompanied the experience.

What is important is the recognition of the symptoms of suffering. When caught in the cycle of suffering, you may notice sensations such as being caught in a spiral, or that life is spinning out of control. You may feel heaviness, emotional or physical pain, or a burden in your body. If you have been witness to a traumatic encounter and felt helpless to react, or if you minimized your experience because it was commonplace or accepted in your environment, the memory of fear can be stored in your body.

In Somatic Archaeology, it is irrelevant whether an experience is real, imagined, or historically imprinted. The important thing is that your body knows that it has been adversely affected by an experience. Due to factors such as your age, levels of dissociation, generational influences, or drug/anesthesia use, your mind may not always remember certain events, especially in a sequential or logical manner. Your body memory, on the other hand, is indisputable. Your body remembers everything. Memories are based on feelings that speak the truth, and each of us *knows* when we have reached a truth. It resonates through every cell in our body. You do not have to get caught up in determining if something really happened or not. Simply focus on your body and follow its lead. Examine how it is affecting your body *now* to bring you into the present.

Emotional Body Suffering

The Wheel of Suffering progresses in a clockwise direction, downward and inward. Many traumatic events originate in the south of the wheel as a result of emotional suffering, but you can enter the wheel from any direction. For the purpose of this diagram and description, we will begin in the south.

The first response to a traumatic event is disempowerment. Your wild, instinctual self feels trapped, and fear escalates. You lose your ability to choose for yourself, your voice, and your will to fight. You succumb to the external threat. Your ability to speak, to respond, or to react appropriately fades. Autonomy is shattered. It is at this point that a flawed context for living is created. Low self-esteem, general irritability, random bursts of anger, and emotional complacency can result.

An emotional imbalance is represented in your body in many ways. Anything that has to do with fluids (water) is primarily emotionally based. Urinary tract infections, kidney infections, water retention, dryness of the skin, weeping wounds, excessive sweating, weight problems, joint restriction, constipation, night sweats, inflammation, and other fluid disturbances represent an emotional imbalance and usually have their origin in emotional withholding, emotional toxicity, emotional avoidance, or emotional deprivation. Certainly other aspects are involved in the creation of a physical symptom, yet it simplifies matters to approach your body from an elemental point of view for the purpose of emotional release.

Somatic or Physical Body Suffering

Traveling around the wheel, and following the emotional withholding, comes the somatic embodiment of trauma. Your body tissues and posture actually begin to adapt to a traumatized belief system. Your body reflects outwardly that which is believed inwardly. This physical adaptation can take on various forms. The most common acute responses are shallow, fast-paced, or non-existent breath patterns; rigidity of tissues; spinal misalignments; significant alteration in movement patterns (e.g., constantly busy versus lethargic); muscle twitching; nervous habits such as grinding of teeth, pulling out hair, biting nails, cutting, etc; nausea; digestive difficulties; headaches; tight jaw; racing heart or blood pressure problems; and addictive tendencies.

The chronic symptoms of somatic embodiment are widespread. They may include arthritis, chronic fatigue syndrome, fibromyalgia, eczema, etc. Your sympathetic nervous system releases adrenalin to employ the fight-or-flight response as a natural reaction to trauma. When trauma occurs repeatedly over long periods of time, your nervous system never has an opportunity to normalize. It remains activated, releasing adrenalin frequently, which can cause depressed immune function, diminished intestinal function, constricted skeletal muscles, decreased liver function, and constriction of the renal artery which leads the kidneys to retain less water, causing frequent urination.

Your musculature may adapt to the emotional stress by restricting movement, causing physical discomfort, lack of coordination, inability to sleep, decreased blood flow, armoring in certain areas, weight gain, joint restriction, poor posture, and body splits (left/right or above/below). All these can eventually evolve into chronic pain, illness, disease, and repetitive injuries.

A primary form of physical adaptation is the numbing of sensation. You may separate yourself so completely from the traumatic memory in your body that you dull all sensation from the neck down. Or, you may have numbed specific areas related to an abuse. It may be difficult to get your picture taken, to look in a mirror, to undress in front of anyone, or to take a bath. Shame, guilt, and embarrassment can be present with images of your body. This may be extremely apparent or may be very subtle.

Mental Body Suffering

As the Wheel of Suffering spins clockwise, your mind takes on the belief that it is a victim. This self-identification limits movement, creates anxiety, obsessive thinking, and fosters hyper-vigilance. You may have nightmares, disorientation, and spaciness. Suffering shifts your perception of yourself in relation to the external world. Your sense of community can deteriorate; you may lose faith in human nature and in your ability to be a good caretaker for yourself or others, becoming isolated and critical. This shatters your sense of worth and self-respect. The foundation for your security becomes obsolete, and consequently you begin to live in a world where there is no safety and few people to trust.

This is especially true for children who are raised in abusive and manipulative environments. It is difficult for someone who believes he or she is a victim to come into relationship with another person with a substantial level of intimacy and vulnerability. The fear of being hurt again becomes stronger than the need for companionship or healing.

Many psychological diagnoses have their roots in long-term mental suffering and are the result of fragmentation from traumatic events. ADHD, dissociative disorders, the inability to concentrate or to stay present, hyperactivity, intrusive thoughts, manic patterns, phobias, circular thinking, depression, and anxiety are all mental body imbalances.

Spiritual Body Suffering

Following the mental embodiment comes the creation of spiritual patterns or repetitive circumstances. This is apparent when you find yourself in life situations that are similar to an original traumatic scenario or when a situation reflects ancestral or familial dynamics. This might mean that a victim of childhood abuse finds himself in an abusive marriage; a victim of rape may find herself interested in pornography; a war veteran may find that the battlefield is in his own backyard; a survivor of hate crimes may find that she becomes abusive through self-mutilation; or the descendant of a holocaust survivor may recreate treacherous living conditions. In each situation, the sufferer is mimicking some aspect of a traumatic event.

Anger and fire are prevalent in this position on the wheel, and therefore creative pursuits may be heightened or dulled. Many brilliant artists have created beautiful and evocative works of art in an effort to communicate the despair of their souls or the anguish of the human condition, only to drown their worries later in a bottle of wine. Inconsistencies reign as we battle light and shadow, seeking to avoid the reestablishment of fear-based familial dynamics.

This pattern of spiritual contradiction is strongly evident in our religious societies as we witness the sexual abuse of young children perpetrated by priests who are thought to be the devoted messengers of God. Prompted by a withholding of power or anger, many attempt to negotiate their losses through addictions, perversions, and politics. Spiritual impotence is translated into heated debates, civil or global wars, religious tyranny, racial intolerance, and blatant lying.

Individually, internalized anger and the loss of power leads to heart attacks and heart disease, strokes, inflammatory conditions, back pain, addictions, or any symptom where heat, redness, irritability, or swelling is present. Violence, manipulation, hatred, verbal abuse, self-importance, humiliation, and cruelty are all manifestations of someone locked into the east on the Wheel of Suffering where they are unable to negotiate effectively with their power. They have lost contact with their true spiritual selves and are determining the use of their energy in an oppressive manner.

Wheel of Suffering Conclusion

Your willingness to remain in dysfunctional or abusive relationships and environments informs you that you are still hypnotized by the Wheel of Suffering. The cyclical pull draws you deeply into the vortex and narrows your perspective. Choices seem minimal, hopelessness is evident, and you experience an emotional payoff with your self-defined reality. Your beliefs are confirmed by your relationships, your environment, and your physical pain, so you continue to attract people and circumstances into your life to confirm your deepest fear that, yes, your perspective is accurate and you are not worthy, and will always remain a victim of circumstance.

This is not typically a conscious belief. It is an underlying embodied belief that you deserve the pain. It becomes an accepted part of life. You become fixated with the belief that you are a victim, and so you create circumstances in your life to give validity to this belief. This may be difficult to fathom. It goes against our nature as a society to accept responsibility for our victimization, but until you acknowledge your responsibility for the pattern, you remain a victim. It is only upon owning your life circumstances that change is possible. When you accept responsibility, you accept the power to change. You can't have power and be a victim as the same time.

Suffering always seeks resolution. This means you also bring into your life your own healing. This is apparent when you have the objectivity and the skills to recognize it. You repeat dysfunctional dynamics in an effort to bring your fear to the surface. Your energy system is constantly looking to achieve balance. Like a splinter that has festered deep under the skin, an emotional or dysfunctional pattern wants to be purged and brought to the surface. Your body's wisdom looks for expression of the withheld emotion by replaying your stuck patterns over and over again, actualizing and exposing your deepest fears.

The principal outcome of repetitive patterns is suffering—a profound loss of love and a disconnection with spiritual reality. Frequently engaging with disempowering situations reinforces your belief system and amplifies emotional toxicity, somatic fixation, and mental isolation. This brings you full circle to the origin, and you feel trapped. You cycle round and round the Wheel of Suffering, strengthening your dysfunctional beliefs, somatically and mentally embodying your fears more and more deeply, suffering without hope of escape. The vortex narrows and survivors become entrenched in the Wheel of Suffering. Life choices become less evident and very limited.

Some of us may live this way for years, others for a short time. The patterns may be overt and obvious or muted and subtle. Your ability to move out of this cyclic whirlpool is dependent upon your ability to accept support, to resource yourself, to end addictive behaviors, to become fed up with your minimal existence, and to seek your spiritual source. Somatic Archaeology takes you to the core of the wheel, for that is where the exit is—in the eye of the storm.

Somatic Archaeology's Wheel of Healing

The following diagram displays step by step how the Wheel of Healing unwinds suffering. Again, it helps to keep this visual in mind because the process can be delicate and you will need perspective. You may move in and out of the Wheels of Healing and Suffering, shuffling from hope to confusion as you progressively recognize deeper patterns that are entrenched in your body. This wobbling feeling is how each person learns to manage his or her energy, and how to accept a leadership role in his or her life and family.

Cyclical or annual patterns such as deaths, births, anniversaries, historical events, religious holidays, seasonal changes, and planetary celebrations can have a great influence on memory. They can trigger feelings such as grief, longing, depression, appreciation or joy; they can bring dreams that awaken our spirits; and they can facilitate movement in our psyche that heightens awareness of buried traumas or illuminates current circumstances. Historical events that occurred on a daily basis can also continue to affect our current patterns of sleep, diet, behavior, memory, and learning. Pay attention to all these patterns, for they can give texture and meaning to the unwinding process.

Somatic Archaeology™ Wheel Diagram
Wheel of Healing

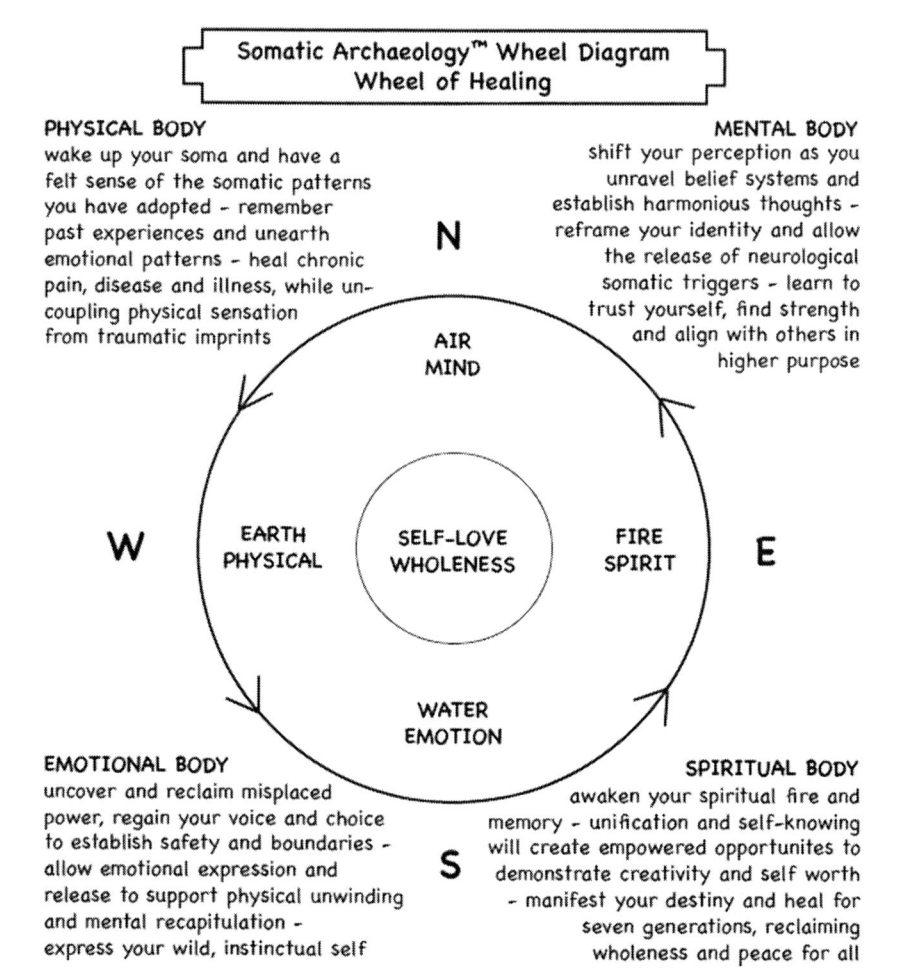

PHYSICAL BODY
wake up your soma and have a felt sense of the somatic patterns you have adopted - remember past experiences and unearth emotional patterns - heal chronic pain, disease and illness, while uncoupling physical sensation from traumatic imprints

MENTAL BODY
shift your perception as you unravel belief systems and establish harmonious thoughts - reframe your identity and allow the release of neurological somatic triggers - learn to trust yourself, find strength and align with others in higher purpose

N — AIR MIND
W — EARTH PHYSICAL
E — FIRE SPIRIT
S — WATER EMOTION

Center: SELF-LOVE WHOLENESS

EMOTIONAL BODY
uncover and reclaim misplaced power, regain your voice and choice to establish safety and boundaries - allow emotional expression and release to support physical unwinding and mental recapitulation - express your wild, instinctual self

SPIRITUAL BODY
awaken your spiritual fire and memory - unification and self-knowing will create empowered opportunites to demonstrate creativity and self worth - manifest your destiny and heal for seven generations, reclaiming wholeness and peace for all

You can enter the Wheel of Healing from any of the four directions. Healing suffering also begins in the center of the wheel through compassion and the rekindling of self-love - becoming aware of your wholeness. The release of somatically fixated fear creates a feeling of safety and unification. Somatic unwinding occurs in a counter-clockwise motion reflecting a gradual and progressive healing cycle. Access to your inherent wisdom and truth is found in all aspects of self with accountability of action, and recognition of cause/effect.

The Wheel of Healing creates gradual consciousness as it unwinds. Take your time as you travel around the wheel, and get to know yourself on all levels. It is a journey of discovery, not a specific destination. You may have identifiable goals that are realized as you heal, but you will find that the deeper you go, the more you will uncover—sometimes unexpectedly. When you have reconciled your personal experiences, your body will create the room to bring forward the patterns you have adopted from your parents. That will lead to more room for healing your grandparents' and great-grandparents' memories, and so on, until eventually you will find yourself as a doorway for the healing of Mother Earth and your tribe or community. Of course you do not need to take healing to this expansive degree; you can excavate and unearth as much history as you are comfortable with. You have your own capacity for healing. Honor it.

Upon emerging from the Wheel of Suffering, you can find that your courage and power are tied up in your fear and helplessness. Because of this duality, it may be important to have a guide to offer objectivity. Since you may have to find resolution with many traumatic events, the healing journey could be long or seem never-ending. A somatic therapist or qualified health care professional that you trust can offer feedback on your progress and become a cheerleader for your healing movement. This will be beneficial to give you a clearer perspective. I recommend that you get support where and when you need it.

Overview of the Wheel of Healing

Begin in the center of the Wheel of Healing with a blossoming awareness of your intrinsic wholeness. Fear begins to release as you remember what it feels like to be unified. The Wheel of Healing spins counterclockwise, pulling energy up and out of the cycle. Whatever has been forced inward with the repetition of suffering now expands outward with love, awareness, and expression. A gradual unwinding occurs, allowing you access to your inherent wisdom and truth. You may have to spiral around the wheel many times in order to break patterns that have been instilled. Each counterclockwise revolution encourages more empowerment and sustained safety, and thus more unwinding and awakening. The Wheel of Healing is steady, measured by your dedication to the process. The speed of healing is dependent upon the severity of your suffering, the accumulation of toxic patterns, and the resources available to you. Mead's story, below, offers a very palpable experience of coming to the center of the wheel.

Mead's Story

"I felt pain in my lower back which, when somatically investigated and breathed into, partially resolved. What was left went to the spleen. I found that my spleen was dreaming. In the dream, I could see a child, seated in the right side of my body, looking through a pane of glass into the left side of my body. The left side was dark and a round face swam up to the window. It was not a human face; it was more like a cross between the full moon and the bole of an ancient tree. It was very loving and the child was drawn to it. With facilitation, she was able to go through the glass. In the other side was all the mystery of the night itself, and I felt roots of light shoot down, down many fathoms and then upward to the sky. Still my spleen was dreaming; it was the window to the right side, dark roots shot up and down through the light, and my heart was washed with joy, like a great wave of song. My elbows and knees began to move, hands, and feet trailing behind in homolateral movements. I was crying. The long exile into fragmentary existence was healed and I was one. In the end, what I experienced was the fragmentary melding into a whole, and life coursing through me. I felt the dismembered parts of myself rise and flow together in my body as a sensation, like a song, the universe itself singing, singing."

Spiritual Body Healing

The first step in healing suffering generally comes in the gift of a spiritual awakening or shift. You may find yourself in circumstances that enliven you—a creative pursuit, an exercise class, a passionate relationship, a church experience, a ceremony, an AA group or recovery community, or possibly a spiritual retreat. It feels like waking up from a trance. This shift can arrive unexpectedly, or can be the outcome of your deliberate efforts or family intervention. Many times an awakening comes as a result of another parallel event, such as the loss of a loved one, giving birth, getting married or divorced, etc.

Shifts in perception establish an awakening of your authentic self. You begin to feel your fire (spirit) and want to fight back. You rebel, so to speak—rethinking the imposed limitations that have come to define you. You become dissatisfied with your existence and begin to imagine your potential. You reconnect with your deepest dreams. You refuse to accept any further abuse or disrespect, and you find your voice. You may realize that it is necessary to change jobs, reconsider friendships, improve your diet, become more creative, and give yourself permission to experience pleasure. Your self-care grows enriched and regular.

You may become aware of generational patterns and threads of influence that are woven into the fabric of your life. Empowerment is a result of this recognition. Change requires you to speak up for yourself, to establish safety, and to define your space. You crave to remember who you are underneath your burdens.

As we previously discussed, this urge is strong in our generation. There is a collective compulsion to find our real power and our truth, yet this shared desire can be experienced as a very personal movement as we address our "stuff." Charitable pursuits become of interest as you hope to recycle your losses to benefit someone else. Prayer becomes important as you learn to trust your relationship to the divine wisdom of a higher source.

Mental Body Healing

Once you have begun the process of waking up, your mental body naturally restructures and adjusts itself, and you begin to challenge your belief systems. Certain ways of thinking lodged in archaic traditions may become revitalized as you translate them into your modern lifestyle, or they may become obsolete as you progress to a more expanded view of yourself.

You may seek out psychotherapy, self-help workshops, meditation classes, or dream circles in order to establish harmonious thoughts and purge yourself of self-loathing. Your desire to align with others in a higher purpose releases feelings of rejection. Affirmations are used to reframe your identity, incorporating themes of abundance, prosperity, self-acceptance, and gratitude.

The symbolic systems of the animal world now give meaning to your life. You notice what animals cross your path and what birds call out to you. Even the smallest interaction has significance. You find the value of your role in the natural world and, therefore, you learn to interact respectfully and thoughtfully. You begin to listen with your other ears and see with your other eyes as you refine how you receive information. Your intuition strengthens, your curiosity grows, and your instinctive self bursts forth.

You find empowerment in being able to control your thoughts. It is easier to stay present with yourself. Your breath deepens and fear no longer keeps you in the stronghold of suffering. You venture out, try new things, open your mind, make healthier decisions, and gravitate toward loving relationships. You are able to have the objectivity to witness your propensity for repetitive patterns before it is too late. You adopt the vision of the hawk or eagle to see the bigger picture.

The future no longer seems dreary, and you fantasize about what it would feel like to make your dreams come true. You articulate these dreams to those you trust, and you are willing to receive feedback. Each rotation around the Wheel of

Healing loosens imbedded thought patterns and beliefs that locked you into psychosomatic symptoms and kept you from your highest potential and divine well being.

Physical Body Healing

As your mind opens and soars, your physical body gains the opportunity to respond to the shifts. Initially there is a felt sense that is uncomfortable. Many describe it like they have outgrown their containers, much like a plant in a pot which has grown too small for its roots. This cramped discomfort urges you to seek change. You stretch and bend in new ways, unraveling your aliveness from the weave of the past. Yoga, aerobics, dance, swimming, or other physical activities call to you. You may get a massage, acupuncture, or chiropractic treatment to release physical pain and to unwind your tissues.

You begin to pay attention to your body and eliminate drugs or activities that numb your awareness or mask your symptoms. Learning to have compassion for yourself and what you have been through, you give your body thanks for all that it has endured. You honor the wonder of your heartbeat, the incredibleness of your digestion, the complexity of your neurology, and the grace of your musculature. You choose to fast or detoxify, cleansing your liver and rejuvenating your blood. You find that you crave fresh foods and eliminate processed foods in order to feel lightness in your body. Cravings diminish and chronic pain subsides.

You may feel drawn to the mineral world, collecting rocks and stones that offer grounding and meaning. Crystals are worn to amplify your intent, protect your heart, and nourish your spirit. You find you have more compassion for the Earth and the waters, and become a steward for the environment and a protector of the mountains, deserts, and canyons. You walk softly on the Earth, respecting the ancestors of the land and the wisdom of indigenous lifestyles.

Breathing into a new way of occupying your body, you begin to uncouple your internal sensations from historical events. This liberates you to realize you are not what has happened to you. You are not your diagnosis or your disease or your dilemma. You are much more. Your body remembers what it feels like to be free, and it spontaneously erupts in joy. It becomes easier to look in the mirror, to accept another's touch, or to be intimate. Reclaiming your body and your power happens as you establish safety and redefine boundaries.

Emotional Body Healing

It is important to give your body a voice. This voice most often takes on an emotional expression. Physical detoxification parallels emotional release when you allow yourself to cry, grieve, laugh, love, holler, and scream. You learn to move your water with gratitude, celebrating your aliveness and passion. Emotional expression is your birthright. It provides you with the courage to honor your instincts and enthusiasm. You cry for your family, for your ancestors, and for your children, becoming a matrix for seven-generational healing.

The tears wash away the darkness from your heart and purge the toxins from your body. Let your tears flow freely down your cheeks, as they have a homeopathic effect. Remember, you cry because you choose to heal, not because you are suffering. You bring it up to let it go! Keep the energy moving through you, recognizing that you are safe now, and can soften. Your motto with emotions: better out than in.

The plant world becomes your ally in the form of essential oils, herbs, tinctures, and flower essences. They are able to clear traumatic memories from your brain, to calm your worry, and to bring you sweetness. You remember that you are good, that you are a miracle, and that you deserve the best that life has to offer. Your beauty erupts and you witness yourself as a treasure.

The emotional burdens of your past lessen, and you are able to laugh at things that once brought dread, to smile at your fortune, and to make sense of what happened to you. Clarity replaces confusion. Each day as you thaw, your emotions move fluidly and you release resistance to being vulnerable. You are able to be seen, and to see others with compassion.

You know that you cannot erase what has happened to you, but your memories no longer carry the charge they once did. Love fills the darkness with light, and forgiveness comes as you acknowledge the accumulated suffering that has caused others to be careless with your heart. With each counterclockwise spin around the Wheel of Healing, you reclaim the wildness of your spirit. You now have permission to stomp your feet, leave tracks, howl at the moon, live for your dreams, and design your future. You are alive and your life has purpose!

Wheel of Healing Conclusion

You exit the Wheel of Healing as you experience a symbolic death and rebirth of your authentic self. The cycle closes with true understanding and a sense of soul infusion, embodying your spirit's legacy and creative potential. Freedom is the outcome, joy the reward.

Circular activities and thinking provide the blueprint for harmonious interaction. When you utilize the wisdom and traditions of your ancestors, along with the elemental balance reflected in nature, then preparing for future Earth changes and paving a way for your personal evolution makes sense. The circle of life is the circle of healing. Allow your newly found wholeness to bless the Earth and all who inhabit her. Own your power by designing passages that draw you into conscious connection with all of creation.

Somatic Archaeology Wheel of Transformation

The Wheel of Transformation bridges the Medicine Wheel and the Five Steps of Somatic Archaeology into a revolutionary ribbon or pathway for conversion on all levels and in all worlds. It forms a horizontal figure eight, the infinity symbol that stands for the unification of masculine and feminine and the life flow that is crucial for harmony in nature. This wheel heals the myth of duality and allows for body evolution—a natural and gradual progression of recreating ourselves while in this physical form. Across cultures and religions, the number eight and its continuous infinite flow is honored as a healing symbol for not only self, but for community, gender, and race.

The infinity symbol has been used by many traditions for spiritual reasons. The Métis flag bears the infinity symbol, representing the coming together of two distinct and vibrant cultures, those of Europe and indigenous North America, to produce a distinctly new culture, the Métis. The Métis Nation is one of the groups of French-speaking peoples in western Canada who are descendants of French explorers, fur-traders, settlers, and native North American peoples in the northwest. Their flag symbolizes the creation, or weaving, of a new society with roots in both aboriginal and European cultures and traditions.

In Buddhism, the number eight represents the Noble Eightfold Path to overcome suffering: 1. Right Knowledge; 2. Right Aspiration; 3. Right Speech; 4. Right Behavior; 5. Right Livelihood; 6. Right Effort; 7. Right Mindfulness; and 8. Right Absorption.

The Jewish religious rite of *brit milah* is held on a baby boy's eighth day of life, and Hanukkah is an eight-day Jewish holiday. The Eight Immortals are Chinese deities, and members of The Church of Jesus Christ of Latter-day Saints believe that humans are responsible for their actions by the age of eight. The *Dharmachakra,* a Buddhist symbol, has eight spokes. In Christianity, eight is allegoric to what is beyond time (because the number seven refers to the days of the week, which repeat themselves), and is the number of Beatitudes. In Islam, eight is the number of angels carrying The Holy Throne of Allah in heaven. In neo-paganism, there are eight sabbats, festivals, seasons, or spokes in the Wheel of the Year. In Hinduism, eight is the number of wealth and abundance.

Follow this circular infinity path for illumination, healing, and transformation in your life, your family, and your tribe—past, present, and future. The diagram below displays the movement of somatic transformation.

Somatic Archaeology™ Wheel Diagram
Wheel of Transformation

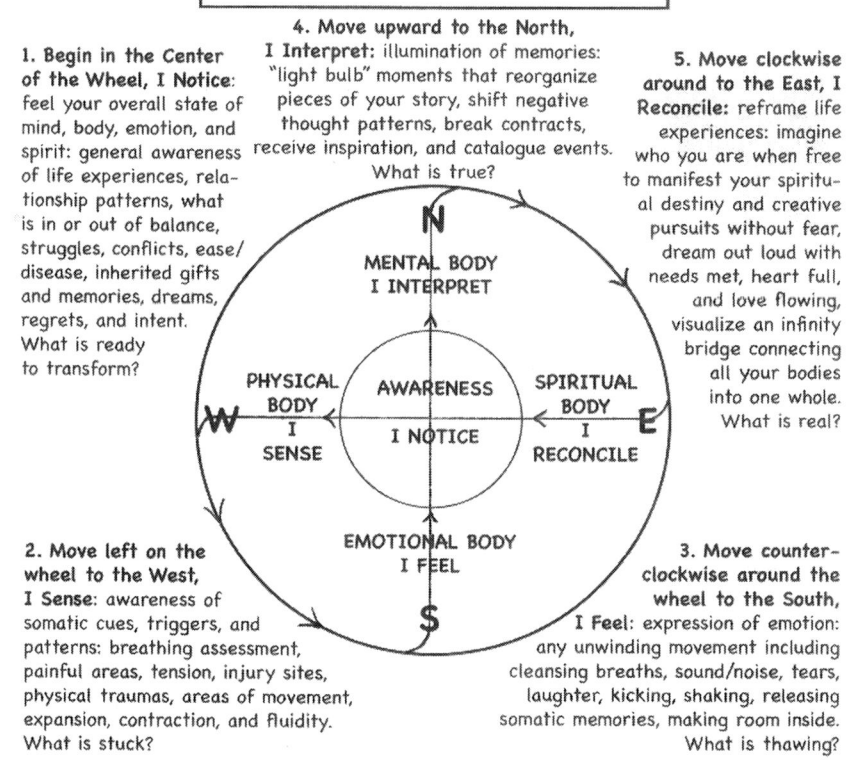

1. Begin in the Center of the Wheel, I Notice: feel your overall state of mind, body, emotion, and spirit: general awareness of life experiences, relationship patterns, what is in or out of balance, struggles, conflicts, ease/disease, inherited gifts and memories, dreams, regrets, and intent. What is ready to transform?

4. Move upward to the North, I Interpret: illumination of memories: "light bulb" moments that reorganize pieces of your story, shift negative thought patterns, break contracts, receive inspiration, and catalogue events. What is true?

5. Move clockwise around to the East, I Reconcile: reframe life experiences: imagine who you are when free to manifest your spiritual destiny and creative pursuits without fear, dream out loud with needs met, heart full, and love flowing, visualize an infinity bridge connecting all your bodies into one whole. What is real?

N — MENTAL BODY / I INTERPRET
W — PHYSICAL BODY / I SENSE
E — SPIRITUAL BODY / I RECONCILE
S — EMOTIONAL BODY / I FEEL
Center — AWARENESS / I NOTICE

2. Move left on the wheel to the West, I Sense: awareness of somatic cues, triggers, and patterns: breathing assessment, painful areas, tension, injury sites, physical traumas, areas of movement, expansion, contraction, and fluidity. What is stuck?

3. Move counter-clockwise around the wheel to the South, I Feel: expression of emotion: any unwinding movement including cleansing breaths, sound/noise, tears, laughter, kicking, shaking, releasing somatic memories, making room inside. What is thawing?

The Wheel of Transformation begins in the center of the wheel and follows the **Five Steps of Somatic Archaeology™** creating a clockwise figure eight, or **infinity**, design. **Infinity** (commonly represented as the symbol ∞) comes from the Latin: infinitas or **"unboundedness."** It refers to several concepts linked to the idea of **"without end"** which arise in philosophy, mathematics, and theology. The **infinity** symbol signifies completeness, being composed of a male, solar, right-handed circle matched with a female, lunar, left-handed circle. The figure eight on its side reflects the divine sexual union and perfection of duality (two becoming one). Since neither circle lies above the other, the infinity design implies equality between male and female powers, leading to balance, self-intimacy, and knowledge of the infinite self.

Recreate Yourself with Earth Passages

Responding to the energies and flows of our natural world, our Earth Mother helps birth our dreams and visions. By being in evolutionary harmony with the four worlds, one can design a life alchemically using the synergistic qualities of the elements that maintain order in our world. This promotes the completion of the lessons and cycles that you are learning, and cultivates the seeding of new intents you are creating, thus mending the circle. Birthing our power separates out the psychological matrixes of the past and creates new ones for the future.

We each have an authentic self that yearns for expression. You may experience it as a passion, a creative ability, a talent, and an unquenchable drive to communicate or exhibit your own unique voice. Reclamation of your authentic self and the capacity for self-expression can be a rite of passage—at any age.

In ancient days, in the cultures of indigenous peoples, young men and women about the age of thirteen undertook rites of passages when their bodies were capable of co-creating life. They would go through certain rituals that were appropriate for their culture, designed by the cycles of Mother Earth. The rites were primarily for the initiation into womanhood or manhood in order to choreograph the important elements that define the individual. The design of the passage took into consideration the individual's age, moon cycle, personal ancestry rules and traditions, climate, familial history, animal kinship, favorite flowers, color attractions, religious appeal, etc.

An Earth Passage brings symbolic death or change to a tradition or belief structure and creates an opportunity to reframe for a new way of being. It is recognized as a passage of reclaiming one's power. In a natural rite of passage, initiates may swim to the bottom of a creek to grab a stone to mark their passage. The stone becomes a signpost that carries a symbolic message of that moment when they embraced or retrieved their power. In this way, the four worlds of Mother Nature witness the passage. It is holistically complete. In the stillness of nature there is no judgment, and this allows the initiates to find their internal authority to define who they are without being driven by external fears or demands of the social culture.

Another important ingredient of a rite of passage is community recognition. The initiate must not only be recognized for this important time in his or her life, but in addition, he or she needs to have witnesses to attend the passage. If one's peers recognize the ceremonial passage, it honored the individual's gifts without others having to go into competition or comparisons with him or her. It left no place for bitterness, because everyone supported what was happening and accepted that this individual was truly changing and growing, benefiting the whole group. A true passage is one that is acknowledged by the familial community and the environment.

An Earth Passage is appropriate for any age or gender, at any cycle or time in one's life. Whether one is thirteen or sixty-three, you have the capacity to bring back together the fragments of self into a cohesive whole, healing the wounds of separateness. Many of us did not have the opportunity to design a deliberate rite of passage during childhood, but it can still be valid at any juncture in your life.

With some coaxing, a friend of mine decided to experience a rite of passage by going skydiving on her sixty-ninth birthday—which also happened to be the same day that she completed chemotherapy treatment for breast cancer. The goal was to leave all her emotional baggage on the plane—fears, worries, illness, anxiety—and jump to her freedom. In a mountain valley of southern Colorado, she gave birth to herself while facing her fear of mortality. Her oncologist is proud to announce that her cancer is still in remission after seven years!

For those who wish to create movement in their life, accentuate somatic exploration, complete a cycle, define their roles, or draw power for self-expression, an Earth Passage can be designed and executed on auspicious days or anniversaries, and include important aspects of your spiritual or religious lifestyle. Create a challenge that helps you break through a primary fear as in Jinji's story below.

Jinji's Story

Jinji stood at the top of the island cliff. A light breeze blew through his hair and the sun beat down on his back. Overhead, a flock of seagulls cried out to him, proclaiming their support. His knees were trembling. His eyes were locked on the scene forty feet below where ocean waves crashed fiercely against the rocks, issuing piles of foam which betrayed the true depth of the channel. He could barely see the waving arms of his two friends beckoning him to jump. They had been treading water for ten minutes now and were growing weary.

"Hurry up! Jump! Come on, it's okay!" they gurgled as seawater sprayed into their open mouths.

Jinji surveyed the landscape once again. Behind him lay the safety and shade of a coconut grove; oh, god, how he wished he could just turn around and retreat! To his left was a steep, rocky incline that he had climbed to reach this height where his aunt and mother patiently sat on a smooth boulder to witness his initiation into manhood. They were unusually quiet and acquiescent. In front of him lay wide-open blue space and a sheer rock cliff forty feet above nowhere. His courage hung precariously on the edge.

Only fourteen years old, Jinji was a strong, virile adolescent with dreams of being a musician. As a mixed blood, he carried the traditions of African, Native American, and Italian ancestry deep within his memory. As he attempted to come to terms with the fear that now rattled his bones, he also yearned to display a bravery that would make his mother proud, that would signify his sexual awakening, and that would dignify his lineage. Inside Jinji's mind, he was ready to be a man, but within his body trembled the insecurity of youth.

When he had agreed to participate in this rite of passage, he did not know he would hesitate. His mother had told him, "As an adult, you will have many important decisions to make. You will have to be responsible for all your actions. The Creator has given you the capacity to create life and to bring a child into this world. It is time to prepare you for this honor." Jinji was feisty and sure of himself as waves of hormones pulsed through his veins, and so he questioned his resistance.

Sitting in the cradle of nature, between sea and sky and Earth, he wavered. Part of him liked being unaccountable. It was easy and carefree to be a child. Jinji wondered, "Can I make it on my own? Do I have what it takes? What does it mean to be an adult?" Jinji recognized that there was a whole world out there that he wanted to experience, that he was part of a larger family beyond his mother, father, brothers, and sisters. More than he needed to be nurtured, he wanted to find his place in society; he wanted to fit in and make a way for himself.

Pleading screams from the ocean below brought him out of his thoughts. *Oh, right—they are still waiting for me. It's now or never,* Jinji knew. He backed up and ran to the edge of the cliff. But instead of jumping, he stopped short, pebbles skipping off the precipice. Although he had measured his personal fear, he was now confronted with his mortality. The terror of impending death reared its unsightly head and he found himself at the mercy of a power he had never had to face. His mind went blank, and he found himself shrouded in darkness. Jinji froze and time stopped.

It could have been a minute, or it could have been an hour; Jinji was unsure how long he journeyed to the archives of his soul. He traveled through memories of unfamiliar scenes and images of fellow warriors, submersed in a collective pool of men who had all taken the plunge into their truth. He saw dozens of men reaching for their identity, embracing their authentic selves, making the passage that defined them as separate from the womb of their mothers. Like a baby bird breaking through its shell, Jinji emerged. He knew that his fear of death was simply a fear of change, and that indeed he was dying to his ego's identification with the sentiment of childhood, but at the same time he was being birthed into the articulation of adulthood.

Out of the shadowy mist of innate survival, Jinji heard his mother's voice. "Let's come back tomorrow. You don't have to do this today, son. There will be other times when you feel more ready."

Guided by ancestral memory, Jinji summoned the courage. If he came back tomorrow, he would feel like a failure. He would be a wimp, and his friends paddling relentlessly in the churning waters would ridicule him. Jinji had his pride. If nothing else, he had to prove to himself that he could face anything, and that he could survive.

Backing way up, as far as he could go, Jinji began running. With long strides he crossed the safety of solid ground and threw himself wildly into the air, arms flapping and legs kicking into his destiny, dreadlocks outstretched like dancing roots. Airborne, his heart fluttered madly and he became fearless, losing touch with the young man who moments before had questioned his capacity. When he unceremoniously plunged into the turbulent waters, he transformed into a warrior of life, and his friends gratefully swam to him, administering praise.

Climbing out of the water, and grinning from ear to ear, Jinji felt full for the first time in his life. Full of himself. His aunt and mother applauded his courage and allowed tears of gratitude to announce his passage. His mother came to him and looked deep into her son's eyes as she said, "Jinji, you are a man now. You may make your own decisions. What will be your first act as an adult?"

Jinji responded joyfully, "Mother, I am going to jump again!" And he did. Jinji made his way up the cliff and boldly jumped his heroic self into the salty love of Mother Earth.

I am the rock, I am the shore
I am the pulse, the ocean roar
I am the wind that sweeps your hair
The breath of love in every prayer
I am alone, I am apart
I am the vein, I am the heart
I am the sun that warms your back
The compassion that you lack
I am the womb, I am the cave
I am the woman, I am the brave

I am the water that you drink
The sounds of peace in thoughts you think
I am the seed, I am the flower
I am the Earth, I am the power.

—Ruby Gibson, original poem

12

A Life Worth Living

You do not have to be good. You do not have to walk on your knees for a hundred miles through the desert, repenting. You only have to let the soft animal of your body love what it loves. Tell me about despair, yours, and I will tell you mine. Meanwhile the world goes on. Meanwhile the sun and the clear pebbles of the rain are moving across the landscapes, over the prairies and the deep trees, the mountains and the rivers. Meanwhile the wild geese, high in the clean blue air, are heading home again. Whoever you are, no matter how lonely, the world offers itself to your imagination, calls to you like the wild geese, harsh and exciting—over and over announcing your place in the family of things.

—Mary Oliver, *Wild Geese Poem*

In nature, change happens as part of a whole; everything is interdependent. The way of life is an interactive exchange between elements that feed, support, and maintain each other. Each action has a reaction; each thought has a consequence; and each life provides fertilizer for the next. The choreography of nature's wisdom is both beautiful and brilliant, establishing a continuous interplay between heaven and Earth. Intentionally living, breathing, and healing within this fantastic continuum is the ultimate goal of Somatic Archaeology, dissolving the illusion of separation that drives our fear and harnesses our passion.

I am reasonably sure that seemingly spontaneous acts of passion are inspired by nature and have nothing to do with calculated plans. True inspiration speaks from the heart of the world, and propels us into action that is not rehearsed or premeditated or even obviously sensible. The eruption of passion is what makes life worth living, and fuels those quintessential moments when we feel part of the whole of creation. Then separation no longer exists and magic can happen. When we give way to passion, we align with nature's wisdom and find certainty in our path.

Divine intervention creates certainty much as nature creates curiosity—both streamline us to Source. I would choose to follow certainty much as one follows the North Star toward the homeland—and not because all is lost. Certainty is the beacon of God's lighthouse on the rocky shores of life. Certainty is the gift of greatness that clears the air around us and allows us to dream out loud. Certainty is a time of deep knowing that is not affected by mental ramblings or by questionable logistics. Moments of certainty are accompanied by a deliberate deed in the world, as if having a body gives us the power to perform our resolve.

Certainty is alchemy—the universal solvent for transformation. Certainty, like alchemy, allows us to convert something into a much brighter form. When our minds and our fears are no long attempting to dictate the outcome of our lives, we can open to enchantment and a deep, internal conversion happens that is outside of our control. This is the sweet mystery of life at work.

Your Life Circle

Your own story is a circle of life within a greater circle of life. This Earth life is impacted and preceded by your spiritual lineage, a larger circle of stories that come from previous or future life experiences and oversee the evolution of your soul. This gradual progression of enlightenment is not dictated by linear time, but rather moves in concentric circles, interlaced with the lives of others, much like the movement of the stars and planets revolve in alignment with the common axis of creation.

Within this life are the remnants of other timelines, reflective of an unwinding, choreographed story that propels you into learning situations to test, challenge, or progress to your spiritual goals. These remnants are carried forward into the present, and they impact your health, relationships, and awareness. As storykeepers, it can be difficult to comprehend mentally the expansiveness of the circle of spiritual life. Again, you can turn to your body for clarity, as it holds not only your family lineage, but also the memories of your spiritual history.

As with personal or familial memories, the spiritual memories most commonly carried forward are those that convey a high degree of emotion—birth or death experiences, tragic memories, unrecognized power issues, and fearful patterns—and therefore they are held as contracted energy in your chakra system. These memories can be unearthed as corresponding present-time memories are brought forward, or as the result of digging more deeply. The world is made up of both large and small circles, and all are valued and vital to the greater movement of the whole.

Each moment is a choice, and each choice creates a cause and effect. Coming to terms or completion with the forces and influences that impact you takes the burden off the whole to manage your story for you. You become part of the solution, adding a harmonious circle of energy to the great hoop of life. This is your story and you get to choose, to a greater or lesser degree, based on what you are willing to excavate, how it gets played out from this point forward.

Healing Between Worlds

Not all somatic excavations happen in one dimension or timeline. Healing seven generations of life occurs whether it is for seven generations of familial lineage, or seven generations of spiritual lineage. Below are two stories that depict how present-day pain and experiences can collide with past traumatic events. Somatic Archaeology unearthed the origin of the pain, allowing Sophia and Ramona to heal generations of their spiritual lineage.

Sophia's Story

"THEN: It was cold outside and I had been lying there for quite some time, feeling the life draining out of my body. I knew I had to hold on. I shivered uncontrollably. The bleeding wound in my back was nothing compared to the pain in my heart. Lying in the snow, I gazed up at stars, bright and flickering as if to calm me. When he finally found me, he gently wrapped his arms around me and lifted me up to his body. His warm tears fell onto my face and pierced my soul. I knew there was nothing anyone could do. I was dying. The pain faded as numbness from the cold and the shock took over. I apologized to him for my choices, letting go. And then there was darkness.

"He could see our small cabin from where he held me, standing in the middle of a dense forest, broken only by a small stream. The smell of smoke permeated the cold crisp air, the quiet deafening, as the faint sound of a baby prompted him to move. He carried the child inside and shut the door.

"He loved me with all of his being. The difference in our cultures didn't seem to matter. When we met, we instantaneously knew that we could not ignore the power of our emotion and attraction. I left my people to be with him, and all that mattered to us was being together. The happiness that filled our lives made all the sacrifices worth it. Then, on that fateful winter night our cultures collided—the elders of my tribe had arranged for me to marry a man, but I had gone against their wishes by leaving my people. This made the man I was supposed to marry very angry. He stabbed me with a knife in the back in a jealous rage. And now all was gone …"

"NOW: I was a confident woman from the day I was born, knowing I was different from the others, but I never really knew why. My life was blessed with a secure family that loved and supported me, and everything fit into place as it should, even though I found myself questioning the universe about my path from an early age. Something wasn't right, but I couldn't put my finger on it. I brushed these feelings aside as I grew, and found a man that loved me for myself and accepted me in every way.

"Driven by my career and the need to succeed, I put my energy into being the best at what I did. This occupied my mind and time, allowing me to continue to put life questions aside for a time. With the birth of my children I found new meaning in my life; but it was then that the visions began to emerge.

"One evening while driving home from work, I came upon a car accident. There were three children in the middle of the highway. A little girl lay lifeless next to a car and as I drove past, I felt the child's spirit rise. Although I didn't understand how it was communicated, the little girl told me, "Tell Mommy it's OK." Later I found that the mother had been drinking at a Christmas party. The little girl died at the scene. I never contacted the mother to tell her what her daughter had told me, but from that day on, my goal was to raise my children lovingly, and to be the best mother I could.

"The daily challenges of raising children were not nearly as glamorous as having a successful career and being recognized for accomplishments. Deep in my heart I knew that it was the right thing to do, that this was my destiny, but always in the back of my mind I felt that I was missing something. I had another vision in which I saw one more child in my life. She had black hair and her name was Raven. The questions began to emerge more regularly.

"One day someone asked me if I knew when I was going to die. It seemed absurd but the question echoed on in my mind until a haunting realization became clear. I did know when I was going to die! It was only a few years off. I even knew the day. I was certain in a way that is unexplainable to the rational mind. Prior to this I had only felt one other time that I was close to death—it was before the C-section of my second child and I experienced a panic attack at the thought of a knife cutting me. I wasn't scared to die, but it changed the way I lived my life. Determined to live each moment to the fullest and do my best to prepare those around me, I shared this burden with no one, and lived this way for almost ten years.

"The back pain I had since being teenager started to worsen. There was always a reasonable present-day explanation for why the pain wouldn't go away. When we started doing Somatic Archaeology sessions, we had the intent of creating clarity about the knowledge of my death date and worked through a powerful session releasing what can only be explained as black particles of energy. I released them through a quivering jaw, tears streaming down my face, unable to comprehend what had just happened. As much as I didn't want the memories to surface, I knew something had changed. It was coming too close.

"A few years went by when something unexpected happened. I was on a family trip to Alaska—the wilderness was exhilarating and familiar, and I was so happy to be there with my family. After landing and exiting the seaplane I was suddenly overwhelmed and feeling faint. I walked into the warm and inviting lodge, still not feeling quite myself, attributing it to a bumpy ride. I went outside to breathe in the cool air and looking up I saw an eagle in a tree next to the bay.

"When I entered the lodge, I was introduced to a man. Our eyes met and I felt strange again. I looked deeper into his eyes and the connection was immediate and confusing. His voice was hauntingly familiar and the sparkle in his eyes made me hesitate, and yet an unseen magnetic force was clear. After spending more time with him, I was captivated by the emotion of not wanting to leave him. How could I have this feeling when I didn't even know this person?

"The feelings intensified over the next few days. One day while flying alone together, three eagles flew beside the helicopter. It was so beautiful and I suddenly had a feeling that we had met before. I asked him why he wasn't married and he answered, 'I guess I just haven't met the right person yet.' In my mind I thought, *You just did.* I felt safe and whole with him, and it scared me. The connection was deep, as if I had known him a lifetime. I kept my distance from him until we left. While leaving, I saw him watching the plane from the lodge and I wondered, 'Will I ever see him again?'

"A year went by. We communicated by phone often and built a friendship. When we talked, I would immediately get cold and start to shake uncontrollably. It happened every time we spoke. It confused me because I was happy with my life, but something was missing and I knew it in the depths of my soul. It was agonizingly painful to try and put the puzzle of my life together. The pieces didn't fit anymore.

"Then he came to visit. My apprehension escalated because I couldn't contain the passion like I had in Alaska. Our union was the most beautiful experience of my existence. The connection was so powerful that I shook with desire. I felt whole for the first time in my life. It filled a void I didn't know existed. It scared me more than anything I had ever gone through. After a few days he left and the feeling of life left with him. Everything meaningful to me meant nothing now. It made no sense. The feeling of hopelessness was pervasive. How could this be? Doing the dishes one day I fell to the floor and wept, completely full of despair and pain. It had to stop. I questioned the universe once again. Why was this happening? It felt as if it was going to break me.

"The day I thought I was going to die came and went. Nothing happened.

"A year or so later I saw him again, and the same thing happened. We both knew the truth and it scared us because there was nothing we could do about it. I began to question if by chance two dimensions had crossed paths. This time when I lay in his arms, tears fell from his eyes. I saw into him and it pierced my soul yet again. Several years went by as we kept our distance, knowing the pain was too much for us to live with. I was not willing to leave my family. It would have to be enough to know that if only for a moment in time, we connected …

"I was finally willing to try Somatic Archaeology again. It was difficult for me to explain or talk about with anyone, so I went into my body. Once again a hot energy was released from my back during the somatic excavation, and I felt one step closer to the truth.

"Over the next few weeks I became very ill and was forced to slow down. This was difficult but at the same time conducive to having time for contemplating what was going on inside my body. One evening I was outside and heard the call of an eagle in the trees. It swooped past me in the dusk and it was then that the memories became clear. I used the Somatic Archaeology techniques to relax my mind and body. I started to tremble, and was able to go back into past memories and relive the vision at the beginning of this story. Questioning the universe had finally paid off and the answers I had been looking for finally came forth during the three somatic excavations I did on my own.

"The last excavation I did finally released the rest of the pain in my back with an enormous amount of heat and a burning sensation at the point of injury. The back pain that I had lived with for almost thirty years was now negligible. Following this clearing of emotional and somatic pain, I have a new-found freedom and clarity to make a choice from my heart without regret; and I have chosen to stay with my family. It is the right thing to do for now. My heart and mind are at peace. This has been a life worth living."

What you can't forgive, you continue to hold in your body. What you hold in your body keeps you stuck and is a constant reminder of what is unloved. Follow the trail of your pain, and do not give up. Listen, love, and pay attention. Eventually it will lead you to the uncovering of your soul and the gifts you have lost or forgotten. The circle of circumstance and suffering that is wedged between our body and soul is so vast that it is unimaginable to our conscious minds. Fortunately, our bodies have the capacity to understand. Trust the wisdom of your body, as it has many stories to tell you. The great circle is always bringing life full around the hoop. All stories will be healed in time.

The next story is somewhat similar in dynamics; both are in alignment with the greater collective story of the healing of the feminine. The common denominator of the stories is the reclaiming of power over one's body in the advent of respect—between gender, race, culture, and nature.

Ramona's Story

"I got pregnant with my boyfriend who was a member of a small indigenous tribe, and we were ecstatic to add to the population of his group. When I was three months along, I happened to encounter an accident where a man had just run over a puppy that was three weeks old. I stopped and picked up the dog that was bleeding from his head. I wrapped the dog in a baby blanket that I had just received for my baby and happened to have in my car. Moments later, the puppy shuddered his last breath and died in my arms. I found his owners and went about my day, crying sadly about this tragic event.

"The very next day, I started bleeding and within three days I had miscarried our baby. It was horribly painful and when I recovered, I buried the placenta in the forest by my home. While praying for understanding and for the baby's swift journey to the spirit world, we looked up on a nearby hill and saw a dog watching us, much like a spirit guardian. When my boyfriend acknowledged the dog, he trotted off, satisfied that his presence had been made. We instinctively knew that the puppy had been our baby's companion to the other side. Soon after that, my relationship ended with my boyfriend and we parted ways.

"Three years later, a Latino man from out of town called me to inquire about doing some healing work. He was suffering from grief because his six-year-old son had died after being run over by a car. He had seen my name in a brochure and intuitively felt that I could help him. On the day he arrived, as I was leaving my house to meet him, I bent down to feed my dog and I felt something strange happen in my lower back. I didn't worry about it, and was in a hurry, so I jumped in my car and drove to my office.

"When I got out of my car, my knees wobbled and I dropped to the ground. My hips and back were in so much pain that I could not walk, and so I crawled down to my office. The man was waiting for me, and because he had flown so far to see me, I was determined to work with him despite my pain. I pulled myself into a chair at my office, and he handed me a gift—a CD he had made called *Ancestors Song*. I thanked him, taking notice of the name, and we began our healing session.

"He grieved profoundly during the session, and I was in so much pain that I wept along with him. This man was familiar, yet I could not place him. We worked together for three days, uprooting much of the pain of losing his special son so young. After he went back home, I was still not better, and spent the next year in physical agony.

"I tried everything—massage, chiropractic, fasting, physical therapy, exercise, hot springs, energy work, sweat lodge ceremonies—you name it, but nothing relieved the pain. I did countless Somatic Archaeology excavations, unearthing pieces of the puzzle, and working through buried emotions, but would only find temporary relief. The grief felt so deep, with multiple layers, and I knew it would take time and life experience to fully heal. I learned to live with the pain in varying degrees, finding other ways to tie my shoes and clean my house because I could not bend over.

"Six months after my injury, I was the recipient of a ceremonial group healing in a class led by an indigenous elder from central Mexico. I had been chosen because I was hurting. The healing automatically led me into body memories of the miscarriage and feelings of loss. Afterward, I felt immediately better, but the next day I was in so much pain that I could not sit still in class. I was feeling very angry and began to cry, so I went off to the bathroom to be by myself. I suddenly started to feel faint and I fell to the floor.

"As I lost consciousness, I was pulled into a deep memory. The bathroom was gone, and I was lying on the ground in a field and felt a dreadful uneasiness in my stomach. I could smell the stench of smoke and blood, and could hear people screaming all around me. Slowly I opened my eyes to a horrifying scene of soldiers on horses riding by me and setting fire to the fields. I watched them decapitating the men and grabbing the women. It was a shocking scene, and panicking, I ran for my life toward the village.

"The people of the tribe were running haphazardly, screaming for their children. Before I could get to safety, a soldier grabbed me, and threw me to the ground, calling out to his comrades. The three men proceeded to brutally rape me, and then one of them spit on my face with disgust as he began to cut my baby out of my womb. I was three months pregnant. He left me to bleed to death in front of a massive fire where bodies were being thrown, and the smell of burning flesh filled the air. I cried and I screamed and I cursed, and I felt the greatest grief imaginable.

"In the far distance, I could make out the voice of a man calling my name, 'Ramona, Ramona.' He sounded so far away from the midst of this terrible scene. I felt someone pick me up, hold me in his arms, and place a cool compress on my brow. It was my friend, Antonio. He had come looking for me when I hadn't returned to the classroom, and he found me lying on the bathroom floor.

"Later he told me that when he entered the bathroom I was breathing spasmodically, at times rapidly, then panting and hyperventilating, while mumbling phrases in another language. It reminded him of the Toltec dialect (which he recognized because our teacher was speaking this language). My hair was disheveled, I was clammy, and drool was coming out my mouth. He couldn't rouse me so he checked my pulse, and it was very weak and thready. As an EMT, he knew this meant that there should be a great deal of blood loss, but he couldn't find any bleeding. Instinctively he knew I was in great danger of dying.

"At first Antonio thought I was having a seizure because I was so rigid. He said that he kept calling me by different names—first my nickname, then my given name, and finally my medicine name. Eventually I responded to this name. I would come in and out of consciousness, and vacillate between screaming and moaning, speaking fluent Spanish and Toltec (I speak only a small amount of both). Antonio followed me from this world to the other world, and he could feel what was happening. He began crying, too, and felt himself pulled into the web of the scene.

"Then the memories came flooding back on him. He remembered that he was my husband, and had gone out hunting, returning only to find the unbearable chaos and my body bleeding and dying by the fire. Antonio was able to keep a link between this world and that one. He did not want to lose me, so he kept sending his love to me, urging me back to present time. It took at least two hours for him to retrieve us from the horrific scene and memory. It was very hard and draining for him to get me back. I believe that it was the power of his love, and of his great heart, that allowed me to survive this memory and to relive this story so that I could heal.

"I was shattered from the experience—cautious, withdrawn, and very shaky. For six months I had trouble concentrating, and felt deep exhaustion as I put the pieces of myself back together and connected the dots of my story. I continued with more Somatic Archaeology sessions to shake out the remaining debris from the long-buried memory.

"Between worlds, I healed—I recognized the Latino man who had lost his son as one of the soldiers who had hurt me, and I forgave him. I reached out to his son with gratitude. I felt the pain of my current miscarriage and its significance in retrieving the memory, and I blessed my baby for her great sacrifice. I felt the grief of my ex-boyfriend who had lost so many of his tribe to cultural genocide, and I prayed for him. I thanked the spirit of the dog who had guarded the path.

"The students in the class who had been in the healing circle had continued to pray for me while I was on the bathroom floor with Antonio. They felt that I had remembered this story for all of us—they had each also felt and seen memories of this massacre. I honored them. My teacher told me that as a traditional keeper of the lands of Mexico, he was familiar with these tragic scenes, and as my father in this memory, he healed right beside me. I cried for him and the ancestry of his people. The present day connections to this archaic memory were more than my mind could comprehend.

"Most of all I honored Antonio, because if wasn't for him, and his courage, love, and insights, I would not be here now. Together, we began to remember the sweetness of our connection and all that we had lost. Our lives had been woven together with such strong joy and suffering that it was the greatest relief to find each other again and remember who we were. Antonio was the gift that the suffering relinquished back to me. It made reliving the pain worthwhile.

"I assumed that the unearthing, processing, and reconciliation of this story would heal my back, but to my surprise, my back still hurt as much as ever. Then, one day, I woke up and I was simply out of pain. I had done nothing different. I looked in my calendar book, and checked the dates—it was exactly one year to the day that the Latino man had come to my office, one year to the day that I had injured my back. I couldn't believe it!

"Two years have passed and the pain has never returned. I have learned to pay attention to the greater cycles that guide my life and my healing. There were certain elements that I could control, and some that were of a higher order. I now recognize that we suffer together as one, and we heal as one. As long as I am doing my part to remember, the intelligence of life will eventually bring all the people and all the fragments of our past full circle to present time. What an honor to witness the grand choreography of the universe. No longer do I fear the mystery of my body, my experiences, and my past."

Archaeology of the Soul

I believe that we were each brought to this life or this planet for a reason, a higher purpose that gives meaning to existence. As you get to know your story, you may catch glimpses of this purpose. The more you relieve yourself of historical limitations and impressions, the more able you are to define and embrace this purpose.

Have you ever seen someone who you thought was doing exactly what they were supposed to be doing, who was right on track and seemed to be in his or her perfect element? Did you notice how his or her entire being was aligned and the air seemed to clear around him or her and he or she flowed easily and effortlessly? This is someone who has matured into spiritual destiny. It is a beautiful sight and feeling, and it is available for all of us.

This is archaeology of the soul. When you excavate your story at this subterranean level, you can transcend self and the myth of duality, becoming a healing vessel for the greater circle. During this *soul dig* you not only look for pieces to give meaning to your life's experiences, or to justify your "karma," but to develop the objective awareness to heal the story of humanity—the collective, ancestral, planetary story. You are doing recovery work for those that cannot do it for themselves. Circular healing extends far beyond the self.

> *It is useless to discuss the peace of the world. What is necessary just now is to create peace in ourselves that we, ourselves, become examples of love, harmony and peace. That is the only way of saving the Earth and ourselves.*
>
> —Pir-o-Murshid Inayat Khan

Closing the Circle

See yourself as healed. Hold a picture, in your imagination, of yourself being whole and loved, and in alignment with your highest potential. There is power in creative visioning—not only the ability to envision your life free from suffering, but to feel it as well. Charge your imagination with your emotion. Feel the goodness inherent in you, and boldly let it shine and expand, charging the particles of your being with love and acceptance for the great circle of life.

You are responsible for leading the way and for keeping your course during the excavation of your story. Keep your eye on the prize—being willing to look forward more than you look back, widening your lens to observe where you are going—using familiar landmarks and goalposts to recognize progress, moving forward while accepting distractions as a consequence of good digging. Pay attention with all of your senses and do the best you can. Let your heart be your compass. Holding onto a healing vision for yourself may mean that you have to keep a grip during rough waters. Don't lose sight. Never give up faith in your ability to heal. Witness the grace of creation and cheer yourself on.

Here are the stages and affirmations to close a circle of healing.

I Banish: "I banish from this time, space, and dimension, any spirit or entity, seen or unseen, that is not in alignment with my highest potential and divine well-being."

I Invite: "I invite into my body and my life all those that support my continued evolution, abundance, and harmony, and work for peace on this planet."

I Release: "I release all resistance and fear, and gratefully give away thoughts, patterns, and habits that no longer serve my growth, my lineage, my community, my Earth, and my love.

I Ground: "I ground myself to Mother Earth, aligning with the rhythm and flows of creation's beauty. I am one with all that is."

I Bless: "I bless the great circle of life, the above and the below, the dreamed and the dreamers, the Earth and the sky, the great and the small, the loved and the unloved, the perfection and the imperfection. I am one in body, mind, heart, and spirit. Ah, ho!"

Advice from Somatic Archaeologists

Mark's Advice

"Somatic Archaeology is the gateway to the body's side of the story. In psychology, the mind tells the story; in somatic therapy, the body tells the story. The mind has a perception, but the body never lies, it tells all. In the depths of me lies a hidden truth that I do not wish to acknowledge—the power of light and love for myself. I was kept away from it by the lies I was taught. Like the overgrown roots of a great gnarled tree holding to the past, I learned to choke out any light that might shine upon the very ground of who I am. Sounds from a distant and primal place within me gave way to bring light upon my space. The essence of a flower drifted into my dark places and awakened the possibilities of who I am. Winds of change come from deep with me, the stirring of sensation, color, smell, and sound. My mind has missed this relationship with my truth; not knowing how to respond, I shut down to find ways to explain what words lack the power to express. Within me now blossoms the joy once trapped by fear, pain, and self-doubt. I advise you to unfold the darkness of your story. Learn to see in the dark. Make the choice to own your power. Receive light. Speak your truth and find safety within. Set your intention, breathe the aromas that stir the soul and awaken memory within your body, being curious about what lies within. Know that the power of joy is right now."

Megan's Advice

"Somatic Archaeology begins for me with a release of tension or holding, and a willingness to let go of attachment to an outcome or an idea of what will unfold. I feel myself soften and surrender into the wisdom of my body. I call for assistance from the world unseen—insights or guidance that my higher self and guides provide. In this space, I feel completely and totally supported. My fear is lessened, and resistance is softened. The process begins. I scan my body for traces of sensation. I encourage myself to stay connected and explore with the utmost reverence and willingness to heal, transform, and grow. There is something tangible that tells me I have found my door in. Within moments, I am taken into a world that is not understandable to my physical reality. It is the imaginative, somatic space where sensation speaks truth. My body opens doors while spirit is the key that unlocks what has been hidden from my sight. I know nothing of the outcome, very little of how I arrived, but for some reason what presents itself is wholly applicable to the essence of my truth and development. What surfaces are layers of my self that are no longer needed—which no longer serve my constantly shifting and evolving sense of self in relationship to the world.

"What I have learned from Somatic Archaeology over and over again is to own myself, honor my power, and give myself permission to be authentically complete in who I am. As I excavate deeper into my soma, I come to identify my path. I understand the reasons I am here and the gifts I have to offer. I own my destiny and my power. This work touches on the place where my body, mind, and spirit overlap. I am no longer afraid of the expansion that lies right before me. I no longer question that I am on the right path, or that I will ever be unseen, unsupported, or unappreciated. I have found a deep and unending love for myself, and a fascination of the process that ensues. I am forever a student of my body, and what a gift it is to have the tools to excavate the meaning of that experience!"

Allyn's Advice

"Somatic Archaeology has transformed my life over the past four years, learning to allow my joy to bubble up and exude out. My body had to scream at me to pay attention. I can't remember when I stopped listening—after the rapes, abortions, or C-sections. It certainly captured my attention in a way that became an all-consuming quest. Slowly but surely, spirit led me down a path to learn that it was never an option for me to have someone else fix it for me. I met many gifted people along my journey that gave me tools to empower myself. It has taken ten years, and even last week I was having doubts if I was hearing my own words, "Breathe and let love fill every cell of your body. Trust the wisdom of your body!" I thought perhaps I was an exception. I feel now that a profound shift has taken place. My belief in myself is renewed and the pain has vanished, leaving the faintest trace of a reminder that there is more work to be done. I give credit and much gratitude to those beings of this world and beyond whose light has touched me as if with a magic wand. The journey continues."

Terri's Advice

"It is funny sometimes in a somatic session how life can unexpectedly be so clear—as if all of a sudden I can see how the chain of my life events has unfolded and how I got to where I am right now. The significance of all the people I am connected to becomes illuminated; it's like someone wrote the formula out on a chalkboard and simultaneously threw the light switch on. It's the beginning of the realization that I can live in a different way. Once a person awakens, once the patterns of behavioral repetition become obvious, then that is when life becomes worth living. Each time I fall back and repeat old patterns, something is triggered, some memory comes forward to warn me that I've entered that door again—the door that has kept me from being who I am. I have a choice to initiate a change in behavior that enables me to move out of the circle of control. Sometimes I like it in that whirlpool and don't even realize that I return to it. I feel safe because it's familiar. But through Somatic Archaeology, I zip off the fear that binds me to that point, then I am free from what has been holding me down, free to open to my unfolding heart, a choreographed dance of osmosis with my true nature. I awaken to a world that looks like a whole new place. Sure, fear raises its ugly head and taps me on the shoulder as if to say, 'Hey, old friend, got an extra place at the table?' That's when the tools I have gathered in my life become a big necessity. Somatic Archaeology has brought me those tools. Like breathing—which alone can bring oxygen to a place of no movement. Then, body movement and sound bring my soul where it can be nurtured and cleansed, and the movement of emotion releases old anchors that hold me under the water. Last but not least, I practice forgiveness for where I have been and where I am going."

Bev's Advice

"Through Somatic Archaeology I have learned that performance anxiety is a huge hurdle for me. I learned that exposing myself is the road to self-improvement. I remember back to kindergarten, at the age of four, when we received stars on our chart for things like knowing our address or phone number or tying our shoes. When we were ready, we demonstrated what we knew, and the goal was to fill in all the blanks with stars. I noticed that other children were bumbling through; not me, though. I practiced on my own, and when I was ready, I performed perfectly. My mom was always so surprised when I would come home and tell her that I got a star, because I had felt so unsure of myself, so inadequate, as a child.

"My lesson as an adult has been to give myself permission to be a student. I now know that I have the words I need, and the confidence to use them. As a student of Somatic Archaeology, I wanted to test my abilities, and found that I can stumble and still be okay. I have learned to dust myself off and move on, focusing on my successes and the things that I could change. I learned that I am adding to my tool belt of recovery skills all the time, and that the goal is not to use all the tools in a particular order, but to have them at hand, allowing the flow of the somatic session to indicate what might be most useful. Somatic Archaeology has touched me in ways that I am only now beginning to connect with, and I feel deep gratitude for the courage to explore the shadow, emerge into light, and to show others the way. The more I process and heal, the more I learn, and the true gifts of Somatic Archaeology are revealed to me.

Bring Joy into Your Story

Expand into your happiness and contentment. Every body has a memory of pleasurable encounters. Encourage it by focusing your attention on areas of comfort, ease, serenity, grace, and fluidity—which are mostly fueled by nature images or being in the wild.

Seek out the areas in your body that are associated with pleasure. Call these memories forward. You may find a pervasive sense of joy throughout your body, or the feeling of joy may be isolated in one specific area. Even if your joy has been subdued for a long time, it doesn't mean that it can't be unearthed. Search for pleasant memories or experiences that have taken root in your body. Focus on "what is right."

Bringing joy into your story leaves you feeling less vacant and more full, giving your ego new meaning to identify with. The next time that you feel overwhelmed or insecure, embody the Magician archetype to access joyful memories and create a bridge to hope and courage. Flood your body with vibrant colors, feelings, and sensations to enhance joy and contentment, offering perspective to widen your circle of healing.

> *Grief can take care of itself, but to get the full value of a joy you must have someone to divide it with.*
>
> —Mark Twain

Take Your Story into the World

As you build strength, protect your newfound joy and power as a precious little seedling, being careful whom you let into your circle. Healing creates vulnerability, which means you may become more susceptible to outside influences. Healing also creates determination. Bring the Warrior archetype to your healing and growth, protecting that little seedling like a mother bear protects her cubs, so that it can blossom into a substantial tree with deep roots.

Healing your story sometimes rocks the boat of relationships because change can be threatening. Healing requires that both parties in the relationship grow. The significant others in your life may not recognize what is happening inside you as you reconstruct your story. Hopefully, there will be some people in your life who can be trusted to encourage your healing movement by watering and fertilizing the new seedling along with you. This is another reason to have a strong support system in your circle.

Surround yourself with people who notice that you are changing, and are willing to evolve as well. Share your experiences together, noticing things such as how your feet touch the ground, where in your body you are moving from, how you are breathing, if you are making eye contact, having healthy boundaries, etc. Friends like this are invaluable to help you recognize that you are not doing this alone. Every day you have the potential to change and grow, and you have the option of stepping into your story with a fresh attitude and powerful presence.

The Gift of Suffering

Like a buried treasure, gifts exist under years of accumulated debris. When excavating, you will find valuable artifacts that belong to you that you thought you had lost. There is such joy in reclaiming these gifts; it is the positive nature of a devastating experience.

As painful as your story may be, it is the force in your life that propels you toward healing. And somehow, the treasures you have lost are much more appreciated when they are rediscovered. Life is an odd and unpredictable series of events, but you can gain the most from it. Use life dramas as stepping-stones for growth, use the tools you have gained dealing with suffering for your personal redemption.

Witness the gift of suffering in the courage to fight for yourself, in the willingness to speak out, in the declaration of your divinity, in the resurgence of creative impulses, and in the uniting of your soul with others. This is embodiment of the Lover archetype. Embrace and witness the joy of suffering while remembering that you are on this Earth to grow and change and love and laugh and explore and procreate and demonstrate and expand and commune. Suffering takes away your choices and your perspective. Somatic Archaeology brings them back. Find joy in your future and the magnificence of your authentic story.

When you view yourself as a beautiful, intricate tapestry woven with strands of delight, sentiment, and dignity, it is only fitting that you display yourself on the wall for all to appreciate. If you find that you are allowing others to trample on your tapestry, or that you are walking on yourself, you do injustice to your divinity. Develop compassion, love, and respect within yourself and it will aid your ability to embody self-enhancing, rather than self-defeating, attributes.

The effectiveness of Somatic Archaeology comes down to the quality of your awareness. Any healing work you do with yourself, or any self-care you practice, benefits your community and the entire world. Be a model of self-love for others. Once you have developed a regard for yourself and have the ability to worship life, you are capable of being courteous, of maintaining appropriate boundaries, of understanding the needs of others, of having compassion for those more or less blessed than yourself, of wisdom and foresight in actions and words, of touching gently, of smiling knowingly, and of honoring the rights of those who are weaker, smaller, remote, unwanted, or discriminated against.

In the advent of respect, you engender an obligation to the Earth, mirroring your internal sense of harmony in your treatment of the environment. Bow to the trees rather than chop them down, pledge your protection rather than exploitation, and walk sensitively and lightly, recognizing the many miracles of creation. Respect enables you to listen to Mother Earth's pleas with an open mind and heart. It gives you the courage to fight for what is right, demanding decent treatment of our water, air, land, and natural resources.

These virtues are the overall outcome of a somatic excavation well explored. Suffering is recycled into salvation. It is the only acceptable solution for what we have endured. In all the negatives, you will find a positive; in all violations you will find dignity; in all losses you will find profits; in all pain you will find joy. Your optimism is your future. The legacy of suffering that you carry in your mind, body, and soul must be excavated, exposed, and reconciled to insure a positive future. External transformation begins through internal exploration. As a somatic archaeologist, you are essentially a peace worker. As a sacred storykeeper, you can change the world.

Conclusion

I had a dream not long ago in which I was in a canoe coming to the end of a long canyon of whitewater. The river opened to a wide, gentle valley where the water was peaceful and easy. A man was paddling the canoe with me, and he said, "You can relax now. Sit back and enjoy the ride."

I said, "Are you sure? What if there is another rapid ahead?"

He replied, "Don't worry, the hard part is over."

What a relief! I leaned back in the canoe and took a deep breath, gazing up at the blue sky and delicate clouds. My heart opened and my body relaxed. Whew! I had made it. Then, I heard the sound of rushing water. I jumped up and looked. Ahead was a huge waterfall, and we were about to go over it in the canoe.

I gasped and said to the man, "I thought you told me that ..." And before I could finish my words, the canoe went over the edge. But instead of crashing down, the canoe floated out into space and there we were, suspended in thin air, gently moving with the currents of the atmosphere.

I looked at him with surprise, and he gently replied, "I told you that you could relax now." I smiled and leaned back again, feeling the love and support of the universal flow.

My story has changed. I am no longer that young girl sitting by the creek, tediously clearing out the sticks, leaves, and debris. Instead, I jumped into the water and became part of the river, floating along with the ebb and flow until I no longer needed the teachings that it had to provide.

Now I soar above the river, big graceful wings guiding me to help others who are in the river below. It is delightful! What a view! From here, I can tell you that transforming your story is possible, and in fact, it's inevitable. Embrace your body and you embrace your story. Shine your truth with fierceness and bravery. I invite you to begin now.

> *I am like the sunrise*
> *coming up over the horizon of tomorrow*
> *illuminating my shadowed eyes*
> *shooting rays of fierce love into my heart*
> *and pulling me into my warmth*
> *like a walking angel in search of her home.*
>
> —Ruby Gibson, original poem

About the Author

Guided by years of spiritual studies and personal healing, Ruby Gibson brings a compassionate heart to her writing and healing practice. Ruby is a woman of mixed descent who embraces many traditions, and she is the mother of three beautiful children. An Earth-centered ceremonialist and traditional pipe carrier, she began her spiritual journey at the age of thirteen and has spent her life in service to the healing of Mother Earth and the betterment of her community. She believes in the power of the circle of life, holding optimism for the peaceful transformation of humanity.

As a certified somatic therapist, Ruby has worked with children and adults for thirty years, specializing in recovery from trauma, abuse, injury, addictions, PTSD, and chronic pain. Ruby is a somatic pioneer who bridges the ancient Medicine Wheel, bodywork, human behavior, and spirituality into a technique she developed called Somatic Archaeology. A national educator for twenty years, she teaches a professional certification program in Somatic Archaeology, along with workshops in Earth-centered healing and essential oil therapy. She is also an instructor at Naropa University's Extended Studies Program in Boulder, Colorado.

Author of the novel *Home is the Heart,* Ruby is a poet and freelance writer and owner of Howling at the Moon Productions, located in the foothills of Colorado. In addition, Ruby is Lead Trainer of Family and Youth Programs for ONE Freedom, a Colorado non-profit group that provides education and training for our nation's warriors and their families regarding the challenges of military deployments and the return home. She is part of a dynamic team offering a powerful framework that places stress mitigation and trauma resolution in the hands of each individual.

Ruby is president of Freedom Lodge non-profit group, whose mission is for the healing and wellness of all people. As a child advocate, she has worked with community youth in recreational sports, violence and date rape prevention programs, and peer support through Talking Stick Circles. Freedom Lodge currently offers ECHO: Earth Centered Healing Outreach for community de-griefing and crisis intervention, providing services for the Wildland Firefighters Foundation. (Visit www.earthcenteredhealing.org for more information.)

A Somatic Archaeology Storykeepers CD designed to enhance the concepts in this book will soon be available. For more information about this and upcoming Somatic Archaeology programs, workshops, and Somatic Storykeepers Circles, visit www.somaticarchaeology.com and www.mybodymyearth.com.

Appendix

Somatic Glossary

ADHD: Attention Deficit Hyperactivity Disorder; any of a range of behavioral disorders occurring primarily in children, including symptoms such as poor concentration, hyperactivity, and impulsivity

Atmosphere of the Invisible: Etheric energetic flows of life and chi that establish the somatic blueprint; including chakras and Earth-generated elemental rhythms; unseen to the human eye but perceptible with psychic vision

Blueprint (Somatic): Figuratively, an invisible guide or image of the physical body which determines health, creates structure, and holds memories; something that acts as a model or template designed by generational imprints and historical experiences

Boundaries: Self-assessed borders designed to maintain personal autonomy, the point at which you end and another begins

Chakra: Sanskrit word meaning wheel or circle; any one of the centers of spiritual power located in the human body which establish the atmosphere of the invisible; somatic memory banks and transformers of energy

Dharma: Sanskrit word meaning decree or custom; Hindu principle of cosmic order, according to social codes and earned by virtue and righteousness; in Buddhism, the truth about the way things are and will always be in the universe and nature.

Dimension: A level of consciousness, existence, or reality; a coordinate used to locate a point in the time/space continuum; multi-dimensional refers to the existence or awareness of multiple realities

Dissociation: The ability to split off or disconnect from your body and/or the present time line; an emotional, mental, or spiritual separation from self

Elements: Primary substances (air, fire, water, earth) that are the materials from which all matter is constructed and through which balance is manifested

Embodiment: Personification of a particular attribute, specifically anchoring it into physical form; the act by which a story is made tangible

Empowerment: To reclaim authority for the co-creation of life; self-esteem or confidence; to make stronger in regards to ownership of life and claiming rights.

Human Law: Rules of conduct recognized by human communities as binding that are enforced by an external authority; a generalized rule to define correct behavior according to conventional or religious doctrines

Intuition: Finely tuned awareness of the body and the mind; to be aware of something without having to think about it; instinctual knowing

Karma: Hindu and Buddhist philosophy which states that the quality of one's current and future lives is determined by their behavior in this and previous lives; cause and effect destiny or fate

Luminous Body: Bright or shining light body emanating from spiritual source; actual energy that establishes glowing vigor, health, and vitality in a person; maintains and holds the somatic blueprint

Parasympathetic Nervous System: One of the two divisions in the part of the nervous system that controls involuntary and unconscious bodily functions (autonomic nervous system or involuntary)

PTSD: Post Traumatic Stress Disorder; diagnosis given to those who experience a devastating event incurring symptoms such as nightmares, night sweats, hypervigilance, anxiety, phobias, loss of boundaries, hallucinations, aggressive behavior, confusion, disorientation, emotional outbursts, dissociation, numbness, loss of identity, chronic pain, and suicidal tendencies

Sacred Law: Rules of cosmic life dictated by a higher law; governed by absolute spiritual principles and natural evolutionary flows

Somatic: Of the body, or affecting the body; physical conditions considered separate from the mind

Somatic Filters: Sieves with which you can sort out memories and feelings; usually developed to cope with stressful situations

Somaticize: To convert into physical symptoms; or to believe mistakenly that an emotional pain is a physical symptom

Sympathetic Nervous System: The part of the autonomic nervous system that is active during stress or danger and is involved in regulating pulse and blood pressure, dilating pupils, and changing muscle tone

Timeline: Spiritual representation of non-linear events represented in significant past, present, generational, and historical experiences

Titrate: A chemistry term meaning to add quantities of two substances together slowly and gradually until a reaction occurs; to continuously measure and adjust the balance of a physiological function or somatic response; gradual integration of breath and awareness into a somatic memory

Tracking: A learned skill to observe changes going on in your body or consciousness during a somatic healing session

Trigger: Any visual, olfactory, sensory, or auditory input that activates the fight/flight/freeze response; to set something off or bring it about

Unwinding: The counterclockwise circular release of energy from your body; to undo something tangled; to relieve your body from tension or worry

Victimization: To embody beliefs that define status as a victim of circumstance or others; to single oneself out unfairly for punishment; helplessness to do anything about unfortunate experiences

- C-SECTION BIRTH
- OVER CUT OR BLISS
- BLISS
- SIEZURE
- SPINAL TAP

- APENDECTOMY
- RE-OPENING
- GAUZE PULL
- IODIDE SOAKS

- HERNIA REPAIR
- SPRAINED WRISTS CAMP
- ROCK TO FACE, STITCHES
- TYROW TACK - HI-FIVE
- GROIN PULL/TEAR/HIP FLEXOR - CAMP

- KNEE SCRAPE ON BIKE
- MASSIVE TOOTH PULL - EPSTEIN
- OCEAN SWIM, HAMPTONS POMMELLED WIND-KNOCKED-OUT
- SKIING & LANDING POLE TO STERNUM
- SOCCER TRAINING, HIPS
- FINGERS BROKEN
- SHOULDERS SUBLUXATION
- GETTING PUMMELED IN GOAL LACROSSE
- CONCUSSION LACROSSE
- TEASED AS CROSS Y - DAD SAYING SO
- SLEEPWALKS HEAD MIDDLE NIGHT
- GO BOOTH, SLEEPING

- INDOOR SOCCER COXIX BONE
- MONONUCLEOSIS
- ANKLE ROLLS, REPEATED
- FEMURS STRESS FRACTURES
- BROKEN NOSE
- POISON IVY - NYC
- SHOULDER SEPARATION w/ BEN QUIGLEY WEDDING
- HAMSTRING TEAR SQUASH
- BMW T-BONE CRASH
- BIKE CRASH SEATTLE - SUNRISE
- BIKE CRASH FONDO - SHOULDER

- GROIN PULL SQUASH SEATTLE
- BACK ISSUE IWCL POP @ SBP
- PUSHING BEYOND ON BIKE
- CALF TEARS, REPEATED
- TWO SINUS SURGERIES
- EYE DAMAGE ON ADAMS & SURGERY
- SLOUCHING
- OVER-DRINKING COLLEGE & AF
- PNEUMONIA
- ASTHMA AS KID
- LIVING W/ CATS - NYC EFAN
- ALLERGY SHOTS AS KID
- CLAUSTROPHIA ATTACK IN NY CAR W/ JEN & VICKI

- DAD GRABBING BY ARM
- MOM TALKING ABOUT MY PENIS
- DAD SPANKINGS
- MOM'S FRIEND WARU GAWKING
- MOM DANCING
- MOM GARDEN BELT @ CATHY'S WEDDING
- DAD & MOM WEIGHT CONCERNS
- FINGER NAIL BITING
- NOSE SELF HATRED
- HAIR SELF HATRED
- NYC ANOREXIA
- HERPES

Essential Oil Information

Young Living therapeutic-grade, organic, FDA-approved products are the essential oils of choice for Somatic Archaeology. (See chapter 5 for Aromatherapy for Balancing Body and Brain.) They can be obtained by mail order only through Young Living Essential Oil Company in Lehi, Utah. To review products, establish your own account, and purchase essential oils with Young Living, go to www.youngliving.com/howlingmoonprod. Follow prompts from there to place an order. Or give them a call at Young Living Essential Oils, 1-800-371-3515. Mention sponsor #168737 when establishing an account.

978-0-595-48823-0
0-595-48823-4

CPSIA information can be obtained at www.ICGtesting.com
Printed in the USA
LVOW08s0254140416

483523LV00001B/5/P